D0278310

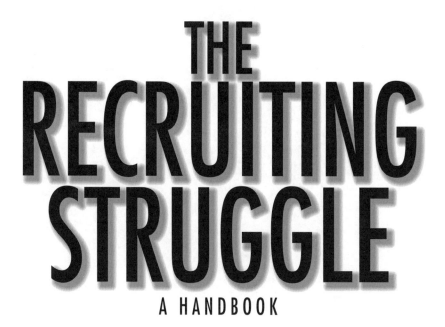

THE RECRUITING STRUGGLE

A HANDBOOK

by Lee Caryer

© Copyright 1996, Lee Caryer

All rights reserved, including the right to reproduce any portion of this book in any form for commercial gain or profit. Use of short quotations in critical reviews or, with attribution, in educational materials for high school athletes is permitted.

Production direction and design: Gary A. Hoffman
Cover design: Gary A. Hoffman
Proofreader: Jeff Phillips

ISBN: 0-9652793-0-8

For worldwide distribution

Printed in the U.S.A.

TABLE OF CONTENTS

SECTION TWO APPLYING THE INSIGHTS

APPENDIX

INTRODUCTION

Jane Smith is a hypothetical composite of a student-athlete in the recruiting process.

Taking the final exam in the most important high school course of her life, she feels the pressure but knows it will be over soon. Fortunately, the exam is brief. All she has to do is decide on one school, the college where she will accept an athletic scholarship.

She has her choice of several; the coach at each assures her, "Ours is best for you," so that part is confusing. Each of those coaches has many scholarship players, and goes through recruiting every year. But Jane hopes she will only make this decision once. If she decides she made a mistake and transfers, she may have to sit out of competition for at least one year. The school she chooses will be the one where she lives, studies, practices, plays (if she is good enough), hopefully graduates from, possibly meets a companion for life, maybe meets the father of her children, and definitely carries on her resume for her entire working career. It's only the name of one school, but it is such an important decision.

Will she make a good choice?

That depends on many things. One is luck, always a part of life. However, there are many other factors; if she manages them skillfully, luck will not be so important.

If she receives adult guidance from people who love her enough to allow her to find what is best for her, that will be a big help. Hopefully, such guidance is clearly available, through parents, other family members, coaches, teachers and guidance counselors. If the help is not clearly present, she must seek it out. There are often adults who would be pleased to help. They may be genuinely concerned about their abilities to "tell you what to do". Good. Due to the impact on her life, nobody is qualified to tell Jane what to do. She must decide. But even someone without a college or an athletic background can be helpful, by asking questions like, "Are you sure you want to study that?" or "Why do you like this coach better than those others?"

Having clear personal goals will give Jane a big advantage. Where does she see herself in 10 years? How do family, income, freedom, stability, travel, opportunity and service to others factor in? Where would she like to be at age 40? 50? Thoughts about the future will improve her present decisions.

By comparing the strengths of various programs to what she wants for herself, she is on her way to a good decision. A strong business school may be critical, or irrelevant. Coaches will list many strengths, and focus on the ones which interest the athlete. Jane must know what is important to her. If not, she is at risk of signing with the best sales person, not the coach who offers the situation which best meets her needs.

Wait a minute. That nice Mr. Johnson down the block used to coach college football; maybe he would help her look at this from a coach's point of view. And Mrs. Anderson from the bank played basketball at the university a few years ago. Jane is a softball player, but isn't recruiting pretty much the same in all sports?

That's the idea behind this book, to listen to the experiences of many people who have been through recruiting in various ways. Coaches at both the high school and college levels, athletes and their parents, some of whom went through it last year, some decades ago. What did they do? Why? Would they do it again? What could have made it better? If they do not always agree, fine. Doctors are highly educated, but patients frequently get a second opinion. Maybe Jane would get some good ideas, some second opinions. Maybe she would avoid a big mistake.

In talking to people who knew about recruiting, I repeatedly asked two questions. First, "What have you experienced?" This led to many interesting stories about the recruiting process. Second, "What do you recommend to young athletes in your sport?" This led to practical guidance, usually pertaining to any sport.

After every interview I sent a copy of the quotes to the person. This is not normal practice, but it is critical to present what they wanted to say. All changes were made as requested. Those interviews make up the first part of the book. Do not skip any of the first section! There are insights from parents, coaches and athletes which apply to any sport. Also, a student may find characteristics or attitudes in a football coach which would be desirable in a gymnastics coach, or vice versa.

There is one aspect of recruiting I wanted to present more fully than you will see here. It is the story of athletes and parents who have been hurt during the recruiting process. It was not difficult to find people who could discuss that, just to find people who would. One parent told me, "It was such a bad experience that I don't want to talk about it. My daughter transferred schools and she never wants to play that sport again." An active coach spoke so candidly that, when she saw her words in print, she did not want to participate. She did not object to what I wrote, she just did not want to be quoted saying what she believed.

Many scholarships result in college degrees, athletic glory, championships and a "happily ever after" ending. Some do not. Coaches say, "It's a business." Most have a sincere concern for the well being of young athletes, but even those coaches are under pressure to win. It is a business. We have warning labels on cigarette packages, maybe we need a warning label on the scholarship forms. But that side is underrepresented in this book because people do not want to talk about unpleasant experiences.

One additional thought on the first part of the book, the interviews. There is a range of stories, including stars and reserves, mothers and fathers, young current players and people who left the sport long ago, experienced high school coaches and younger ones, revenue and non-revenue sports, as well as D-I, D-II, D-III and junior college coaches. While the college coaches mentioned in this book are all outstanding at their level of competition, and I deeply appreciate their contribution of time and insights, it is important to say that there are other excellent coaches at each level who should be considered in any recruiting decision.

As for the second part of the book, parents, athletes, or high school coaches looking for ideas to use in helping athletes and parents may not need to read it. Your experience, coupled with those of more than 170 experts, may be all you need. But in case you want some opinions on applying all of these thoughts, read on. Just do not adopt anything you see there, or even in the first part, as totally and absolutely correct. They are merely ideas. Pick through them, adjust some to fit your situation, toss away the rest. Nobody can offer the correct process for every situation because it does not exist. You have to make your own. The goal is to provide tools for the construction.

Because talent evaluation, salesmanship, academic comparison and deciding on a college are more like an art than a science, you will see different points of view throughout the book. I particularly like the times coaches acknowledge mistakenly evaluating the ability of a player. In addition to the examples you will read, Penn State Coach Joe Paterno recruited Eddie George, Heisman Trophy winning running back, as a linebacker. NBA No. 1 selection Joe Smith wanted to go to North Carolina, but Dean Smith didn't recruit him. Anyone think Joe Paterno and Dean Smith can't coach? Of course not, but they make mistakes. So have our experts. But the college coaches who gave their time so that readers could learn about recruiting have collectively won nearly 100 NCAA championships.

Finally, don't just read this book—use it. Mark it up, underline it, extract the appropriate information. While athletes and their parents may read it from one specific perspective, coaches and other adults who provide guidance to students at different times need another approach. Try to organize the suggestions and stories in order to locate them in the future. One athlete will need help in promotion, another will need advice in screening the offers; someone will need a reminder to take core courses early, another will need to find the right AAU team. Every athlete will benefit from adult guidance through this process. Though the book is written to the athlete, it is written for the teachers and coaches who dedicate their lives to students and athletes as well.

Readers will not adopt every idea; there are too many and sometimes they conflict. Pick up a question here, an idea there and add them to what you believe. Put together the best approach for yourself, or your players, after considering what is in this book.

Think of a smorgasbord. You will not be able to apply (eat) the whole thing, but there is plenty for everyone, from highly recruited athletes to those hoping to find a place as a program player, from D-I level to D-III, from experienced coaches trying to gain another perspective to parents overwhelmed by what is happening to their children, to fans who have followed recruiting for years and now want to see it from the athlete's point of view.

The starting point is to make students aware of college at an early age. It is sad to hear an athlete say, "When I was younger, I never thought there was life after high school sports. I never thought about college. I didn't know there was such a thing as a scholarship." Adults can help young people see college as real, and sports can help make education important to them.

No high school student knows enough about college, much less college athletics, to go through recruiting alone. Athletes who have adults to offer ideas and support possess the best chance to succeed; remember the African proverb that "it takes a village to raise a child."

"This book is a wonderful idea because it is part of the educational process," said Ken Hall, a man who will be introduced in the first chapter. "Hopefully Mom and Dad will discuss it, and sit down to listen to the coaches. Parents can listen better than the child, to the coaches and to the stories in the book."

He understood the idea.

Some very knowledgeable people are skeptical about this book. They told me, "Athletes don't care about perspective, they only care about playing on television today...Parents want to go on their own ego trip in recruiting, not face the real thing...Coaches won't want to bother guiding their players through even parts of a book...Fans don't care about the recruiting process, they only care about players their schools signed."

They may be right, but I hope not. I do know it has been very difficult for athletes, parents, coaches and fans to obtain access to experts on recruiting before this. Now varied expert opinions are available in one place. Will people open the book? Will they take the time to sort through the ideas? Time will tell.

Jane Smith, I hope you ace your exam, but more for my sake than yours. While I may watch you play, in college or even professionally, the odds are much higher that one day you will prepare my tax return, fix my computer, write in my favorite magazine, decide how much I pay for food, vote on my Social Security, prescribe how much medicine I have to take, or teach people who will do those things for me. You will go to college for four or five years, but your influence on my life may be 10 times that long. I prefer that you get an education and a degree, so you can use that education in a valuable job which you do well. So I'm wishing both of us luck with your decision.

Lee Caryer

SECTION 1

INSIGHTS FROM THE EXPERTS

Chapter I
FOOTBALL

"Recruiting is the most important job a college coach has. The X's and O's are pretty much the same around the country, but if your X's and O's are bigger, faster and stronger, you have a better chance of being successful."

Bill Conley
Ohio State University Recruiting Coordinator

Many states select a Mr. Football, the best high school football player in the state that year. *USA TODAY* and others even choose a national player of the year.

Come on, who's kidding who? How could anyone do that? Is it possible to compare the caliber of football in East St. Louis, Illinois to Valdosta, Georgia? Or to decide if a quarterback here is better than a linebacker there? Is this receiver better than that defensive lineman? There are no reliable answers.

Since a national player of the year is unreasonable, naming the best player of all time is beyond consideration. Was Dick Butkus at Chicago Vocational a better linebacker than Chris Spielman at Massillon? Spielman was on a Wheaties box. How about Herschel Walker of Wrightsville Johnson County, Georgia compared to Billy Sims of Hooks, Texas? Todd Marinovich put up some great passing numbers at Santa Ana Mater Dei and Mission Viejo Capistrano Valley in California, but did the competition compare to what Koy and Ty Detmer faced, or Jeff George or Ron Powlus? For that matter, a baseball player ranks ahead of all those passers. Josh Booty of Shreveport Evangelical Christian, Louisiana, signed to play quarterback for Louisiana State University in 1993, but decided to join the Florida Marlins organization as a shortstop. In 1995, Kentuckian Tim

Couch of Leslie County moved ahead of Booty in setting national records for completions, yardage and touchdown passes.

No one can be completely serious about selecting the all-time best high school football player. The job is too big, with too many variables. But parents and athletes looking at the college scholarship process have to have a sense of humor, or the rules and stress will drive them crazy. They are entering the world of amateur athletics, where college football teams buy out home games for $850,000 a shot, the schools have a $1 billion contract to televise the NCAA basketball tournament and coaches make more money on a shoe contract than most people do for their life's work. Amateur athletics? Everyone gets paid except the athletes. This is not a world which can survive close scrutiny. If any group would accept the concept of the "best high school football player of all time," this might be the one.

The football section of the *National High School Sports Record Book* contains many familiar names. The "Wheaton Iceman," Harold "Red" Grange, averaged 31.9 points per game in the 1920 season, still third in history. Dallas Cowboy Emmitt Smith of Pensacola, Fla., Escambia rushed for 8,804 yards in his high school career, third-best. Walker gained 3,167 yards in 1979, the seventh best year in high school history. Max McGee, wide receiver for the Green Bay Packers who won the first Super Bowl, gained 254 yards rushing per game for White Oak (Texas) to set the national record in 1949. Only nine players have exceeded McGee's mark since then. Actually there have been seven different players, because one did it as a sophomore, junior and senior. That person also surpassed every other record mentioned in this paragraph. That person is Ken Hall.

KEN HALL, HIGH SCHOOL LEGEND

Ken Hall gained 669 yards as a freshman running back in Sugar Land, Texas, in 1950. Not bad for a freshman, particularly since he didn't join the team until the sixth game. The next year he rushed for 3,160 yards in 12 games, an average of 263.3 per game, still the eighth best rushing average in history. He topped it with 288.2 as a junior (to rank third) and 337.1 as a senior (first, by over 40 yards, with 4,045 yards in 12 games). As a senior, he gained 520 yards on 11 attempts against Houston Lutheran. Sugar Land won three straight regional titles, which was as far as they could go. Usually they were so far ahead that Hall played little in the second half. Some games he only played a quarter.

"We played a single wing, using the old Notre Dame box," said the man known as "The Sugar Land Express." "I played tailback and handled the ball every play." Usually he ran with it. Despite not appearing in the records for rushing attempts in a game, season or career, Hall totaled 11,232 yards rushing in four years. Brad Hocker of Archie, Mo. gained 9,193 yards (1988-91) to rank second.

Occasionally Hall passed the ball, throwing for 3,326 yards. His career offense of 14,558 yards is the best in history, as is his total of 5,146 yards in the 1953 season.

Hall also led Sugar Land to state track and field championships as a sophomore and junior. He scored 38 points the first year, 36 the next. His events included the 100-yard dash, the 220, the 440, the long jump, the shot put, the 440-relay and, at times, the discus and the high jump. As a senior, he began to prepare for the 1956 Olympics in the 10-event decathlon until he suffered a hamstring injury, which also prevented him from leading Sugar Land to a third state track title.

He started on the basketball team.

Ken Hall may not be the best high school player of all time, but no one has better credentials. If he is, what can be learned from his life in sports? As he said, "I'm not sure I understand what all this has to do with recruiting."

After a brilliant high school athletic career, Hall went through a recruitment process as intense as anyone would today. He played at a high level college program, then had a pro career. He faced life after sports and found happiness. After turning 60 in December 1995, he was in the perfect position to reflect on a life which initially revolved around sports and which eventually had almost nothing to do with them.

"I was from a small town with limited exposure," he recalls. "Everything was fine in Sugar Land. Some of the townspeople and the coaches were talking about records (my) junior year, but there were never any problems within the team. Then the recruiting started. Tens of thousands of letters. There were about 250 offers.

"My parents were wonderful, and I loved them both. But my mother had a tenth grade education, my father fourth grade. I was an only child. My coach was overwhelmed. He tried to help but he didn't know what to do. We wanted to do the right thing, but what was right? Unless you have adults who have experienced it, recruiting can be overwhelming. Now the world is much smaller through communication, and young people are better able to handle it, but it still must be difficult."

The decision came down to the size of the school and its distance from home.

"Texas was too big. I learned that going to the state track meet four years," Hall said. "Texas A&M had about 7,000 students, small compared to Texas, and was close to Madisonville, where we lived before moving to Sugar Land. I had followed them, they had a strong tradition, so I decided to go there. Rice was closest, about 20 miles away, and their coach came to see me every week. They were second choice. Notre Dame was third. Frank Leahy was there, but that was too far away."

The new Aggie coach had just arrived at A&M from Kentucky, where he won 60 games in eight years but never learned to co-exist with Wildcat basketball coach Adolph Rupp, the Baron of the Bluegrass. That coach, Paul "Bear" Bryant, was ready to cast his own shadow. He and his staff immediately brought in 120 recruits, an amazing number. Today football programs are allowed a maximum of 85 scholarship athletes for all four classes. Bryant recruited almost 50 percent more, in just one class. In addition, those were the days of single platoon football and limited substitution. Players were full-back/linebackers and quarterback/safeties. The athlete who could not play both ways simply didn't play. With kicking specialists an unknown term, a football team had 11 first stringers as opposed to at least 24 today. Now a large recruiting class would be 24-25 players.

Bryant brought in 11 teams in one year.

Hall and several of those recruits were introduced to an over-flow crowd of A&M boosters at a special gathering. When Hall was introduced he received a standing ovation, almost as if he were a messiah. Bryant said, "I'm damned happy to hear Kenneth Hall is coming to A&M. I hope he goes out for football." The boosters roared, Hall blushed, and Bryant made clear who the messiah was at Texas A&M.

In 1954, freshmen were not eligible to play varsity ball, so Hall and his classmates played in a Southwest Conference freshman league. Though moved from tailback, he was second in the league in rushing and first in scoring as a fullback. The tailback was John David Crow, the outstanding player in Louisiana the year before. Crow went on to win the Heisman Trophy his senior year, be chosen second in the NFL Draft and eventually be inducted into the Pro Football Hall of Fame. He was a Bear Bryant type of player.

Sophomore year "everything changed," Hall remembers. "I learned about the word 'more'. On the varsity there were more play-ers, more competition, they had more weight, there were more plays, the offense was more sophisticated, there were more classes, more pressure and more strangers. I wasn't around friends I had known all my life, but people on a mission. A player has to have his priorities,

6

or someone will take his place. Coaches don't care, because they have their priorities, their job to do. It's like that any time you move up a level in athletics or school or business, and that's when I learned it. Bear Bryant knew what he wanted to do. He was going to win, and nothing was going to stop him."

That fact had been made clear to everyone in the football program the year before when Bryant took the varsity to a Texas dust bowl called Junction, about 300 miles away from campus. Bryant wanted to teach football his way, and didn't want boosters stopping by, much less anyone who might be interested in the welfare of student-athletes. When current Alabama Coach Gene Stallings was asked if Junction was tough he said, "All I know is we went out there with two buses and we came back with one." Players hitchhiked back to campus alone and in small groups, often late at night so they wouldn't have to face Bryant. The next year the NCAA passed a rule to prohibit such trips. Texas A&M played the 1954 season with 29 players, going 1-9. It was Bryant's only losing season in 38 as head coach.

For Ken Hall, playing fullback in Bryant's system caused two huge problems. On defense he had to play linebacker, where he was small and completely inexperienced. He had always played defensive back. On offense he was primarily a blocker, something else he was trying to learn. Meanwhile, the varsity had an excellent junior fullback returning. Jack Pardee was a good runner, a very good blocker and eventually an NFL linebacker and head coach.

Hall practiced hard but made little progress until midway through the season.

"Before the Baylor game the coaches said I'd be starting. When I didn't, and hardly played, I quit the team and went home to marry Gloria," his high school sweetheart to whom he has been married for nearly 40 years. Later he asked Bryant to return, joined the team for spring ball and appeared to be challenging Pardee.

"People saw me as the starter at fullback," said Hall. "But the next year the same thing happened. I hardly played during the first half of the season. Then, before the Baylor game, Pardee was injured and I was going to start. Just before the kickoff Bryant said he was going to start Jack. When I played I did well, I had a run for 15 yards and one for 18 I think, but I only had the two carries. After that I told Coach Bryant I was through. There was nothing more to say. I had come to school hoping to be a three-time All-American like Doak Walker [at SMU] but it wasn't to be. It was a disappointment."

The difficulty of translating high school success to college glory continues. Of the 73 first-team college All-Americans selected by the

Associated Press in 1993-5, only 12 had been either first—or second—team All-USA choices by *USA TODAY*. But back to Ken Hall's athletic journey.

After the 9-0-1 season in 1956, Aggie assistant Jim Owens was named head coach at the University of Washington.

"He called, said, 'let's see if we can work things out for you to go with me,'" recalls Hall. "I really wanted to play, we met and had a good discussion. I thought everything was set until he sent me a telegram which said I would lose a year's eligibility by transferring. Since I only had one year left, I couldn't go. Now the rule is different—you sit out a year, but don't lose it. I was through with college, and the NFL had the rule that you couldn't play until your college class graduated. I wanted to play to prove that I could, and my only option was the Canadian Football League. So I went there and played for a $7,000 salary and $700 travel money. It doesn't sound like much, but we bought a house and had money left. I played 26 games in Edmonton, mostly wingback and some safety, and missed Rookie of the Year by one vote." He had a rushing average of 7.8 yards, caught passes and punted.

Now eligible for the NFL, the Baltimore Colts drafted Hall in the 14th round. So in 1958 he went to try to make the Colts of Johnny Unitas, Lenny Moore, Raymond Berry, Jim Parker, Gino Marchetti and Art Donovan, and those are just the members of the Hall of Fame. Heisman Trophy winner Alan Ameche was also in the backfield. This team was on its way to an overtime victory against the New York Giants in the NFL Championship game.

"They only carried 33 players then, but I had the team made," recalls Hall. "You know how they cut you by saying, 'The coach wants to see you and bring your playbook?' Well, the other thing that happens is they say, 'The coach wants to see you' and the coach said, 'Tell the trainer to issue shoes'." After five exhibition games Hall had his shoes, but unfortunately the Colts played six exhibition games. "I went up the middle against the Giants and lost my footing. As I tried to regain my balance [Hall of Fame middle linebacker] Sam Huff hit me in the back of my neck. The blow cracked the sixth vertebra in my neck in five places."

Hall missed the 1958 season and was traded to the Chicago Cardinals in 1959. "That was a happy time," said Hall. "The team had seven former Aggies," including John David Crow. Hall was fifth on the team in rushing, first in yards per attempt with 5.8.

The 2-10 Cardinals cut Ken Hall in the 1960 pre-season. He signed with the Houston Oilers of the new American Football League, which featured veteran George Blanda and Billy Cannon of LSU.

"I always seemed to be around those guys," mused Hall, thinking of Heisman Trophy winners Crow, Ameche and Cannon. The Oilers won the first AFL Championship, defeating Republican quarterback Jack Kemp's Los Angeles team, 24-16. Hall was a valuable cog, finishing fourth on the team in rushing, second in punt returns and first in kick-off returns with a flashy 31.7 average.

Before the 1961 season started, Hall separated his shoulder and Houston cut him. He played his last season with the St. Louis Cardinals, who had just moved from Chicago.

"My pro career soothed some wounds, but it didn't heal them. It was not satisfying, but it was OK. Nothing could measure up to high school."

Sports Illustrated published a major article on Hall September 27, 1982 titled, "Whatever Happened To The Sugar Land Express?" In it Bear Bryant said, "I was stupid. You're a fool to think, as I did as a young coach, that you can treat them all alike. He should have been an All-America for me. With him, we'd have won the National Championship in 1957. Without him, we lost it." That year A&M was 8-3, with narrow losses to Rice (7-6), Texas (9-7) and Tennessee (3-0). *UPI* named Ohio State No. 1, *AP* selected Auburn. Maybe Ken Hall would have made the difference.

In the same article John David Crow said, "Lord knows I love Coach Bryant to death but I'll say this, if Kenneth Hall had gone to play under someone like Bud Wilkinson at Oklahoma, the world never would have heard of John David Crow." Jack Pardee added, "I looked at (Ken Hall) and figured I had just been demoted to second string. He was the prototype back, (but) Coach Bryant believed that you played defense first and then found a position on offense. So Ken Hall had his skills reversed."

Bryant eventually wrote Hall a letter saying he had been wrong not to play him at tailback and Crow at fullback. Teammates agreed Crow would have excelled at linebacker. Hall graciously replied. He had dealt with the situation long before.

In 1984, Hall left the prestige, security and salary of his vice-presidency with Los Angeles-based Sweetener Products, a sucrose distribution firm, to pursue a dream of 30 years. "I wanted to get a piece of God's green earth, have my own business and be my own boss. I took a year looking around before opening Ken Hall's Barbeque," in Fredricksburg, Texas. He may embark on another venture before retirement, maybe not. For now, when asked, he is glad to offer his expertise on the subject of choosing a college.

"If someone asked me about being a student-athlete," he said, "the first thing I'd say is, 'You've got the order right. Make school the first priority and get the degree that you need.' I never got a degree. I had over 170 hours, some medical, some engineering, some psychology, but not enough in the same field. Then I'd say that not everybody is college material. Some should go to trade school. With the amount of money available, some kids may not need to work after the NFL. That's if everything goes well."

Ken Hall is living proof that things don't always go well. Players are not always used correctly by even the best of coaches, sometimes they end up at the same position as a great talent or there are injuries. Hall experienced all of that. "Third, I'd say, 'the body will give way, the mind will not give way—don't neglect the mind.'"

Hall had one final thought: "Strangers don't know you, you have to earn your spurs in a new league. That's true in sports or business. When athletes go to college I'd encourage them to close the book [on high school] and open a new one to a blank page."

TIM COUCH, THE NEWEST LEGEND

In 1995, the Gatorade National Player of the Year was Tim Couch of Leslie County in tiny Hyden (pop. 375), Kentucky. Like Hall, Couch set national records in key career categories and moved into the top 10 on almost every season and career list. Like Hall, he went to a small high school and was a multi-sport athlete. Couch averaged 36 points-per-game in basketball as a junior.

Like Hall, he chose an in-state school after being nationally recruited. Unlike Hall, Couch announced his choice at a press conference before several hundred people, but then this is the '90s.

Tim Couch chose Kentucky over Tennessee, after considering Florida State, Florida, Auburn, Notre Dame and others, but before going on any official visits. "I had been to Tennessee's camp and stuff, and at Kentucky's camp. I'd seen their campuses and pretty much everything you'd see on an official visit," he explained. He had also received home visits, and plenty of phone calls. In the end it came down to longtime UK loyalty and a desire to "start a big tradition at Kentucky rather than just be another name in a great line of quarterbacks." (Like Tennessee, where one of those great quarterbacks, Peyton Manning, would be pre-season favorite for the Heisman Trophy during Tim Couch's freshman year.) Couch also announced early to influence other high school recruits to join him at Kentucky. His approach was, "They could go somewhere else and be part of a long line or come to Kentucky and be remembered forever."

Elbert Couch, Tim's father, said, "A lot of coaches will tell you anything to get your kid to go to their school. Most of them said Tim would start right away. When [Kentucky Coach] Bill Curry came in here and said Tim would start out second string [behind returning starter Billy Jack Haskins], we felt comfortable with that. Honesty is the most important thing."

Tim Couch is rated as the best Kentucky high school football player since Paul Hornung of Louisville Flaget. Before a great NFL career with the Green Bay Packers, Hornung won the Heisman Trophy for a Notre Dame team that only won two games in 1956. At UK, Couch joined a football team which was 5-17 the two years before he arrived. It will not be easy to separate himself from further comparisons to Paul Hornung and Ken Hall, though there are instances when he will want to do that. But then, Tim Couch chose Kentucky to make a new mold rather than break an old one anyway.

RECRUITING NEWSLETTERS

One change in recruiting since the days of Ken Hall is the newsletter business. Many men make a living by talking with coaches about prospects and prospects about colleges, then selling the information to subscribers. Sports talk shows invite these men as guests, and the information becomes available to anyone listening. Representatives of two national publications added their perspective to the process.

The term "blue chip" athlete has been around for decades. In poker, the blue chips are worth more than the white, red, and yellow ones. So in athletics, the "blue chipper" is considered to be the best, the star of stars.

Fourteen years ago *BLUECHIP ILLUSTRATED* magazine was launched to help fans follow the achievements of the best high school football players in the country. Since talent evaluation is an imperfect process at best, *BCI* leaves a margin for error. While a typical football team has 11 on offense, 11 on defense and a couple of kickers, *BCI* selected 1,305 members on their 1995 team. Recognition began with the *BCI* Dream Team, which included 100 players, and continued with *BCI* All-America, 2nd Team All-America, All-Region and Honorable Mention All-Region. With height, weight, time in the 40-yard dash, and early colleges part of a paragraph on each of the players, and pictures of many of them, a *BCI* subscriber received a 98-page book of information on players who are early favorites to receive coveted Division I scholarships.

There are 108 D-I colleges, which give a maximum of 25 grants per year, that's 2,700 scholarships available. But Army and Navy are unique situations and all schools do not offer 25 each year, either because they are limited by the maximum of 85 total or because they are "banking" scholarships for the following year. It's probably safe to conclude that about 2,600 D-I opportunities exist in a given year. If the *BCI* network of reporters and coaches does a good job of evaluation, they identify about half of the recipients. Viewed from the other direction, if a player wasn't selected, he is probably competing for the "other" 1,300 scholarship offers. His chances have been reduced by one half.

"No problem," any parent and many high school coaches would counter. "This boy is easily one of the 2,600 best seniors in the country." However, about 1 million boys play high school football in America. Assuming about 26 per cent are seniors, that calculates to 260,000 senior football players in the country. With 2,600 scholarships, that means only the top one percent receive one. With junior colleges and players from other countries, the reality is worse.

And, of the less than one percent who do receive a scholarship, most will be disappointed.

That is not a typographical error. *BCI* asked their top college prospects for their top five colleges, the schools they wanted to visit. Some had already received and accepted scholarship offers, but most were not so far along in the process. Their top schools were subject to change, yet included the one or two 'dreams' each player hoped would become a reality.

Most of those dreams will vanish. Nebraska and Notre Dame were mentioned by more than 10 kids for every one who will get a scholarship. The Cornhuskers were named 286 times and the Fighting Irish 257. Neither school could give more than 25 scholarships. Florida State, Michigan and Penn State were chosen by over 200 hopeful boys, 14 other colleges were mentioned 100 times.

Rick Kimbrel is the Managing Editor of *BLUECHIP ILLUS-TRATED*. In that capacity he said he speaks with "500 to 800" kids in a given year. He is still amazed by the confidence recruits have. "When Todd Helton went to Tennessee he thought was going to beat out Heath Schuler at quarterback." He never did. Schuler is now quarterback for the Washington Redskins and Helton is working his way up the professional baseball ladder. Things didn't work out badly, just not as expected.

Kimbrel also spoke about athletes not considering their talents as they would fit into the coach's system. He cited a high profile example but asked not to be quoted, realizing some colleges define negativity and objectivity pretty much the same. No sense making an

THE RECRUITING STRUGGLE

enemy of a source you will need in the future. Unfortunately, he could have used dozens of instances where a defensive player wants to be more aggressive while the coaches teach containment; or the drop-back passer plays for a coach who prefers someone who can run the option and scramble; or the wide receiver chose a school which believes in ground control.

Bob Griese, ABC television announcer and former NFL and Purdue University quarterback, spoke about this on the record when he said, during the September 30, 1995 broadcast of the Notre Dame—Ohio State football game, "I just don't think (head coach) Lou Holtz and (quarterback) Ron Powlus compliment each other when they play the option. (Former Notre Dame quarterback) Tony Rice ran the option better; Ron Powlus is more of a drop-back passer."

Kimbrel's final thought sums up the uncertainty of the entire recruiting process: "The athlete can go through a mature decision making process, make the right choice of school, but there just may be somebody better at his position."

Bobby Burton and his associates started NATIONAL RECRUIT-ING ADVISOR out of Austin, Texas in 1993, to compete with BCI and others. From late August through early February they try to call 100 football players per week to obtain recruiting information, for their subscribers and to "trade" to college coaches for more information. Through this wide variety of contacts Burton has a unique look at the recruiting process.

"Some coaches prey on perceived differences between schools," he said. "When kids tell me a large state school is going on probation, I can often guess who they've been talking to. Imagine what it would be like to be 17 years old and have Lou Holtz, John Robinson, Joe Paterno and people like that calling you. All quality people, all quality schools, all great stories to tell." Plus they are great story tellers as well.

"I think it's important for an adult to take an active role in guiding the student through the process. It could be a parent, a coach, a teacher—but someone who has the best interests of the kid at heart. The student has to determine what he wants, then the adult can help him get it," Burton said.

If the student just listens to the stories, recruiting can be overwhelming; if he actively seeks specific information needed to decide how to reach his goals, the coaches tell him what he needs to know rather than a lot of impressive, but irrelevant stuff.

"When you think about it, what do Notre Dame, Texas A&M, and Florida State have in common except good football teams?" asks

Burton. "Notre Dame is a liberal arts school, Texas A&M an agricultural and engineering school, while Florida State was born out of a teachers college. Yet those may be the top choices of a star football player."

Burton's point is, any of the three may be a great choice, but the others shouldn't be in contention for that same student. If the student wants, say liberal arts, choose among several good ones with sound football programs. Or if attending a Florida school is important, look at several there. Selecting from among similar universities makes more sense.

STEVE PEDERSON, NEBRASKA RECRUITING COORDINATOR

Years ago, fans of many universities began to proclaim, "around here the two main sports are football and spring football." In cases like these, football recruiting may now be third, maybe second. Interest in potential recruits, both locally and nationally, seems to build every year.

According to analysts, the University of Nebraska hasn't done very well in the sport of football recruiting. After two straight national championships on the field, the Cornhuskers did have a consensus top ten class in 1996, a rare achievement for them. Yet receiving recognition for their incoming players does not seem to be a priority for Steve Pederson, Associate Athletic Director for Football Operations and recruiting coordinator, when he discusses the process of building winning football teams at Nebraska.

"A good evaluation program is the key to successful recruiting," he said, "not national rating, publicity or what the public thinks. A few years ago, our coach found a 6-foot-5, 190-pound defensive lineman in Louisiana who was all over the field making plays. The coaches thought he could be a 'difference maker' in college, but the other major schools were not recruiting him. We took a lot of local criticism for signing Neil Smith, who went on to make All-American for us. He was second pick in the NFL draft after the 1988 season and now is a Pro Bowl defensive lineman at about 285 pounds. But I have to say, for coaches and fans alike, it is very hard to gauge the growth and development of a 17-year-old football player, or his desire to play."

Nebraska is well known for a walk-on program which has repeatedly generated outstanding players on highly ranked teams. With scholarships down to 85, and academic requirements up, other schools call frequently to find out how to develop a similar program.

14

"Schools call and say, 'We want to start a walk-on program because we need people to play on our scout team.' I say, 'Don't bother, because no one wants to be limited to the scout team.' Kids call us because they think they can play if they have a chance, and believe they will be treated as equals here. A walk-on in our program has the same access to study table, training table or the weight room as a scholarship player, and the best players play. The greatest mistake a coach can make is to assume walk-ons are lesser players," said Pederson.

"Maybe 90 percent of our walk-ons come from Nebraska. A few success stories, like I. M. Hipp from South Carolina and Jimmy and Toby Williams from Washington, D.C., may have given people an incorrect impression. The cost of in-state versus out-of-state tuition makes an out-of-state walk-on very unusual," he continues. "Being the only state university which plays Division I football helps us, but at 1.5 million people, the size of the state hurts."

Nebraska always evaluates players before they walk on, through film and the high school coach's recommendation, to make sure they have a chance to help the program. After all, the player will be taking up space at the study table and in the weight room.

"A potential walk-on should analyze the situation much like any other recruit would," said Pederson. "Aside from football, what does the school have to offer me? Has the coaching staff evaluated me? Where could I fit into the program? Will I be given equal access to assistance, and an equal opportunity to play?"

Coach Tom Osborne said, "Walk-ons have been a very important part of our program for the past 30 years. Roughly one-third of our starters and travel squad players originally started as walk-ons."

Of course, other schools have success stories as well. Iowa's Hayden Fry has developed nine former walk-ons into All-Big Ten selections. Florida State's Bobby Bowden said he averaged two scholarships to former walk-ons each of his 20 seasons. Colorado's Rick Neuheisel walked-on at UCLA and became the starting quarterback.

When asked to change his thinking completely, to comment on the star talent at tailback or quarterback who would suddenly find himself competing with equals for playing time, Pederson did not make a major distinction between media darlings and walk-ons.

"Every athlete has to try to find the best situation overall," he said. "It is a big mistake for people to try to pinpoint their position on a team. The player who expects to redshirt, then play in spots, may find himself in the starting line-up when someone gets hurt. [Just like the star who wants a starting position may be beaten out by a walk-on.] A more important question is, 'If you are injured the second day of practice, which would be the best school?' If someone is happy in the classroom and in the dorm, he'll be productive on the field.

"Of course, everyone is different," Pederson continues. "For some, playing is not as important as being in a good situation, on a winning program. If playing time is your biggest concern, go to a program which is down, where there is less talent.

"A majority of people know what they want to do before recruiting starts," adds Pederson, "yet it is important to wait to commit until you meet with the coaches. After that, don't be too analytical, just do it.

"After you decide, don't waste people's time. As for visits, with the limit of 56 visits for each school, the athlete who takes a visit without a sincere interest in the school may be taking a visit away from another player. Be considerate of the school and the other student-athletes. Besides, when a player goes to a school without a genuine interest, it seems like he doesn't have fun on the visit anyway. Also, the player who is serious about three schools but takes five visits runs the risk of getting confused, or of the right school running out of scholarships. With earlier commitments and fewer scholarships, that seems to be happening more often."

LINDA RICE, FOOTBALL MOTHER

While Nebraska was the team of the year in college football in 1995, the Northwestern Wildcats were the story of the year, or maybe the decade.

Northwestern's 10-2 record was the first time since 1971 (7-4) the school had won more than four games. During that period, the team averaged two victories per year. After going through the Big Ten with an 8-0 mark, the Wildcats went to the Rose Bowl for the first time since January 1, 1949. Despite their loss to the University of Southern California, Northwestern had defeated Notre Dame, Michigan and Penn State in the same season.

To the delight of their alumni, Northwestern did it without relaxing academic standards. "We recruit the best football players who can do the work at Northwestern," said Coach Gary Barnett. "That reduces the pool to 20 percent of what other schools work with. Admissions determines if a student gets in."

According to a 1995 NCAA study, the grade-point average for incoming Northwestern football players was 3.21, compared to 2.71 for all of Division I-A. Their average SAT score was 1,037, while the national average was 851 for football players. A separate NCAA study showed Northwestern first in the conference in graduation rate of freshman recruits entering from 1985-88, to which an athletic director from another conference school said, "None of us is going to have the graduation rate Northwestern has. It's a different kind of place, with different admissions standards."

Academic standards notwithstanding, four years after Gary Barnett had announced at a Northwestern basketball game that he would "take the Purple to Pasadena," he had fulfilled his promise. It was the ultimate turnaround in collegiate sports.

Most recruits are told to come here and you'll be a part of building (or rebuilding, or establishing, or improving) something. Sometimes Tennesseee women's basketball, or Iowa wrestling is on the phone, but usually it's a school which aspires to the top position. Gary Barnett and his coaches were in that role. While it can be fun to join a coach with a dream and help achieve it, how does the athlete know the coach can deliver? It is far easier to promise success than to keep the promise. Since Northwestern football had delivered, maybe there were some lessons to be learned.

When Matt Rice, a junior All-Big Ten defensive tackle in 1995, took his first official recruiting visit in December, 1992, "Honest to goodness, we saw it in Gary Barnett's eyes," remembers Matt's mother, Linda Rice. "He said, 'Matthew, we are going to the Rose Bowl while you are here.' The players Matt talked to felt the same way. We met many coaches that year, but we didn't see another coach like Gary Barnett."

When Matt decided not to take his other visits and commit to Northwestern immediately, his parents were surprised. A process they thought was just starting had ended.

"But we were happy, too," said Linda. "Matt had always been a serious student, even at an early age. We wanted the best possible school. Most athletes don't continue their sport after college, and the time comes when they have to get a job. The academics at Northwestern were outstanding, and we sincerely believed in Coach Barnett. We sensed that the Northwestern coaches were different, maybe because of the kind of players they are required to recruit. My husband was comfortable, and he's not an easy person to convince. He knows his football."

Actually, everyone in the family knows football.

Matt's paternal grandfather, Fred Rice, was head coach at Colgate, assistant at Marquette, and a longtime high school coach and athletic director. His mother's father, Frank Howe, coached high school football for 46 years, 35 as head coach, winning more than 200 games. Having turned 78 shortly after the Rose Bowl game, Howe took credit for the two shovel passes Coach Barnett used against the Trojans and hoped the Wildcats would try some of his single-wing plays soon.

Matt's father, Eric, played defensive end at Wisconsin from 1964-66, and was a graduate assistant coach at Ohio State before deciding on a career in engineering. Managing his aerospace engineering firm did not keep him from taking the Rice family to the Rose Bowl, to follow the Wildcats after the 1995 season and to watch his alma mater two years before.

"Eric wanted Matt to go to Wisconsin before Coach Barnett won him over. When Wisconsin went to the Rose Bowl Matt's freshman year, Eric took the whole family. Matt was adamant about not going, because they were opponents now. But Matt's line coach, Vince Okruch, told him, 'Go, learn, then come back and tell us what we need to do to go as a team.' The vision of Northwestern going to the Rose Bowl was genuine," remembers Linda.

One more member of the family played a role in Matt ending up at Northwestern.

"His older brother, Scott, really wanted to go there," said their mother. "He was accepted, but there wasn't much demand for 150-pound running backs in the Big Ten, and we couldn't spend $25,000 per year to send him. He went to Lawrence, a Division III school, where he lettered in track, but had to give up football because of a fractured back. He later transferred to Wisconsin. There's no question that Scott's early interest pointed us toward thinking about Northwestern."

After a high school career that included All-Wisconsin and *BLUECHIP* All-America recognition for football, playing basketball and competing in the 100-yard dash, shot put and discus in track, the phone calls started coming to Matt.

"Wisconsin and Northwestern were the early leaders," said Linda. "There was a lot of early interest from Washington, too, because Randy Hart, one of their assistants, had known Eric at Ohio State. But we wanted Matt close. We took unofficial visits to Wisconsin, Iowa and Northwestern. For us, Evanston is perfect. About a 2-hour and 45-minute drive, it's definitely away, but it's also accessible."

After arriving on campus, the demands of college sports and the rigors of academics collided for Matt.

"He had enrolled in engineering, and later switched to economics," said his mother. "We had to talk about the value of the degrees, to be sure he was making the decision for the right reasons. Should he quit football to have more time to study? Was he in the wrong major? We now believe he was making the change for the right reasons."

Looking back on her son's first three years at Northwestern, this football mother felt a variety of emotions, from pride to joy, satisfaction to enthusiasm, but there was one emotion she did not feel. Linda Rice was not surprised by the success of the team.

"The parents all thought it could happen. People watching closely could see the progress, like the game they almost beat Ohio State (15-17) the year before. Over the summer most of the team stayed in Evanston, and seemed to develop a greater closeness. Then when Marcel Price, who was Matt's calisthenics partner, was accidentally shot and killed [at home in Nashville], that further unified players from different backgrounds." Black patches with the words "Big Six" were worn by the players throughout the season to honor Price.

When asked what other parents should consider during recruitment, Linda Rice suggests, "Focus on getting a great education in college. Don't just grab a scholarship; it might be better to turn down a scholarship to go to a better school.

"The coaches are very important," she adds. "The head coach doesn't necessarily interact with each player each day, but they do have contact and he sets the overall tone. The position coach relates more to the players day to day, but assistants leave and positions change. Matt was recruited as a linebacker at 240 pounds, but he's added weight and now plays defensive line. We've been lucky because only one assistant has left Northwestern since Coach Barnett has been there, and they are all great."

While the 1995 Northwestern season made for a wonderful story, what about the future?

When Gary Barnett applied for the job, "I looked at the situation and saw a diamond." When he arrived, he found only three players who had received other Division I offers, not counting the Mid-American Conference (whose Miami Redskins gave the Wildcats their only regular season loss in 1995).

Recruiting analysts did not foretell the spectacular Northwestern improvement. For example, *SuperPrep* in California rated the 1995 class 49th nationally, the 1994 class 35th, the 1993 class 26th and the 1992 class below the top 50. However, it takes good players to win 10 football games against the teams Northwestern played. As Barnett puts it, "Some of the flowers don't look so good by themselves, but put next to the others, they look a lot better."

Since 37 of the top 48 players would return from the Rose Bowl team, their 1996 recruiting class was small. Yet Barnett said, "This class is probably the most talented class we have recruited. We have filled all our needs." Most analysts rank the class in the middle of the conference, with the kind of grade they used to give Nebraska.

One of those recruits, offensive lineman Jack Harnedy, was thinking about Michigan, Stanford, Oklahoma and Illinois when he took his first visit to Northwestern. He liked what he saw and committed without making any other visits. He agreed with the Barnett philosophy that, "Playing for Michigan or Notre Dame is like renting a home. At Northwestern, you can be a part of building something."

Matt Rice would understand.

HIGH SCHOOL COACHES DISCUSS RECRUITING

The first person most players turn to for advice about college teams is their high school coach. If the player is lucky, the coach knows what he is talking about. If the player is very lucky, the coach is willing to help find the right school, not just the best football program.

Gregg Miller took Columbus (Ohio) Brookhaven to four straight City League championships from 1989-92, including three trips to the state play-offs. He sent players to Northwestern, Ohio State and Kansas, some of the best college teams in the country in 1995. But the look on his face as he talks about his players, the ones who became stars and the ones who didn't, shows that he is in coaching for the relationships, not the honors.

The weekend after Brookhaven's 1995 season ended, Miller traveled to the Kansas-Nebraska game.

"I see my players play. When they graduate I'm not done with them," explains Miller. "Kansas had the better team."

Possibly not an impartial observation of a 41-3 game, but Kansas had Brookhaven's June Henley. Most of Miller's guys end up closer to home.

"Some people say I send Ohio State players," said Miller. "I love Ohio State, but that's not true. I want my players to go where they'll be happy and have a chance for success."

Charles Henley, Jr. (who prefers June, short for Junior) would have had a chance for success anywhere after rushing for 2,582 yards and 35 touchdowns as a senior.

"The year before he split time at tailback and started at defensive back," remembers Miller. "Then June had a great summer camp at Ohio State. He was ready to commit. When he broke out as a tailback senior year, he wanted to play there in college, but thought

Ohio State wanted him for defense. They said he could play tailback, but he wasn't sure they meant it. Kansas wasn't in on him early, recruited him solely as a tailback and he went there."

After gaining 1,160 yards as a freshman, Henley's attempts and yards decreased by almost half as a sophomore. After seeing him carry only seven times against Nebraska, Miller reported, "They aren't using him the way they said they would during recruiting." However, Henley rushed for 107 yards and two touchdowns in leading Kansas to a victory over UCLA in the Aloha Bowl one month later.

In high school, Henley's family gave shelter to a 13-year-old teammate whose single-parent mother had been murdered. "Terry Glenn asked to stay overnight one night," said Miller, "and stayed three years. He had nowhere else to go, because things hadn't worked out with other relatives. The Henleys are a hard-working family, and all their kids delivered papers. Terry was welcome to stay, but he had to get a paper route too. Mr. Henley always kept up the heat."

Still, Glenn wasn't sure he'd be able to go to college.

"His grades were acceptable, but he didn't pass the test by the time scholarship offers were made in February," said Miller. "Schools wanted him to walk on, but he couldn't get a scholarship. We had to convince him how good he was, he just had no confidence. Walking on at Ohio State was the simplest solution. It was close to his support group, the Henley's, myself, some other Brookhaven teachers, and the cost was low until he got the scholarship."

Explaining his relationship with Glenn, Miller said, "Sometimes he needs a pat on the back, sometimes a little advice, sometimes a fatherly scolding. I do those things for him." And because of the involvement of people like Miller and the Henleys, Terry Glenn became a Fred Biletnikoff Award winner as the best receiver in the country and the seventh choice in the 1996 NFL Draft.

With Marlon Kerner and Jayson and Anthony Gwinn also playing at Ohio State, people could think of Brookhaven as "Buckeye territory." But what about Henley, or Shawn Harris?

"Playing close to home is important to most of our players," said Miller. "When Jayson Gwinn flew to Indiana for a visit he was scared to death, never having been in a plane before. Shawn Harris wanted to go to Ohio State and they wanted him, but it wasn't a good situation for him. They had too many linebackers in the program." Harris became a starter for Hawaii.

Miller has more influence in recruiting than he did earlier in his career. Every letter comes to him. He decides when announcements will be made, and who will make it.

"My first year, Anthony Thornton came back from visiting Kent State, and told me he was going there. I told the coaches recruiting was over. Then one day he came to school wearing an Ohio University jersey with his name on it. (Head Coach) Cleve Bryant had backdoored us. I learned. Now when a kid tells me something, I make him call all the schools on my phone. If he won't call, recruiting is not over.

"Actually it worked out well. Anthony is the second leading passer in OU history, to Cleve Bryant." But things don't always work out so well.

"Wilbert Brown graduated in 1990," recalls Miller. "He set the Franklin County career rushing record with almost 5,000 yards, and may have been the best back I've ever seen," high praise from a man who played high school football with Archie Griffin. "Academics were just not a priority for Wilbert. He went to a junior college, but didn't have the discipline to succeed. It took me a while to figure out that you can't do it for players. They have got to want it themselves. Some see your philosophy, some don't.

"We had an excellent tight end a couple of years ago who had college ability but was way behind in school," remembers Miller. "I spoke with his parents between his junior and senior years, and he really got turned around. He took two classes in the summer. Then he went to night school his senior year, on top of a regular schedule. Plus he had a good senior year in football. He graduated, with a Division I scholarship. When he got to college, out on his own, it was 'party time' and he lost it all.

"Most kids struggle their first term at school," said Miller. "I warn them, but it still happens. I would like to see freshmen ineligible. Some can do the athletic and academic work, but it's a problem for most."

Coach Miller has a tradition that former players are invited to stop by his home to eat pizza and watch football when they are home from school the Saturday after Thanksgiving. Though the pizza bill gets larger every year, he enjoys the occasion so much the tradition may last a long time. He will never forget Thanksgiving weekend, 1993.

"Jayson Gwinn got lost, and got there about 8:30 p.m. The pizza was gone and the other players had left, but he sat and talked with my family. One of the teachers at Brookhaven had taken him to Cleveland for a Browns game and he sat in the 'Dawg Pound', so he was excited about that. He had had a good year (as defensive end at Ohio State), but I remember he said he wouldn't want to leave school early because of all Ohio State had done for him. Then December 12,

Jayson Gwinn died in an automobile accident."

After wiping his eye, Miller said, "One guy to talk to about getting kids into college is Doug Smith at East High School. It's completely different selling city kids to colleges than suburban kids. The city kids may have more developing ahead, as they gain experience and work on weight training. Usually our freshmen haven't played organized football or lifted weights. Doug Smith has 35 players show up for practice, the team may go 1-9 but two of his guys get scholarships."

Smith, a teacher at Columbus East since 1973 and head football coach since 1983, said, "It takes old-fashioned hard work to put kids into college. The entire staff at the school works individually with a kid, talking about life, that you can't play football forever but that you can use football as a means to an end. We set the tone early, ninth grade if possible. Coaches, teachers, guidance counselors and parents have the message to get ready for college in case an athletic scholarship comes along. If it doesn't, they are ready for society, or maybe to get to college on their own. We show kids what they have to do. Some coaches feel 'Mom and Dad will get them ready.' We feel if we don't do it, it won't get done."

Just weeks before, Smith and Lee Williams (a college football letterman, former East coach and Doug Smith's mentor) had taken three players 80 miles to visit Ohio University.

"When the kids see a campus, the whole idea of college becomes more real," Smith explains. "If the parents don't have the dream, they can't pass it on to the kids. The players begin to see themselves as college students, then become more serious about preparing to go to school. Lee Williams said, 'One year of college is good, two better, three is better still and a degree the best. If he'll take a chance, he'll grow through the experience.' With city kids, if they aren't productive, they'll get into trouble."

Or maybe that's true of any kid, or anyone.

East has a storied athletic tradition, which includes state championships, NFL players like Jim Marshall of the Minnesota Vikings and NBA stars like Houston's Ed Ratleff. Recently, though, open enrollment throughout the city has meant smaller turnout for East athletic teams. Tradition doesn't mean a great deal to a teenager, particularly when a coach at another school is telling him how good he is in order to entice him to change schools.

Though recruiting of high school athletes in some parts of the country is so bad coaches refer to it as "The R-word," Smith doesn't have time to compete there. He's too busy trying to see that his players are recruited by colleges.

"The toughest thing is predicting how a high school player will play in college. Because of our low numbers, we play kids at different positions and get to know the kids pretty well. The better you know the kid, the better your projection. Is he willing to redshirt? Would he be lost on a big campus? Then we get input from his teachers. I don't tell kids where to go, but I'll give my opinion if they ask.

"You've got to get to know the college coaches," Smith continues. "They used to think Ohio State got all the Columbus players. Now they know there are a lot of players in Columbus, and they may take a chance on an East player because of past experiences," such as Jeff Sydner, the 5-foot-6, 170-pound NFL veteran.

"Jeff's story really illustrates how important it is to meet people, go to clinics and network," smiles Smith. "Penn State invited me to work their football camp. One summer I took a tape of Jeff's junior year.

"A scout for the [Pittsburgh] Steelers saw the tape and was so impressed he called his son, an assistant at Arizona. They were set, but that coach knew a coach at Hawaii. Some time passed, then the Hawaii assistant called. He was in Atlanta, and was willing to stop in Columbus on the way home. When he got here he didn't have a school ID. I began to suspect somebody was playing a joke. But he was for real. Jeff liked them because they were rebuilding; he thought he could help them and play a lot. It was a great decision for him." And for Hawaii as well.

After a redshirt year to recover from a knee injury, Sydner made first team All-WAC as a return specialist once and second team twice. In 1990, he was fifth in the nation in all-purpose running, setting a school record. Sydner is first in school history for total yards in a game, a season and for average yards-per-game for a career.

A sixth-round draft choice by the NFL Philadelphia Eagles in 1992, Sydner was tenth in the league in punt returns in 1994. He returns to East to talk to present players about college. An NFL player, particularly one so small, makes a powerful impression on teenagers.

"Legally, I'm through with the kid after football," said Smith. "But we tell them they never leave us. We push for the college degree. We tell them, 'We'll come visit you in college. We won't care about football, but we'll care about school.' Luckily most of them stay in Ohio. It's easier to see them play on Saturday after a Friday night game.

"Our society has to make some decisions," concludes the coach who even helps players from other schools go to college. "It costs more to incarcerate a kid than to educate him. We—it's a team approach at East—realize someone made it possible for us to have a chance in college, so we try to give other kids that opportunity."

While Gregg Miller and Doug Smith worked to win games and send their players from the Columbus City League to college, Coach Brian Deal was meeting some of the same challenges, and some very different ones, in the Columbus suburb of Dublin.

After a 10-2 record and a rank of seventh in the state in 1994, Deal and his many returning starters for Dublin High School looked forward to the 1995 season. Then came the announcement that after four years as head coach, Deal would be reassigned to the new, smaller Dublin Scioto High School opening that year.

Nineteen seniors decided to change schools with him. One returning starter decided to stay at the "old school" because he had a greater allegiance to the baseball team there than to the football team at Scioto. What a choice to have to make.

At the first-year school, "new" coach Deal welcomed some strong returning talent. Running back Nick Goings was all-state as a junior, when he gained 1,501 yards rushing and received a scholarship offer from Ohio State after his third game. Rolland Steele had remarkable speed. Lineman Brad King's brother started at Ohio University as a freshman. Shawn Bannon was the son of Bruce, linebacker for the Miami Dolphins Super Bowl Champion "No Name Defense."

All would start both ways for the smaller school, which was now classified Division II. The smaller classification might be an advantage in the state play-offs, but to qualify Scioto had to play eight larger Division I schools and two schools of comparable size.

Lack of numbers did not seem to be a problem as Scioto won the first seven games. The season was Going(s) well. At 6-foot, 213-pounds, Goings had consecutive games of 292; 284; and 261 yards rushing. While he was being recruited by all the powerhouses, teammate Rolland Steele committed to Ohio State.

"Rolland went to their camp and opened their eyes. They timed him at 4.4 in the 40. Penn State contacted him this week, but Ohio State has always been his first choice. We have a policy here that if their No. 1 choice offers them a scholarship, let's be fair to everyone and not waste anybody's time," Deal said.

In the middle of his ninth year as a head coach, Deal had learned most of what he knows about recruiting after his college playing days ended. "At 6-foot, 170-pounds, with a 4.9 40, there weren't any scholarship offers. I went Division III and had a great experience. The difference between D-I, D-II and D-III is 25 pounds, 2 inches and .2 seconds each," smiles the former quarterback.

"It's difficult to learn about recruiting as a high school assistant, because colleges want to talk to the head coach. My assistants do so much, it's hard to ask them to do more anyway. But the biggest problem a coach faces is when the parents think their son can play Division I and I know better," Deal sighs.

"When it comes to evaluating college talent, experience is essential. The young coach thinks he knows, but the older coach realizes he didn't know back then.

"After their junior year I meet with players and their parents to explain the recruiting process, academic requirements and what I will do to promote their sons. If parents have better ideas, they have to tell me.

"Camps are good for the in-between player who knows the school he wants. He can go prove himself. Increasingly, camps put together staffs of coaches from various levels, which widens the exposure. The blue-chip player can hurt his stock at a camp, so I might not recommend one for him," said Deal.

"The single best way I have found to sell a player is video tape. A suburban school like ours has the time, technology and the money to make tapes for kids. If a coach can't or won't, parents should do it themselves. Video stores can do it; some college scholarship marketing organizations do it for a fee."

With that he jumps out of his chair, grabs a tape and takes it to the VCR.

"Game tapes are fine, but put the highlights at the front. Here's one play of Nick Goings that would get an offer from anyone." The tape shows Goings make a leaping, one-handed catch of a screen pass, immediately avoid a tackler, then quickly separate himself from the defense. "See his speed—two strides every five yards," praises Deal.

"Rolland and Nick are different cases," states Deal. "Nick is a blue-chip, blue-chip who wants to take his visits, Rolland is a good Division I prospect who got his first choice. It's good for Rolland to commit, and good for Nick to wait."

After a late October loss to Westerville South, ranked second in Division I in the state, Scioto beat two more large teams to finish 9-1, and finish second in Division II.

Behind eight touchdowns from Goings, Scioto won their first two play-off games. In the semi-finals they met Celina, voted the top Division II team in Ohio. Celina's defense and a second half ankle injury limited Goings to 110 yards rushing, but Scioto's defense won the game. Against a team which had averaged 45.5 points-per-game, the Scioto Irish won 28-14 to meet Akron Buchtel in the state finals.

Ricky Powers, the Michigan tailback, had taken Buchtel to state championships in 1988 and 1989, but this year a stingy defense was their strength. They had seven shutouts in 12 games and led Scioto after three quarters, 14-6.

During the quarter break, Coach Deal walked over to Nick Goings and said, "You know somebody's going to have to make a big play." With less than five minutes to go in the game, Goings raced 57 yards with a punt to set up his own touchdown plunge. A two-point conversion forced overtime, where Dublin won 21-14.

Though 216 yards short of breaking the Ohio single-season rushing record, Goings had led his team to a state championship. But it was far from a one-man show. The rest of the offense had been so productive most of the season, the rest of the defense had won the semi-final game and the rest of the special teams had turned the final game around. Everyone earned a piece of this championship.

In January, Nick Goings accepted a scholarship to Ohio State. In March, Coach Deal met with the parents of junior football players, starting the recruiting process again. He went through the steps in the process, had a guidance counselor available to discuss entrance requirements, and recommended their sons consider academics, people (coaches and players) in the athletic program, other students, proximity and "what attending the university will do for me five years from now, ten years from now" in making their decision about college.

Miller, Smith and Deal agreed that the high school coach had to be brutally honest in evaluating a player, or lose credibility with colleges for the future. Also, they said the coach could not be personally offended if a college decided on another player.

JIM TRESSEL, DIVISION I-AA YOUNGSTOWN STATE

Three Division I-AA national championships in the last four years was impressive. So was the fact that Youngstown State had 61 victories in football in the 1990s, most in the country. Florida State was second with 54. But the picture of the 1995 team meeting President Clinton at the White House after repeating as national champs was the single most dominant impression that a recruit must take away from Youngstown State.

Coach Jim Tressel has built a Division I-AA powerhouse at Youngstown State. In his first nine years there he won 11 coach-of-the-year honors, including the Eddie Robinson Award as National Coach of the Year in 1994. He and his father, the late Lee Tressel, who was 155-52-6 at Baldwin-Wallace College, form the only father-son coaching combination to win national football championships.

To achieve this record he's had to be able to "sign mid-major athletes who could play for Division I teams." As a D I-AA coach, he has to do it with six coaches instead of nine, using 63 scholarships instead of 85. Some of those scholarships are divided, in order to attract more than 63 players. This man can recruit; he also remembers what it is like to be recruited.

"When I got letters as a recruited athlete, I wanted to believe I was that good. My parents helped me deal with the initial rush. When I got a letter from an alum then playing for the Minnesota Vikings and I saw that Viking stationary, my mind jumped past college to the pros," said Tressel, who went on to play quarterback for four years at D-III Baldwin-Wallace.

"One of the big problems recruiting causes is distracting the athletes. We tell our players, 'don't think about the NFL,' but then we call high school players and cause them to think about college. We try to reduce in-season recruiting, but I'm not proud of my place in this," he said. "The high school coach is really caught in between. If he shuts out recruiters, the parents are mad because there are no scholarships; if he's too open, the players are distracted from the task at hand and the team is not successful.

"The system leads kids astray, like society leads people astray," Tressel said. "We are shown success on television, but not the travail that leads to the success. People don't see what it takes to become (Michael) Jordan or (Sylvester) Stallone. The mail is mind-boggling. Some kids and parents think a letter means they are being recruited. Schools mail to 1,000 people to sign 20-25. Phone calls, invitations to campus and scholarship offers, that's recruiting, those three, in that order. Until the head coach says, 'I have a scholarship for you,' nothing is definite. Letters are marketing, not recruiting."

After putting letters into perspective, Tressel said, "The biggest problem for recruits is finding out soon enough where they fit. If you are an Ohio State- or Michigan-level player, contacted by 20 schools like that, choose the best one. The major, majors make recruiting decisions early. In September, Penn State is close to being finished."

But often a player is at the lower end of one level, or the upper end of the next.

"My dad recommended to me," said Tressel, "'If you make an error, make it too small rather than too large.' I suggest that to high school coaches. Parents don't always realize that everything is affected by their son's success in sports: self-image, social, academic. If we bring in a player who can't contribute it hurts us, but it hurts the player more. If you're not good enough to sign at one level, have your coach call colleges at the next level. I love those calls.

"We all make mistakes in recruiting," he adds. "When I was an assistant at Syracuse, I told Shane Conlin he couldn't play for us." Instead Conlin starred at Penn State and in the NFL.

"We say the player has to control recruiting. To keep schools from manipulating you, decide what you want. Evaluate schools by setting criteria based on your goals. Also, there has to be real evaluation of what is said, not just acceptance. A lot of talk about academics is just that. I always wondered how many people really ended up in Michigan's school of business," he continues. "But maturity is a problem at that age. The person with the best chance to monitor recruiting is the high school coach, but their time is a huge problem."

"High school coaches put in a great deal of time on recruiting, but all their players don't get scholarships. Some parents don't understand," said Tressel. "A coach in Cleveland has college coaches fill out a brief evaluation on his players. If a parent feels that his son wasn't helped, the coach would pull out the cards and say, 'I did try to help but I didn't broadcast that 25 schools weren't interested.'"

"Like society, there's not much reality in recruiting," he said. "It doesn't result in a happy ending for the majority, after all the expectations. From February to September is rough for many kids. After about two weeks of football, things change and they're happy to be here. Teammates jumping on you after a touchdown is fun, no matter where you are."

Tressel's secretary for nine years, Lynn Cadle, has a "behind the scenes" role in the recruiting process. She is responsible for sending out questionnaires, logging them into the computer with copies to recruiting coordinator Ron Brown and the coach responsible for the geographic area, requesting tapes, organizing solicited and unsolicited tapes, assembling a mailing list of about 800 names, narrowing it to about 450 active names and handling all the details of official and unofficial visits. That's the easy part. She also is a direct contact for parents who want to promote their son, the football player.

"The number and length of the calls is amazing," she said. "They want to tell me all about their son, partly because they are proud and partly because I will listen. But that doesn't help them. I send out a questionnaire but always recommend their son talk with his coach. The sad part is the calls after signing day. Their kid didn't get picked up and, based on one letter, they thought he would. You can be proud of your son, but you have to see the reality."

BOBBY WALLACE,
DIVISION II UNIVERSITY OF NORTH ALABAMA

As head coach of the only team in collegiate football history to win 40 games in three years (41-1 from 1993-95), the first school in the history of NCAA scholarship football to win three consecutive national championships, Bobby Wallace of the University of North Alabama is not exactly a household name. Yet, he is on the list of 18 football coaches to ever win three national titles, with legends like Bear Bryant, John McKay, Knute Rockne and Bud Wilkinson.

Division II does not have the publicity of Notre Dame and Alabama, but "to win at this level we have to get great football players, the kind who can play in the NFL," states Wallace.

In fact, North Alabama receives more television exposure on Sundays than Saturdays. Three players were drafted in 1996, and five have played in the Super Bowl. Back when UNA was known as Florence State Teachers College, graduate Harlon Hill went on to recognition as NFL Rookie of the Year in 1954 and NFL MVP in 1955 with the Chicago Bears. The Harlon Hill Trophy is now presented to the Division II Player of the Year. In 1995, the winner was UNA linebacker Ronald McKinnon.

"Our whole key is to find great football players who have been overlooked. We recruit junior college players during the season, because for players who want to enroll second semester, the signing period starts around Christmas. For high school players, we have somewhat of a waiting process. After Christmas, our coaches go out to high schools in our recruiting area, a radius of about a 2 1/2 hour drive from Florence, Alabama. They spend two weeks talking with coaches, looking for players who might not have come to the attention of the top teams. We don't compete with Alabama, Auburn, Georgia or the other SEC powers, but we do go against other Division I, Division I-AA or Division II schools," said Wallace.

When D-I schools went to the sliding scale for initial eligibility, D-II did not.

"We still require a 2.0 grade point on 13 core courses and a 17 ACT for high school graduates," said Wallace. "For junior colleges, a non-qualifier out of high school has to graduate to go to a D-I school now. We require 24 hours of transferable work at 2.0. It seems like we should have more players available under their tightened requirements, but this is the first year and it's too soon to tell now."

A Division II football program is permitted 36 equivalent scholarships, which are calculated by dividing the financial aid given by the cost of attendance. Because out-of-state tuition is higher, a .5

equivalent scholarship to an Alabama athlete is less expensive to the university than one to a player from across the state line. But to compete with schools from bigger divisions, UNA has to offer full rides most of the time. "We signed 15 players on signing day," said Wallace in early 1996, "and most of them were full. Every player we signed had at least one offer from a D-I or D I-AA school."

Yet D-I schools have 85 scholarships available, DI-AA schools have 63. That makes walk-on players critical to North Alabama and other D-II programs. "Most of the partial scholarships we give go to walk-ons who play. They might get full tuition, then tuition and room and board, then possibly a full-ride," said Wallace. "We also like to leave room for transfers. There are some successful transfer stories, though there are more stories where it is unsuccessful."

Asked to help a high school senior make a good choice of a college, Wallace said, "Play hard and enjoy your senior year. Although a lot of money is spent to send materials out to colleges, we seldom look at any of it. Why would a kid come here from California? The way recruiting works here is, we contact high school coaches for recommendations, then we contact players who can help us.

"I'd tell a player that walking on is not bad. There are a lot of walk-ons playing college football. But if you are being recruited, select the kind of schools to visit which you would want to attend even if they didn't have a football program. Distance, academics, atmosphere, these are the kinds of things to consider before the visit. On the visit you will learn about the program. I've generally found that players tell the truth, and you will feel the atmosphere when you arrive. If there is pressure, anxiety, animosity, you will feel it in the air.

"The hardest thing about recuiting is telling people 'No.' Most places are good. I was highly recruited out of high school [a prep All-American at Callaway High School in Jackson, Mississippi before lettering three years at Mississippi State], so I've seen it from every side.

"Always remember, do what's best for you. Don't be afraid to tell a coach 'No,' because he has heard it before," concludes the man who recruited Bo Jackson as an assistant at Auburn.

Bobby Wallace really has seen it from every side.

BOB MACDOUGALL,
35 STRAIGHT JUNIOR COLLEGE VICTORIES

Following a 59-0 victory over Vermillion (9-1) in the Midwest Bowl, the College of DuPage (Ill.) football team concluded the 1995 season 12-0 and stretched the nation's longest winning streak to 35 games. With 10 state championships, eight bowl victories and three other bowl appearances in the last 13 seasons, Coach Bob MacDougall had created a junior college power. To sustain it, a significant portion of his time is devoted to bringing in the type of players who can keep the program at such a high level.

"The average fan would expect a good high school player to star at a community college," states MacDougall. "However, there are a lot of offensive linemen for good high school programs who are two-year starters weighing 225 pounds. Here, our offensive line averages 6-foot-5, 313 pounds. How fast can a kid get bigger and stronger? Can he develop the skills to change positions? What about other players already experienced at those positions? To win, I need the kind of kid who wants to play for Michigan or Penn State, that level of talent and desire. Now, to play at schools like that requires a select kid. Maybe he can't play quite that high, but he has a high aspiration to succeed. For every 15 calls I get, one can play."

With academic standards rising, junior colleges are an increasing consideration for many student-athletes. "A lot of us didn't take academics seriously our freshman or sophomore year in high school," said MacDougall. "A divorce in the family, immaturity, a problem with a girl friend, there are many possible reasons why we didn't get the job done, but we didn't.

"So what's next? Go to college as a Prop 48 and sit out, or go to junior college and play? The best decision is what is best for the individual; no one choice is best for everyone.

"Twenty-five years ago community colleges were thought of as having secretarial science and building and trades courses. At the College of DuPage you can take the same English, history or philosophy class you can at Michigan. Less than 10 percent of the population is made up of non-predictors," students who do not meet grade and test score requirements for a scholarship.

"While that figure does not apply to the football team, athletes have to compete with other students in the classroom. Zero-level classes and tutors help them make up for what they missed in high school, so they can graduate from a four-year college. We want kids who have college graduation as a goal, and who will work to achieve it," he said.

Not all junior college players were unable to receive college scholarships. Some wanted to play at a level higher than they were recruited.

"Joe Bergin wanted to play in the Big Ten but the only scholarships he was offered were in the MAC. He came here for two years, then got a scholarship to Michigan State. He achieved his dream and started for them in the [1988] Rose Bowl," recalls MacDougall.

Maybe Michigan State and other schools at that level made a mistake on Bergin. Evaluation is an inexact science. On the other hand, two years of practice, weight lifting and college competition should make a player bigger, stronger and more skilled.

"Colleges can't recruit all junior college players, but they can use them to fill in, to replace kids who left the program. Besides, very seldom can a high school senior turn a college program around—maybe a junior college player can. We've had three players become captains of Big Ten teams," said a proud coach.

Predictors can leave junior college after one year and 36 credit hours. Some benefit by staying for that second year.

"Billy Lobenstein came to us from a rural area," said MacDougall. "He was a back-up defensive end for us as a freshman, started as a sophomore, then played two years at Wisconsin and two years for Denver in the NFL. Some players keep improving."

From his unique vantage point of recruiting high school players for the College of DuPage, then watching them be recruited by four-year schools, MacDougall has had a comprehensive look at the recruitment process. He saw four key issues to consider:

"First is the academics. How do kids from there do at four-year schools? Do the classes transfer? How does the tutorial support work? Use different sources to evaluate this, not just the coach. Your ultimate goal is a college degree for a career," he said. "Second is the environment. Is this where you want to park your hat for two years? We talk about our new library and new fine arts building and small average class size as important educational benefits. But we are all different, so what's important to you?

"Third is the athletic program. Do the athletic facilities, the coaches, the off-season program meet your needs? Fourth is the location. We promote access to exhibits and culture in the local community and in Chicago. We aren't out in the middle of no where. Distance from home is a part of this. Too near? Too far? Put it all together, 'Are you happy in the environment?'"

MEDIA OBSERVATIONS

Former players and coaches who stay involved with the game as members of the media are no longer involved in recruiting, but observe developments today in terms of what they experienced personally. A recent Big Ten quarterback and a former Pitt head coach added their unique perspectives.

In college sports, it is possible to decide on a school by following your heart instead of your head, encounter adversity along the way, and still be very pleased with the final result. That's the way Kirk Herbstreit of ESPN's *College Football GameDay* remembers his career at Ohio State.

Kirk was born to be a Buckeye. His father, Jim, lettered three years under Woody Hayes, serving as Buckeye captain in 1960. But "like most kids, I wanted to be a part of it, to be recruited," he recalls. "You might say I lied to Bo, Joe and the coaches," who asked if he would really consider any school except Ohio State.

Herbstreit was only lying to himself. He didn't accept any paid visits other than OSU's, though he unofficially visited Michigan.

"Bo Schembechler was an assistant when Dad was at Ohio State, both as a player and assistant, and Dad coached for him at Miami (Ohio). Michigan's offense suited me well. Bo saw Jim Harbaugh in me. If my heart hadn't been all Ohio State, I would have gone to Michigan," he remembers.

"I had to change my entire offensive style as a quarterback to play at Ohio State. It's not easy to change from a roll-out and option quarterback [in high school] to a pro-style, drop-back quarterback. It takes time and experience. Eight years later, in terms of offensive philosophy, my best choice would have been Michigan or Notre Dame," he said.

Herbstreit never saw himself as an NFL quarterback.

"At the time my ultimate goal was not pro football. I wanted college football and the Rose Bowl, but I thought I could play major league baseball. My final four schools—Ohio State, USC, Michigan and Penn State—all said it was OK for me to play baseball in the spring. Schools tell you what you want to hear.

"When I was a freshman, there were two other freshman quarterbacks, plus all the upper-classmen," he recalls. "The coaches said, 'It's OK to play baseball, but who knows where you'll be on the depth chart by fall?' Every year I played spring football."

But giving up baseball didn't seem to help.

"My third year I was a redshirt sophomore. Greg Frey was a senior, starting for his third year, and Kent Graham had transferred in from Notre Dame. [Quarterback coach Ron] Hudson liked Graham. It was his first year eligible and they were pushing him toward Greg. My future was non-existent," Herbstreit said.

"Once I talked myself into being sick to miss practice. I went to the trainer, who sent me to the student health center. They found something, made me take a week off and sent me to the team physician. He took some blood and told me I had mono. I thought, 'What

THE RECRUITING STRUGGLE

the heck, I'm riding this out.' I had a few more weeks off."

Herbstreit returned to play quarterback for the scout team as Ohio State prepared for Air Force's option attack in the Liberty Bowl. "After that loss, I was discouraged. The hand writing was on the wall, and [highly touted freshman] Joe Pickens was coming up behind me. On the plane, Coach Cooper said, 'I want you to know you're going to have a chance this spring.' I was skeptical, but [the coaches] convinced Dad and me that I'd be given an opportunity."

In 1991, Kent Graham started as Ohio State had an 8-4 record.

"Kent was a pro-type NFL quarterback, but he just was not a leader that the team responded to," recalls Herbstreit. "He made mechanical mistakes in calling signals which hurt. The players thought I should have started, which helped me."

In his fifth year, Herbstreit started, led Ohio State to an 8-3-1 record, a Florida Citrus date with Georgia and had 1,904 yards passing to Graham's 1,018 the year before. Kirk was selected co-captain before the season started and Most Valuable Player when it ended.

"After my senior year, Coach Cooper told me if he had it to do over he would have started me as a junior," said Herbstreit.

Today the former captain is completely at ease with his college experience.

"I'm most proud of what I overcame and what I achieved," he said. "As for advice to high school players about college, don't let coaches push you away from your dream."

While Kirk Herbstreit observes football for ESPN as a player, Mike Gottfried provides a coach's point of view.

As a player at Morehead State, an assistant at several schools, and head coach at Murray State, Cincinnati, Kansas and Pittsburgh, Gottfried has an extensive knowledge of football recruiting over the last three decades. The ESPN analyst has a detached perspective to offer.

"What happens to kids in recruiting is they get over-powered," said Gottfried. "People start calling, and it's nice to be wanted. Pretty soon there are so many calls the players don't know who they are talking to. Some enjoy the process so much they go down to the wire, and they sign with the last coach to talk with them."

To make the best choice, athletes have to take charge of the process.

"They should start thinking about college their sophomore year in high school, though it is difficult to know how good they are that early," states Gottfried. "They need to ask a lot of questions, and not just on their official visit. Then everybody puts their best foot forward, and time goes by too quickly to get all the information you need. Unofficial visits are a good idea. If distance is a problem, write letters to players and schools. Get information any way you can. On an official visit they'll put you in a nice hotel, feed you better food. I always thought the kids should ask to stay in a dorm, and eat cafeteria food, but I never had a player do that," he said with a slight smile.

"Some of the rule changes have hurt recruits by limiting their exposure to the coaches," Gottfried recalls. "Back in 1984-85, big name coaches called me at Pittsburgh, very excited about their chances to pass rules to keep the head coach on campus more. I didn't like it, because they had established reputations and I had to sell myself. Also, kids are more likely to make a bad choice if they don't know the coach well."

The ex-coach also cites the reduction in scholarships as a mistake.

"I think 85 football scholarships is too few. This year [1995] is the first year I saw the quality of college football go down from the previous year. I think 95 is about the right number. The players aren't professionals. They lose interest or transfer or get hurt. There are no trades."

In addition, there is the difficult task of evaluation.

"The NFL brings their top picks to Indianapolis to run them through drills, and they still miss," said Gottfried. "In college, you can't do that. Penn State and Michigan have a big advantage with their camps, which are probably the best in the country. They bring in 900 kids and figure out who they want that week. But with so many kids, even that may not be a true evaluation. Some of the best kids I had nobody wanted, but they were hungry. For others, the scholarship was their goal. When they got one, that was the end.

"Look at Phil Simms, a great NFL quarterback for the Giants. He went to Morehead State. No D-I school recruited him. There is a long list of guys like that. Having done it, I can see why coaches miss."

In giving guidance to players, Gottfried said, "Don't get caught up in the name of the school. After the press conference and the party, you have got to go there and live with the decision. Don't let someone else decide for you.

"When you ask questions, carry a notebook and write down the answers. It gets confusing, and hard to remember who said what. Coaches select the best kids to host recruits, so make a point to talk to other players as well. And talk to them one-on-one, not in a group where they might be very careful what they say. Also, remember that not everyone will tell you the truth. A guy at your position may not want you to come. The best source of information is the head coach, but you have to bear down on them. You also have to try to figure out his standing at the school. Is he likely to get fired, or leave for a better job?

"If you go to a football camp, be ready to perform well. If coaches find out you went to Penn State's camp and they don't offer you, it hurts. And a school like Michigan brings in MAC coaches, from schools which don't compete with the Wolverines for the same players. Even if you know you aren't a Michigan-level player, your camp affects the schools which recruit you," he said.

"In almost every case, your high school coach has to sell you, to promote you to colleges. Some can't do a good job of that, and some won't. But if your size or your 40-yard dash time are not good, that can get you eliminated anyway."

Gottfried had one final word for the player who doesn't get a scholarship, but is encouraged to walk-on and try to earn one. "Watch out. That is really tough. Once you are labeled a walk-on, you may stay there forever. Schools are usually tight on scholarships, so they hate to use one when they have the player already. If a coach makes a promise of a future scholarship, ask for something in writing. Tell him, 'It's for Mom and Dad to see.' Then you'll know how real the offer is."

Chapter II

WOMEN'S BASKETBALL

"We look for good people. I refer to the three A's,

attitude, academics and athletic ability."

Pat Summitt
Head Coach, Tennessee Lady Vols

In 1969, Immaculata College won the first National Intercollegiate Women's Basketball tournament. Most historians proclaim it was the beginning of the modern era in women's collegiate basketball.

That same year one of the early powers of the women's game, Nashville Business College, gave up the sport. NBC had won eight straight AAU championships from 1962-69, when the rules called for a "roving" game, with two stationary forwards, two stationary guards and two players who played the whole court as rovers. The roving game was a big change from the two-court game, with stationary guards and forwards, for those concerned about the gentility of young ladies. Interest in the "five-player" game was growing, and NBC sponsor H. O. Balls withdrew his support because he did not agree with the radical change. The "five-player" game would be used on an experimental basis during the 1969-70 season and officially adopted in 1970.

In 1972, Congress passed legislation known as Title IX, which required funding for women's athletics identical to men's. In 1976, women's basketball was added to the Summer Olympics as a medal sport, and the United States took the silver. The first women's Top 20 ranking was published, in *The Philadelphia Enquirer.* Two years later the *Associated Press* began to carry the ranking. Occasionally, articles appeared about great players like Ann Meyers of UCLA, Carol Blazejowski of Montclair State, Nancy Lieberman of Old Dominion, Lynette Woodward of Kansas and Cheryl Miller of Southern Cal. When Meyers signed with the NBA Indianapolis Pacers and Woodard played for the Harlem Globetrotters, the attention increased. Maybe these women could really play. Apparently, many people already realized that they could. Tennessee drew 24,563 fans to a game with Texas in 1987. Pat Head Summitt led the Olympic team to gold in 1984, and Kay Yow repeated in 1988.

Then came television. The women's finals had been televised before, but in 1991 NBC signed a package deal to broadcast three regular season games, plus both semi-finals. A CBS game between Texas and Tennessee drew a record 2.5 million viewers.

ESPN got involved in an increasing way each year. With ESPN2, there were 64 women's games available in 1996, the most extensive women's NCAA basketball schedule ever featured on national television. The final game between Tennessee and Georgia was the highest-rated women's game in ESPN history. It was their second highest-rated basketball game of the year, behind only the men's Big East Conference final.

In 1996, more than 5.2 million spectators attended women's NCAA basketball games, the 15th consecutive record year.

Throughout the year, Robin Roberts was at the forefront of ESPN's coverage of women's basketball. She had prepared for the role by having an outstanding playing career at Southeastern Louisiana University, where she decided to go after a trip to another college.

"I was on the way home from Louisiana State, which was too big for me at that time in my life," she recalls. "A sign said 'Southeast Louisiana University next right,' and I took it. I liked what I saw, went home and called them." They hadn't called her earlier because bigger schools like Ole Miss, Mississippi State and LSU were involved.

"I wanted to study communications and they didn't offer it, but the coach promised they would. There were two of us in the first classes, a guy who was a photographer and myself, the journalist. I had a lot of great experiences. Also, they let me play both tennis and basketball, which the other schools didn't want me to do."

So now Roberts, in addition to her duties as host of ABC's *Wide World of Sports* and ESPN's *SportsCenter,* is a leading media personality for the booming sport of women's basketball. While pleased with the growth, she sees coaches under pressure to win, which begins with recruiting.

"When coaches called me, I was smart enough to know that everybody wasn't my best friend," she said. "Still, when we had a scrimmage in college and I went up to a coach who recruited me pretty hard, it hurt when she was absolutely rude to me. We're talking about kids here. That's why I praise the good ones [in the profession].

"Two things strike me about the women's game. First, there is such a depth of talent, not just one great player like a Nancy Lieberman or an Ann Meyers. Second, the core of why women play the game is not to get to the NBA. I knew the NBA wasn't after me, so I went to my 8 a.m. class. Even if the new professional leagues develop for women, that won't change," Roberts concludes.

PAT SUMMITT,
YOU DON'T HAVE TO RETIRE TO BE A LEGEND

The best way to introduce Coach Pat Summitt of Tennessee is to say, "She needs no introduction." Consider a few of her impressive credentials.

As a player, she set several records at the University of Tennessee at Martin. She was co-captain of the 1976 U. S. Olympic women's team which won the silver medal in Montreal, and represented her country as a player on four other international teams. She coached the U. S. Olympic team to the gold medal in 1984, and compiled a 63-4 record in international competition. As a college coach she has 596 victories and four NCAA championships at Tennessee, as of 1996. She has taken the Lady Vols to the Final Four nine times, compiling a record of 49-11 while playing in every NCAA tournament. Every player who has been at Tennessee for four years has gone to the Final Four, at least once. Pat Summitt is the E. F. Hutton of women's college basketball—when she talks, people listen.

"Obviously, the women's game has changed tremendously over the years," said the woman who became Tennessee head coach after graduating from UT Martin in 1974. "It began when administrations across the country made a commitment to women's basketball. That had to happen first. They provided resources, which allowed programs to assemble quality coaching staffs, which began to recruit nationally, which served as motivation for young players. With more quality players came more quality teams. When women were placed under the NCAA umbrella for national championships, that was a huge step [in 1982]. It led to national television exposure, which took the game to more players, coaches, fans and media.

"I hope we are ready for the next step, a successful women's pro league. You have to crawl before you walk, and walk before you run. The high school and college games have to be in place first; look how long it took the men. But this is the best time we have had for women's professional basketball, and I would like to believe it will be successful."

After a brief overview of the women's game, Summitt describes the recruiting philosophy at Tennessee, a subject of interest to players throughout the country.

"We look for good people. I refer to the three A's. Most important is Attitude. She must have good character and a solid background. Is she a team player? Unselfish? We want givers, winners, fighters who are goal-oriented. Do they want to compete every day at practice? Do they want a college degree? This is someone who is going to be here for four or five years, so she has to fit in. I have asked the best players, 'Do you want to be the showboat, or be on the showboat?' If they want to be the center of attraction, they probably won't enjoy it here.

"The second A is for Academics. Does she have the potential to be a successful college student? The primary purpose of college coaches is to educate young women, and men. We check into her background. We see the transcript as well as the game film.

"The third A stands for Athletic Ability, and basketball skills. We recruit specific to our needs. There is no point to bring in a player who doesn't have a role in the program, to bring in a player if there is no opportunity at her position. Also, not every player is alike. Some are recruited as role players, some we expect to be starters. Then they determine their position on the team after they get here. We are allowed 15 scholarships, but only have 11 players right now. We lost one recruit late last year and decided not to offer that scholarship, or we would have 12. I think 12 or 13 is about right, considering injuries, playing time and everything.

"There is a myth about Tennessee that we have great players. I've had high school coaches say, 'Do you really think she can play at Tennessee?', almost in awe, because of our presence in the game and our four national championships. We've lost recruits because college coaches told them they would sit on our bench. At 17, they believed what they were told. People form opinions and have perceptions that are not true. Our players are human. Last year we were not the most talented team in the country. We do hope to be top five in talent, but we really want to be the best team.

"We do most of our talent assessment in the summer. We see the athletic ability then, and do our homework in the fall on academics and attitude. AAU play is the single most important place for us to evaluate talent. Because the pool is so large, we usually see the best talent at the AAU nationals. We go to high school games, but AAU is more efficient for us. I've heard about problems with AAU coaches in the men's game, but we haven't seen that. We see people who unselfishly give of their time in the summer. However, the potential for a problem does exist."

After explaining recruiting from the Tennessee point of view, Summitt was asked to reverse roles, and offer guidance to a young athlete facing the recruiting process.

"First, it is real important for the student-athlete to determine the right level of play. A high school coach, or some basketball person, would be helpful here. What is the skill level? Be realistic. I hear from people all the time about 'the best player in the history of the state, or the region, or the county.' There are not as many players who can compete at a high Division I level as people think.

"Second, the player has to establish what is important to her. That is hard for a 17-year-old to know. This is where parents can be very helpful. For example, distance from home either opens or closes a lot of doors. The area of academics is critical. What do you want to do when you grow up? Which schools are strong in that area? How important is playing time? Winning? What kind of coach do you want to play for? Male or female, or does that matter? Demanding? Do you want to play for an established program, or one that is building? What about returning personnel, at your position and at others? The type of climate may be important, or it may not."

With all but two players returning from the 1996 NCAA champions, talented freshmen arriving and outstanding high school players very interested in the Lady Vols, the "climate" in Knoxville, Tennessee looks like it will be attractive for a while.

NANCY LIEBERMAN-CLINE, "LADY MAGIC"

"Lady Magic" is the name fans gave her after Earvin "Magic" Johnson came to town with Michigan State. "He passes the ball just like Nancy," said Old Dominion fans of their 5-foot-10 star. But if Nancy Lieberman had been a Native-American instead of a girl from Queens, she probably would have been called "Pathfinder." In the sport of basketball, she often went where no girl or woman had been, making a path for others to follow.

After her mother forbid football, Nancy turned to basketball. "Boys played football and basketball, girls played kickball and punchball," she recalls. "I knew there were no professional kickball leagues." Her mother said, "Sports are for boys, not girls." Nancy replied, "I'll show you. I'll make history."

Then she began to take the subway, alone, to play for the New York Chuckles AAU team, and the Harlem Hellraisers in a summer league. She got a paper route, to pay for subway tokens and athletic equipment.

Nancy particularly needed money for basketballs, because she worked on her ballhandling all the time. During bad weather, she dribbled in the house, ignoring her mother's complaints about the pounding. Her mother finally took a screwdriver and punctured the ball. Nancy went out and bought another ball, resuming the cycle, which once lasted through five balls. That home was not a place for quitters.

At age 15, Lieberman went to an open try-out for the USA women's basketball team. "There were 150 girls there," she recalls. "I wasn't so strange after all. Other girls loved sports too."

She made the group of 10 players invited to train with athletes from three other sites in Albuquerque, New Mexico, making her one of the 40 best players in the country. But she had to leave when she finally admitted she had been hurt. Fractured ribs and an enlarged spleen were too much to overcome. Her coach said, "Get ready for the 1980 Olympics," in six years. Lieberman was thinking about 1976.

The next year she made the Pan-Am team, which won the gold medal in Mexico City. She was the twelfth player, but this was before her senior year in high school. Then, recruiting started.

Two decades ago in women's basketball might compare to the 1950s in the men's game. Recruiting was regional, because there was no way to find out about players. Schools could not pay for campus visits, and had no budget to travel to visit players. Scholarships were not plentiful; if any, aid was usually limited to quarter- or half-scholarships. However, none of this applied to the recruitment of Nancy Lieberman.

Every coach knew about the high school girl who could outplay All-Americans. Many had seen her in person, so she was more than a legend. She had seen many campuses, and met many coaches, during her travels with USA basketball. About 100 schools had no problem finding a full scholarship for her.

"At 16 or 17, with people telling you how wonderful you are, it's hard to stay away from an ego trip. When you're young, it's hard to know who's for real and who's phony," she said 20 years later. "I never met a coach who didn't have the best school, the best academics and the biggest and newest facilities."

Some things haven't changed.

"Coaches had different techniques," she recalls. "Some went through my mother, some through my friends, some direct to me. Mostly it was talking on the phone. They had unlimited access to me, but I had difficulty getting any reliable information about them. Yet I had a life changing decision to make.

"I seriously considered Cal State-Fullerton, UCLA and Old Dominion. I wanted to play for Billie Moore [one of her Pan-Am coaches], who was at Fullerton at the time. I wanted to go away from home, but I was concerned about going that far. And there was a rumor that she was going to another school, possibly Arizona. I knew I didn't want to transfer and sit out a year. She ended up at UCLA, but I had to decide before she did."

As it turned out, Nancy made the mistake most common in recruiting—signing with the best recruiter.

"Every time I turned around, Pam Parsons of Old Dominion was there. She called me five, six, seven times a day. I have never seen someone work so hard. It was far enough away from home to grow up, but not too far to get back. People said I should go to Delta State or Fullerton to win a championship, but I always liked being with the underdog." It would be Old Dominion's first year as a Division I women's basketball program.

"I remember being in Warrensburg, Missouri, in April for try-outs for the 1976 Olympic team," said Lieberman. "I put my signed letter (of intent) in the mail box. As soon as I let go, I wanted to reach in and pull it back." Too late.

She missed her high school graduation to play for the silver medalists in the Olympics, and remains the youngest member ever to play for the U. S. women's team. Then Nancy Lieberman began college.

After a 23-9 season made difficult by what she calls "mind games" from her coach, Lieberman wanted to leave ODU.

"After that year I wanted to transfer to Tennessee, to play for Pat (Summitt) and to get away from a coach I didn't like," Lieberman remembers. "But Parsons went to South Carolina, and Pat suggested I stay and play for the new coach, Marianne Crawford Stanley [an All-American point guard at Immaculata College in 1976, who Lieberman beat out for a spot on the Olympic team]. Pat thought she had an unfair advantage recruiting me, because she had been head coach at Tennessee for two years when we were teammates on the Olympic team. She told me 'your word is your honor.' I'm glad she convinced me to stay, because Marianne was great. She was a brilliant coach, one of the best I ever played for."

Marianne Stanley is now head coach at California.

Under Stanley's direction, Lieberman learned how to be a point guard. Her scoring went down every year, but assists and team victories went up. She led ODU to a 30-4 record and a National Women's Invitational Tournament title as a sophomore in 1978, then predicted a national championship before the next season began. The

Lady Monarchs won 26 straight before winning the national title with a 35-1 record. They repeated as champions with a 37-1 slate in 1980, when Lieberman won her second Wade Trophy as the outstanding player in the country.

President Carter's boycott of the 1980 Olympics prevented her from seeking her dream of a gold medal, but she continued finding new paths. She played in the New York City Summer League in the backcourt with Nate Archibald and Charlie Criss, generating enormous media attention as a woman playing against NBA players and hopefuls. That led to the Southern California Pro League, where she played for the Lakers and their soon-to-be coach, Pat Riley.

When she arrived at the first practice, she was given the standard Laker bag of equipment and was pointed to the locker room to change "with the rest of the team." She opened the bag, pulled out her official Laker jock and yelled to the trainer, "What do you want me to do with thing? It's way too small for me." The players looked to see what was going on and saw her waving the jock. She was adopted.

At age 22, Nancy Lieberman signed to play for the Dallas Diamonds in the Women's Professional Basketball League. She starred, but the league failed. The same thing happened in 1984. In between, she worked as trainer to Martina Navratilova and revolutionized the approach to training in women's tennis. At age 28, she played in the United States Basketball League with men like Hot Rod Williams and Michael Adams, and for the Utah Jazz in their summer league with Karl Malone. In 1987, she joined the Washington Generals and toured with the Harlem Globetrotters. That led her to do something *really* unusual; she married a teammate on the Generals, Tim Cline. They have a son, T. J., and live in Dallas, where they are involved in athletic promotions.

Nancy Lieberman-Cline was elected to the Basketball Hall of Fame in 1996. She works as color commentator on women's games for several networks, and will probably have something to do with the latest effort for professional women's basketball in the United States. Too bad Rod Serling is no longer with us. He could write a script for "The Twilight Zone" so she could go into a time machine and play in that league. It seems like she has done everything else.

THE USA BASKETBALL NATIONAL TEAM REMEMBERS RECRUITING

Jennifer Azzi, 1990 Naismith Player of the Year when she led Stanford to the national championship, was representing the 1995-96

USA Basketball Women's National Team when she spoke to a group of elementary school students.

"All my life I wanted to be a forest ranger," she said. "When I was about your age, we had an assembly something like this. The speaker asked what we wanted to be when we grew up. When he called on me, I stood up and said I wanted to be a nurse.

"My mother was there. When I got home, she said, 'Did you change your mind after all these years, or did you lie in front of all those people?'

"I said, 'Mom, you know girls aren't supposed to be forest rangers, they are supposed to be teachers or nurses.' You need to know that you can be anything you want to be," said Azzi to her captivated audience.

Then Teresa Edwards, a three-time Olympian who would make her fourth trip in 1996, said, "Don't let anyone tell you you can't reach your goals, or achieve your dreams. The players on the National Team have a dream of setting a path for little girls. I hope that some day, when I'm walking with a cane, a woman will come up to me and say, 'Thanks'."

If those students are lucky, they will not only remember meeting two of the best women basketball players in the world, but also what they said.

In addition to preparing for the 1996 Olympics by winning 52 straight games, for which they logged 100,000 air miles in nine countries; practicing and lifting weights virtually daily; and promoting women's basketball in a variety of ways as they crossed the country to play the nation's best college teams, several members of the team took time to reflect on their recruiting experiences.

"I had a good experience," said team veteran Edwards. "My mother and my coach were very helpful. If colleges are recruiting you hard, they may make promises. The student needs to get advice from people who have her best interests at heart."

One thing these women have in common, in addition to basketball skill and a mission to win the Gold Medal in 1996, is their intense recruitment. They had to select from among a number of outstanding situations when they were in high school.

Azzi went to Stanford from Oak Ridge, Tennessee, deep in the heart of the SEC. "I wanted the best possible education, and I wanted a program where I could come in and make a difference," she recalls. Since Stanford was 13-15 the year before Azzi got there, and 32-1 her senior year, she certainly didn't hurt the program.

"You want to match your goals to what each school has to offer. It's really pretty easy to do, if you have goals," emphasizes the holder of a degree in economics from Stanford.

Carla McGhee went from Peoria, Ill., to the University of Tennessee.

"The player has to know what's important, and for me it was important to get away from the cold," she said with only a slight smile. "Trust is important, too. I had my high school coach handle everything. He told some schools I wasn't interested and I didn't even know they called. I found out he was trying to arrange a package deal for both of us, so I stopped that.

"For me, the most important decision was whether to play on a national championship team or be an All-American. Sometimes you can do both, but usually the best teams have several good players while the All-Americans are the featured player on their teams." The 6-foot-2 McGhee never averaged more than nine points at Tennessee, but was on two national champions. As a member of several international and professional teams, her individual skills have been repeatedly confirmed.

"What do you think, Dawn? You were player of the year. Would you trade that for a national championship?" McGhee asks Dawn Staley, the best player in the country in 1991 and 1992.

"National championship," quickly replies the point guard who patterned her game after NBA star Maurice Cheeks and took Virginia to three NCAA Final Fours. "Easily."

Staley recalls, "I handled the whole thing, because I was afraid to trust anyone. I had a great experience at Virginia, but if I had it to do over I'd put it off on someone else, someone I could trust. I had people coming at me from all over the place, and had to learn to say, 'No,' to have any time. It's best to have an advisor to help."

Rebecca Lobo, the 1995 Player of the Year and the *Associated Press* Female Athlete of the Year in 1996, the "rookie" of the National Team, said, "The rules have changed since I was recruited. The phone calls started during my sophomore year. My mother helped by telling the coaches not to call until after Christmas of my junior year.

"I'd tell young players two things. First, be wary of people who promise you things. I liked Coach Auriemma [who led Connecticut to a 35-0 national championship season in 1995 with Lobo, then the semi-finals without her] because he said, 'I won't promise you you'll start. I'll give you the same opportunity, but you will have to earn your time on the floor.' Second, in making your decision consider things beside basketball, but basketball will be a bigger part of your life than you can imagine. If you have a problem with basketball, whether it's playing time or a problem with a teammate, it will carry over to school."

Ruthie Bolton helped Auburn to four NCAA tournaments (twice runner-up) by the time she graduated in 1989, and continued to expand her game in professional and international competition after that. A transportation specialist as a First Lieutenant in the Army Reserves, she had a special waiver which allowed her to participate with the National team.

"Have an idea what you want to major in," said Bolton. "Basketball may be your No. 1 priority, but school is important too. Some coaches may want you to take easy courses to stay eligible, but if you do that you can't get a job after basketball is over. Also, go where you can help the team, but not too far from home. I was four hours from home (McClain, Miss.). That was close enough that my family got to see me play about 10 times a year, and it helped when I got homesick, particularly freshman year. You go 10 hours away from home, what do you do when you get homesick?"

"Yes, homesick freshman year. I remember that," comments Nikki McCray. "I was six hours away from home. My parents came to every home game played on a weekend.

"I wanted to go where I would become a better player and a better person," continues McCray. "You look at the history of women's basketball, you see [Tennessee Coach] Pat Summitt everywhere. She helped me understand recruiting, because I didn't know what was going on. I wanted to learn from the best, and the SEC is the best conference in women's basketball. Some people are afraid to go there because of all the good players, but Pat's motto is 'defense and effort'. If you play defense, you'll play there," emphasizes the 1994 and 1995 SEC Player of the Year.

"When we played Tennessee, it was the biggest game of the year," interjects Bolton, who finished her career three years before McCray started hers.

Having gained the floor, Bolton said, "Recruits should talk to the seniors, the players who have been at the school for several years. Then try to find one you are comfortable with, and ask about the advantages and disadvantages of the school. No place is perfect, there are always things that are not what you want. The question is, 'What can you deal with?' Ask questions of everyone.

"And," adds Bolton, "don't believe coaches who tell you you will start. They all say that to everyone. My coach said I probably wouldn't play until junior year. I saw that as a challenge, and went anyway. And I started."

"The Tennessee players told me not to expect to start as a freshman," adds McCray, "even though I scored 35 points a game in high school. I didn't expect to start." After sitting out her first year with a torn anterior cruciate ligament, she started the next four years.

The 11 women united in the common purpose of winning in the 1996 Olympics had a lot to say to athletes being heavily recruited in any sport. Additionally, their past actions speak loudly. All 11 have college degrees, as well as gold medals earned through their triumph in Atlanta.

KATIE SMITH, MS. EVERYTHING

Katie Smith from tiny Logan, Ohio, was heavily recruited in high school.

That's what happens when someone is selected Gatorade and Dial National Female Student-Athlete of the Year, after averaging 29 points per game her senior year and 26 points for a four-year career. During that career, Logan High School was 90-14. Her AAU 18-and-under team won the girls basketball national championship. She was all-state in volleyball twice, and won the state shotput (state record) and discus (meet record) titles. Also class valedictorian with a 4.0 average, she received stacks and stacks of letters.

Dr. John Smith, her father, remembers, "The early letters were complimentary; we were glad to get them. They motivated Katie. We saved them all. They will be something for her kids to enjoy."

She started playing organized basketball in fifth grade. "The letters started in eighth grade," she said. "I had gone to the Ohio State and Ohio University camps, and played AAU." Her 13-and-under team went to the nationals that year, something all her AAU teams would do.

The Smith family is very close, and very athletic. Dr. Smith, a graduate of the Ohio State College of Dentistry, received a football scholarship to Ohio University, located about 25 miles from Logan. Katie's older brother, John, played center for Mt. Union's 1993 Division III national football champions. Tom, less than one year younger than she is, is on track scholarship at Ohio University, where he also plays football. As a family, they got an early start on the recruiting process.

"Freshman and sophomore year my parents and I went on unofficial visits," Smith recalls. "We went to Virginia, Tennessee, North Carolina and North Carolina State. I went to Ohio State and OU many times. We wanted to have a manageable number of home visits. I think it turned out to be eight."

But long before the home visits were the phone calls.

"Katie would talk about 20 seconds, then hand the phone to

me," said her father. "She was business-like. She set her goals and worked to accomplish them. I enjoyed talking with the coaches."

Smith remembers, "I wasn't very good at asking questions. My parents helped with that. They also helped me keep from getting a big head. They wanted the best choice for me. They played 'devil's advocate'; whatever I said, they came back with another point of view.

"I was always totally honest with coaches. Now when I see coaches who recruited me, it's great to see them," she said.

The Smith entourage of Katie, her parents, her younger brother, her grandmother and her boyfriend went on official visits to Virginia, Kentucky and Ohio State. "The schools didn't pay for everyone," said Dr. Smith, "but they arranged activities. At Virginia we had 10 people at the table for dinner."

Due to the distance involved, only her father accompanied Katie on her other official visit, to Stanford. "They went all out," he recalled. "They had Stanford jerseys in our hotel rooms, and a video tape of their national championship season. At the game they passed out buttons to the fans with 30 (her number) on them."

"The only negative I can remember from a visit was when one of the coaches tried to pin Katie down to a commitment. She didn't appreciate the pressure," he said.

"The final decision came down to Stanford, with its academic reputation and beautiful campus, or Ohio State, which was close to home and where I wanted to go to dental school," said Smith.

As the adopted daughter of the city of Logan (pop. 7,000 where nearly 2,000 would jam into the high school gymnasium for her games), she made a lot of people happy by selecting Ohio State.

"I wanted to have an impact, contribute if not start," she said years later. She contributed by leading the team in scoring, shooting percentage from the floor, the 3-point line and the foul line, and starting every game. She was named *SI* National Freshman of the Year and made the Kodak All-America team. Quite a contribution, particularly on a team which finished second in the nation.

With hundreds of fans regularly making the trip from Logan, Ohio State led the nation in attendance per game the next year. But the inability to replace three senior starters resulted in a 14-14 record in 1993, followed by a 17-13 mark her junior year. As a senior, Smith set the Big Ten career scoring record, established nine Ohio State records, led the Lady Buckeyes back to the NCAA, was named conference MVP and made several All-America teams. In her final home game, 9,583 fans came to say good-bye to her and her classmates, "including the whole town of Logan," according to the public address announcer.

After Smith scored 20 points against a variety of Penn State defenders and defenses in that last game, visiting coach Rene Portland said, "It's a privilege to play defense on Katie Smith. When you're told to play defense on her, you know you're the best defensive player I have. It does bring out the best in opponents, but they can't do it very long."

Looking back, Katie Smith shared some thoughts with aspiring athletes.

"From high school to AAU to college to USA Basketball, the competition gets more intense. The harder you work, particularly on conditioning, the more you can achieve. Even if you are the best player on the team, you have to push yourself to be a better player. If you and your teammates play each other hard, everyone gets better. In college everyone is athletic, so the mental aspect becomes more important and the game is more physical. Just remember that the yelling from the coaches is not personal."

Regarding recruiting, she said, "Don't pay attention to the letters. Coaches tell you you are good, but it's hard to know. Know what you want to accomplish, have goals and steps along the way, and stay on your path. My parents helped me set goals. For example, they said, 'Don't be a dental hygienist, be a dentist.' With time management you can do things that are important. If you don't pursue your goals, you'll feel like you let yourself down.

"Take unofficial visits. If you are in the area, call the coach even if they don't know you," she continues. "Some questions that might be good to ask during recruiting would be about the academic side, priority scheduling, counseling, your major. What about travel? Our (Big Ten) league games were Friday and Sunday, so we didn't miss much school. Do you travel by bus or charter? Is the housing convenient to the gym and to classes? When and where are meals? What if there is a conflict between class and practice?"

"Of course your teammates are important," she said. "The basketball program is where we spend our life. I didn't expect to have 'best friends' on the team, but I wanted to get along and feel comfortable with them. Playing for different coaches helped me. When I think, 'Nancy [Darsch, head coach at Ohio State] isn't perfect,' I know the others aren't either.

"Most of all, enjoy recruiting. Don't try to do it yourself. No one can do that. One mistake people make is working to get a scholarship. You would be better off working because it is fun to get better. By getting better, hopefully you will deserve a scholarship," she said.

"If you end up in a situation you don't like, find the positives and work hard. It's easy to transfer, but it's seldom the best thing to do."

Katie Smith wanted to make the Olympic team in 1996, but was named an alternate. The next Olympic goal is 2000. In between, she intends to play professional basketball, either in the new U. S. league or overseas. Basketball will be over after the year 2000, replaced by dental school.

Dr. Smith adds his thoughts for the benefit of parents:

"We wanted Katie to look at a lot of different schools, so informal visits were good before she started to reduce the number. AAU was good because it helped her judge her ability. It can be a weeding out process, for girls who decide not to continue. Parents need to know college [athletics] is a tremendous commitment, a big change from high school. It's not as big a shock if you are involved in AAU, especially nationals where the standards are high. Girls need to know colleges contact many to recruit a very few. A marginal girl cannot afford to say 'No' to anybody, because colleges will drop you in a minute. I think it's usually a good idea to stay close to home.

"As a parent, I would ask questions about the eating and living arrangements at a school, particularly when school is not in session [quarter breaks or vacation times, during the athletic season]. Also, are the parents integrated into the athletic program, are there get togethers or brunches so they can meet each other, or are they on the outside?"

Dr. Smith recalls the most difficult aspect of the recruiting process for Katie was notifying the coaches of her decision not to visit their school.

"It was an honor to have been recruited by these successful coaches. In reality, Katie could not have made a bad choice," he concludes.

CARLY FUNICELLO, UCLA RECRUIT

Carly Funicello may aspire to a career like Katie Smith had, but she did not receive letters from college basketball coaches before her freshman year in high school. That's not surprising, since she hadn't begun playing the game before then.

"From the time I was six I played soccer," said the all-state center from Alemony High School in Mission Hills, Calif. "I didn't stop until I was 13."

The footwork developed on the soccer field carried over to basketball. "She's 6-foot-4, but she plays like she's 5-10," said her high school coach, Melissa Hearlihy. In fact, Funicello moves so well, defending her opponent and helping teammates, screening and going to the boards, that her 15 points a game is just one aspect of her total game.

As "sophomore state player of the year, and all-state as a junior," according to her proud mother, Katy, Carly was not hampered by lack of early basketball training. In 1995, the fall of her senior year, she chose UCLA over Connecticut as the best place to continue her athletic improvement while earning a college degree.

Thinking back to her recruitment, Carly said, "That first letter made me feel important, and made me realize there were college scholarships out there. It also made me nervous, because I knew it was special."

Her mother adds, "It was a long process. Every day, every week, it was a different school, depending on who was winning, or who her friends suggested.

"In the summer after her junior year, I remember a big let down," continues Katy. "Everyone had told us about all the phone calls she would get, but there were only a few that first day. It took a while to build up, because all the coaches were at a tournament."

The phone calls led to home visits, which quickly lost their appeal.

"They were stressful," remembers Mrs. Funicello. (No relation to Annette, for anyone remembering the Mouseketeers.) "They lasted three to four hours. I didn't realize they were so long. The coaches were guests in your house, so you felt like you had to fix them something. Carly's three brothers and her sisters were ignored while the coaches were there, and the discussion was all pretty much the same."

Carly took prompt action, cutting 13 scheduled home visits to three, then visiting those three. "I didn't think I needed to spend any more time on it. Not only are you looking at them, they are looking at you. It takes a lot out of you." Connecticut was too far for the self-professed "California girl," and University of California at Santa Barbara "Didn't feel right," so she choose UCLA. "But not because of the men's team," which had won the NCAA championship the previous spring.

"You have to go to the school for yourself," said the future Lady Bruin. "It's not what your friends want, it's what's right for you. I liked UCLA's coaches, the campus and they are strong in my major, which is child development. That's why I signed there."

KRISTEN CLEMENT,
THE LATEST MAGIC JOHNSON COMPARISON

For one long-time basketball fan, watching Kristen Clement play for the first time was a three step process.

During warm-ups the fan said, "So that's her? She's pretty. I wonder if I could introduce her to my son." When the game started, the initial, superficial reaction was replaced by, "She is good. Look at that drive. Look at that pass." By the second quarter the observer was trying to think of a comparable player to the 5-foot-11 junior point guard. Who played with that combination of skill, poise and command of the game? The only answer was a young Magic Johnson, the all-time standard for point guards with the size of an inside player.

"That's what I said, 'Magic Johnson,' when a writer asked me who to compare her to," said Linus McGinty, her coach at Springfield Cardinal O'Hara High School near Philadelphia. "Only she's a better shooter."

While that may sound like just a proud coach, the man with over 300 high school victories found agreement among elite college coaches pursuing Clement. "You can't quote me, due to NCAA rules, but she is a very special player," said one head coach.

Kristen's nickname has long been "Ace". She averaged 22+ points, seven assists and about five steals, setting the school career scoring record in her junior year in 1996. But O'Hara started five girls who projected as Division I college players, so they frequently won blow-outs and pulled their starters. The best way to evaluate her, for those who didn't see her in person, was to look at her performance in big games.

When O'Hara suffered its only loss of the season at No. 2 ranked Christ the King (Queens, NY), she had 22 points and seven rebounds in a low scoring 49-46 game.

At the prestigious Pickerington (Ohio) Holiday Classic, in a field of outstanding teams from across the country, O'Hara rode Clement's diverse game to a championship, and No. 2 ranking in the country at that time.

In the first game, a 65-48 victory over nationally ranked Georgia power Sequoyah, Clement was the leader for the game in scoring and assists. Opposing star LaShonda Stephens, who had already signed to attend Tennessee, said, "In Georgia, we don't have teams that play defense like that." Sequoyah went on to a 26-1 record and their second straight Class 4A state title. In the semi-finals, Clement again led both teams in assists, and added 15 points and eight rebounds.

For the finals, against the host Pickerington Lady Tigers and their partisan fans, Clement threw a change-up. "Coaches scout," she said after a 57-51 victory, "and they saw me pass in the first two games. I thought the passing lanes would be shut down, so I decided to shoot more."

That explained 33 points, on nine of 20 from the field, four of nine from behind the arc, and 11 of 13 at the foul line. She still added game high totals for assists and steals.

Opposing coach Dave Butcher, winner of four Ohio state championships at Pickerington, said, "Kristen Clement is a great player. She played with poise and court presence. Late in the game she got herself to the foul line. She is the complete package."

Asked about her poise and maturity after the game, Clement, County Player of the Year as a freshman, said, "I love to play. I have five older brothers and sisters, and saw some of them make choices which caused them to leave athletics. I have other goals to accomplish in basketball." She is focused on reaching those goals.

In December, Coach McGinty said she was looking for "a Top 20 school, a national contender, one that needed a point guard where she could play soon. She's an honor student, so she can go anywhere she wants. If she finds the right situation she'll probably sign early. That's often better for the player, and definitely better for the coach."

"Our players earn the scholarships with their play, but the exposure Kristen generates is great for all of us," said McGinty. "We had over 2,000 people show up for a regular league game on a Tuesday night."

O'Hara closed their season 27-1, ranked fifth in *USA TODAY's* Super 25, by winning the Philadelphia Catholic League tournament before 8,300 fans. Soon after the end of her season, Clement announced she would "verbally commit to Pat Summitt and the Tennessee Lady Volunteers," then watched her new team win their fourth NCAA title.

"She and her mother did a lot of work the previous year," said McGinty, "taking informal visits to several schools. I thought it would come down to Tennessee and Connecticut, and she always liked Tennessee."

RENE PORTLAND REPLACES A BACKCOURT AT PENN STATE

Penn State went into the 1996 season with a senior backcourt of Tina Nicholson, a talented passer at the point, and Katina Mack, a reliable scorer on the wing. They would lead the Lady Lions to a 25-6 record, a Big Ten tournament title and an NCAA berth. The only thing wrong with such an outstanding combination is that they would have to be replaced the next year.

"Chrissy Falcone and Helen Darling were the two we wanted to replace them," said Coach Rene Portland when recruiting had ended. "Chrissy came to a game with her parents during her junior season. We're like a close family here, we spend a lot of time together as a team and she decided early. I fell in love with Helen before she fell in love with us. She came when we played at Ohio State (Helen's junior year). We lost the game. Since she was there, I felt especially bad that night. She likes our style of play, and decided she wanted to go away from home.

"We saw Chrissy and Helen play together in an all-star game, and sold the combination to them. They both can play point, they both can play '2' and they will do both at Penn State. Chrissy has a lot of spunk, has been running a great high school team for three years and is an excellent three-point shooter. Helen, she has a game face on 24 hours a day. She is physical, can post-up and will be a defensive stopper in the Big Ten for us." The fact that both were National Honor Society students, and both were liked and respected enough at their schools to be elected homecoming queen, didn't hurt either.

For Chrissy Falcone, deciding to play college basketball at Penn State was the easy part of recruiting. The hard part was waiting for them to decide to take her.

"Since seventh grade I've dreamed of playing college basketball," said Falcone after committing. "I visited Penn State informally in February of my junior year, then went to their basketball camp in the summer. When they called in early July, Rene said they were trying to decide who to take, me or three others. She said they would call in two weeks and let me know. Well, it was longer than two weeks," remembers Falcone, who must have suffered waiting for Christmas as a child, "but they called July 29 and asked me to commit. I did."

A three-year starter for Trinity High School in Garfield Heights, near Cleveland, she had a 44 percent career record from the three-point arc and 82 percent mark from the foul line before losing almost her entire senior year to an anterior cruciate ligament injury.

To Falcone, Penn State was in a class by itself because "of their tradition, their success and their history of top-notch point guards. Also their academics are strong in the fields that interest me, either communications or education."

Referred to by Coach Pat Diulus as "the essence of Trinity High School," Falcone advises young athletes to, "work hard. Don't settle for less than your dreams. People tell me I'm short (5-foot-6) but I don't listen to them. At the same time, make sure your academics are good. Basketball will come to an end sometime. Maybe you get injured. When you turn 30, basketball won't be there no matter how good you are."

As the 1996 season approached, Coach Diulus had led the Trojan girls to Ohio state titles in 1990 and 1994, state final-four berths in 1989, 1992 and 1995, and national ranking in *USA TODAY* for eight straight years, while sending players to Purdue, Tennessee, Vanderbilt, Iowa and other Division I schools.

"The last nine years we've had 23 D-I players," said Diulus. "Our program has a reputation for producing quality athletes who produce in high school and college. Colleges know our kids play AAU and lift weights. Colleges tell us if kids don't have that background they are a year behind when they arrive. We tell our kids we strive to give them choices. The better athletes have a cross-section of different schools."

Diulus coaches AAU in the summer, but rather than putting together players from other schools, he coaches the Trinity High School team as an AAU entry. "I care about developing the high school team in the summer," he said.

"AAU is an extremely important off-season activity for a player's development," states Diulus. "But parents need to check with the school and their coach before getting involved in AAU. There are a lot of very good people [coaching AAU], and a lot of frustrated coaches who couldn't get a high school job. I call them '90 day wonders'. They have players out of position, play too many tournaments and may not know the rules. The [athletic] program belongs to the school, not the head coach or the AAU coach."

But as Pat Diulus got the word that Chrissy Falcone would be lost for the season, he wasn't thinking about summer basketball. He had to decide how to compete without one of the best guards in the state. He didn't have to look very far, only to the other side of the backcourt where junior Semeka Randall had starred as a first team All-Ohio sophomore.

"She is faster dribbling the ball than most players are running without it, " Diulus said when he still hoped Falcone would return to set-up Randall and their teammates. But Falcone never returned to regular play and Randall moved to point.

By any standard of measure, the move was a success. Against a schedule including teams from five different states, Trinity went 25-3. Randall averaged 30 points, more than eight rebounds, six assists and an amazing 8.2 steals per game. She was only the second junior to be named Ms. Basketball in the nine year history of the award.

Semeka Randall was at her best during the state tournament. In the semi-finals, she scored 32 points in only 25 minutes. The opposing coach said, "She is wasting her time at Trinity. She should be playing in the NCAA tournament for someone tomorrow." In the finals, Randall scored four lay-ups and a free throw the first four times she touched the ball. Later in the quarter she got out on a break, made a 360-degree spin move to lose the last defender, but flew past the basket. Somehow she slowed her progress in mid-air, kept her head underneath the backboard, reached back and lofted the ball into the basket. It was beyond awesome, it was impossible. When opposing Lima Bath, 27-0 at the time, refused to go away, Randall and teammate Sasha King ran a two-player game throughout the fourth quarter. Randall's two free throws iced the game, which she led in scoring and rebounding.

After her work was done, Randall had some preliminary thoughts about her upcoming choice of college.

"I want to be an impact player," she said. "I'm willing to work my butt off to earn a role, to stay in the gym to improve. I think my skills are better at two-guard, but I'm willing to play any position the coach wants. Right now I'm iffy on my major, maybe physical training or engineering. I came from Cleveland public schools as a freshman, and struggled at first. I've been improving every year, and I've been promising everyone I'll be in the 3.0 area as a senior.

"I think a nice distance would be about an eight hour drive, at the most. I want the overall college experience," she concludes.

With Semeka Randall on the floor, Trinity had a 76-7 record. In 1997, despite the loss of three D-I players, that record may improve.

Only one girl compared to Semeka Randall as the top player in Ohio in 1996, Division I Player of the Year Helen Darling. Her Columbus Brookhaven and AAU Coach Reggie Lee said, "Helen faced the best players in the nation last summer in National AAU competition, and always outplayed her opponent. In high school, it's impossible to find anybody who would work harder. You may find players who are more skilled, but I'd take Helen because of her heart and her will to win. She won't let you down because she wants to win so much. She's very skilled, but her work ethic is exceptional.

"She will be better in college," Lee continues. "Her natural strength is a big plus, but we don't have the facilities for weight training. When she goes to college, that will help her. She'll have time to take 500-600 shots a day, and she'll be playing with better players, so opponents can't concentrate on her."

Deciding on a college was much more difficult for Helen Darling than it was for Chrissy Falcone. After reducing the list to four schools, she had a strong attraction to each one.

"The coach at North Carolina-Charlotte is a lot like Coach Lee, and I've always played for black males," said Darling. "My teammate from last year, Anitra Perry, is at Dayton. I've always liked Penn State, and Ohio State has watched me play since the eighth grade." Two months before signing, Helen sounded like she would be happy at any of the four schools.

Ohio State assistant Melissa McFerrin saw her in that eighth grade game. The Buckeye coaches liked her then and wanted her now, for many reasons.

In the three years since Katie Smith signed, OSU has encountered difficulties in recruiting Ohio players, normally the backbone of the program. "Those three years have not been too good in the state," said McFerrin. "There have only been two or three players a year who could help us."

Besides being a player from Ohio State's backyard, they saw Darling as a point guard and had her a the top of that list. Also, they wanted to bring a defensive presence to the backcourt; she was exactly what the Buckeyes wanted.

Often colleges group two or more players as having similar ability at a position, and decide to take the first one who commits. When abilities are close, this is sound strategy because it prevents being shutout by passing on the others, then finishing second on their first choice. When Ohio State's second-rated point guard recruit, an out-of-state athlete rated ahead of Darling by some observers, wanted to commit, the coaches decided not to accept her. It might send the wrong message to Darling, and they really didn't need two point guards. In the minds of the coaches, Helen was worth the risk. Then, apparent disaster struck.

On their home visit to Darling in September 1995, two assistants accompanied Ohio State Coach Nancy Darsch. In 1994 or before, that would have been allowable because the university was not in session. However, the rule had been changed to prevent schools on the quarter system, which started later than semester schools, from having an advantage. The revised rule stated that schools could send three coaches out only during the July evaluation period. Ohio State had made an illegal contact, and reported it to the NCAA.

The NCAA interpreted the violation as minor, and did not prohibit Darling's recruitment. No disaster after all. Things looked better when Helen announced that she had reduced her list to Ohio

State and Penn State, especially since the Lady Lions had already signed point guard Chrissy Falcone.

Then Helen Darling decided to go to Penn State, "to grow up on my own and be more independent".

After choosing her college, Darling led Brookhaven to a 28-0 season, a state title and No. 8 ranking nationally. Their closest game was a seven point win over perennial power Pickerington in the regionals. She ended her career holding school records for points, assists and steals, and began to think about her future at Penn State.

The future coach of Falcone and Darling, Rene Muth Portland was a member of the 1972-4 Immaculata College teams which won three straight AIAW championships. The 1974 team was inducted into the Basketball Hall of Fame. After coaching two years at St. Joseph's and two at Colorado, she came to Penn State in 1981. Since it was first held in 1982, she has taken the Penn State Lady Lions to every NCAA women's tournament except one. After addressing Penn State's backcourt needs for the 1997 season, she was asked to help girls with college recruiting.

"It is essential to play AAU because July is the key time for colleges," she began. "We only have 20 days during the season, and don't always schedule all of those. The AAU coach has more influence than the high school coach; that's who we talk to in July. And it's important to pick an established team, one that wins and goes to nationals. The summer after sophomore year and the summer after junior years are crucial. Be in the right place at the right time, so coaches see you."

Portland offered some other thoughts on the process:

- "Don't hesitate to send film to colleges. We watch every film that comes in. Send an entire game tape, two if you like. Athleticism shows up more in the flow of the game, and the game is headed in that direction.
- "Be proactive. There are more scholarships out there than there are players, so go get them. If you are interested in a school, let them know. They might be interested in you.
- "Set limits, so you have time to seriously consider your serious choices. Get your list down to, say, 15 by August 1, and seven by September 1. Only accept phone calls on Monday and Wednesday, or Tuesday and Thursday, and have a time limit for each conversation.
- "Finally, when you pick a school, be decent enough to call and tell the other coaches. We had a plane ticket for a girl to visit, she picked another school and never told us. Once a high school coach called to tell me a player was going to

another school. I had a year and one half of my life invested in recruiting her, and she wouldn't call herself.

"The problem [college] coaches have is, sometimes they blow the kid away. We have to improve that. When it happens to me, I always ask [the recruit] why and wish her luck. If the coach is rude, that just proves the player made the right decision," Portland concludes.

PICKERINGTON HIGH SCHOOL, NATIONAL POWER

The 1995 season was disappointing for the Pickerington Lady Tigers basketball team. A No. 5 national ranking by *USA TODAY* with a 25-2 record would be a dream season most places, but fans of this suburban school, located 20 miles east of downtown Columbus, had intended to be first in the nation. Except for an overtime loss to fourth-ranked Stevenson High School in Chicago and a one-point loss in the state semi-finals, they could have been.

With all five starters gone, four to college on scholarship, would 1996 bring a rebuilding season? Not even a consideration. You don't win 92 percent of the time over 12 years, as Coach Dave Butcher had, by rebuilding. Since 1988, the team had only nine losses; there wouldn't be time for rebuilding.

An early indication of the season's success took place at a scrimmage in mid-November, when Columbus Brookhaven stopped over with a team which later won the state title.

James Stocks arrived before the opening tip. The father of two daughters, last year's starter, Amber, on scholarship at Cincinnati, and 6-foot-4 junior Tamara, a priority for many college already, said, "This is the one you wanted to sell tickets to see."

Each team won three quarters. In the final quarter, clock winding down, there was a tournament atmosphere in the sizable crowd. The Lady Tigers were back, never really having left.

Butcher, head coach at Pickerington since 1983, has seen many players recruited by colleges. "Beth Ostendorf was our highest regarded recruit ever," he said without hesitation. In 1995, Ostendorf won every honor in Ohio and made numerous prep All-America teams. It was only her second year at Pickerington, though her fourth as a varsity player.

"At the end of her sophomore year, Urbana [located about 60 miles west of Columbus] was voting on a levy to eliminate athletics," Butcher remembers. "Her parents weren't sure the levy would pass, and didn't want to wait. They called four schools, spoke to guidance counselors and decided on Pickerington.

"Both parents worked in the Urbana area, her father as an assistant principal and her mother as owner of a beauty shop. Since Pickerington has no open enrollment, it was not possible for them to pay tuition to send her here. They had to live here. They put their home in Urbana up for sale, and lived in an apartment here until their house sold. Then they bought a house in Pickerington. They commuted for two years while Beth was in school, and have not moved.

"Her college recruitment was a high stress, high profile situation," said Butcher. "She had hundreds of contacts initially. The parents asked me to be involved. Beth and I talked about things like the pros and cons of signing early. She agonized over not going to Ohio State, so we talked about that a lot, too.

"It finally came down to Vanderbilt, Ohio State, Iowa, Penn State and Virginia. Penn State signed another player, and Virginia decided Beth wasn't interested enough, so they dropped out. Vivian Stringer at Iowa [since moved to Rutgers] went around me, which hurt them with the Ostendorfs. The final two were Vanderbilt and Ohio State," said Butcher.

"Beth wanted to study pharmacy, and both schools were good there. She had goals of being at a Top 10 program, playing on national television, being in the Final Four and possibly playing in the Olympics. At Ohio State, she would have had to follow Katie Smith and be compared to her. Also, their program was not at the same level nationally as Vanderbilt's [28-7 in 1995, versus Ohio State's 17-13]. She liked the idea of going away to school, and chose Vanderbilt," Butcher said.

"The other very high profile recruit from Pickerington was Nicole Sanchez, many years ago. Her father was very involved in the process and the family wanted her to go to Ohio State," Butcher remembers. The Ohio 1986 Player of the Year helped Ohio State win two Big Ten championships, playing in 118 games while she was there.

Susie Cassell was four years behind Sanchez at Pickerington. Ohio Player of the Year in 1990, Cassell led the Lady Tigers to a state title and set school records for free throw shooting and assist average which still stand.

"Ohio State visited in her home, but decided not to recruit her," said Butcher. "I said, 'She's just got it, the fans will love her,' but they thought they had too many point guards. The next year they had injuries and were forced to recruit a point guard." Cassell went to Bowling Green where she started for four years, leading the team to a 75-14 record the last three.

"Then Kim Van Kannal came along," said Butcher. After playing behind Cassell in 1990, Kim started at point for two years. During that time Pickerington was 52-2, with a state championship. "She was comfortable playing behind Susie, then stepping in as a junior, but Bowling Green didn't think she was good enough. She went to Ohio University, where they lost more games in one month than she had since seventh grade, but they turned it around." Ohio University went to the NCAA tournament in 1995.

Butcher's most interesting story came from that year.

"Jenny Anderton is a Mormon. When she was here, she wasn't allowed to practice on Sunday. College coaches would call and say, 'What do we have to do to recruit Jenny?' I'd say, 'Do you have a Mormon church? Do you have Mormon boys?' They'd say 'I don't know.' There were a lot of conversations like that," he smiles.

"In general, I see my role as having an open, helpful discussion with every coach who asks about a player," said Butcher. "I'll have a critical evaluation about the school and the player. I'll try to predict the appropriate level for the player. As for the final decision, that's up to her and her parents.

"Colleges have scholarships," he said. "They are fighting for program players," not just stars.

Pickerington got through its "rebuilding" year with a 23-2 record. One loss was to Cardinal O'Hara, the other to unbeaten state champion Brookhaven. Both opponents were ranked Top 10 nationally. With all five starters returning, Pickerington's Lady Tigers are looking to be one of the best teams in the nation in 1997. Their key player would again be Tamara Stocks, an All-Ohio selection who scored 40 points in leading her team into the regionals.

"I grew up in the projects, the ghetto," said James Stocks, Tamara's father. "We called it 'Brick City.'"

There wasn't much to do except play basketball and get into trouble. Stocks played basketball, at Akron North High School and on the outdoor courts. "Pro players would come by," he remembers. "Gus Johnson was a regular [and an All-Pro in the NBA]. He could dominate when he wanted, but he also taught. He'd beat you on a play, then after the game he'd say, 'Here's what happened and here's what you need to do next time.' It was an education."

That education led to a basketball scholarship to Murray State, and a college degree. As assistant principal with the Columbus Board of Education and a part-time research director for a local radio station, James and his wife, Debby, now live in suburban Pickerington, where their three children have many choices of things to do. They all chose basketball.

Their first child, James, "rebelled against basketball at first, became interested later. It helped the girls to hear us talk about playing," said Stocks.

"I never guessed Amber [born one year after James] would be athletic," said her father. "She was born prematurely, spent the first three or four weeks of her life in an incubator. We thought she could die, but she became very strong physically."

She played on the Pickerington varsity for three years, during which time the team won a state championship, finished second once and lost in the semi-finals once. But college interest started long before that through AAU play, when Cincinnati's 14-and-under team won the state tournament and added her to their team for the national tournament.

"When she went to nationals with them, the mail started to come in truckloads," said Stocks. "She started, played most of the game and they finished in the top 20 out of 70-some teams. The next year they asked her to play with them. They practiced on the weekend, so I dropped her off on Friday, she stayed with the family of one of the players and I picked her up on Sunday.

"The University of Cincinnati got in early on Amber, made a good impression and signed her," said her father. "She had about 100 schools to choose from, and about 50 firm offers."

Now comes Tamara, two years younger than Amber but with 48 varsity games before her junior year.

"I wanted her to play with Amber on the Cincinnati AAU team, but their coach, Deb Gentile, talked me out of it. She said, 'Tamara could play for us, but I don't want her to do it. Because of the two year age difference she'd be ordinary. Let her play with girls her own age and be a star. When basketball is over for the day, she can spend time with her peers, talking about things girls her age are interested in.' It was good advice," Stocks said.

Instead, Tamara teamed with Helen Darling on a team which went to the nationals.

"Tamara had no early interest in basketball, she started as a dancer, ballet and tap. Today she has the attitude of a dancer, to be graceful. Even at 6-foot-4, she looks like everything is effortless, like she's not working hard. She has to add strength, because she'll be the focal point of the team, and there is a lot of contact in the paint," said the former post player.

With Coach Dave Butcher reporting "constant calls, far more than any junior we have had," what are some of the important questions to ask during her recruitment?

"I want to know that the women have parity with the men,"

Stocks said. "Do they have the support of the athletic department? What are the travel accommodations? Are there limits on the books that are provided? When are tutors available? Is summer school paid? Is there a full-time trainer? Is there equal access to weight and strength training and coaching for men and women? Is there a nutritionist? If not, who watches their diet?

"I'll tell Tamara as I told Amber, it wouldn't make sense to try to consider more than 25 schools. Then she can eliminate more based on geography, facilities and players at her position. It's important to ask the school how you fit in. Kentucky wanted Amber as a role player, which wasn't what she wanted."

Asked for advice for other parents, Stocks, part way through his third recruiting cycle, immediately said, "I'm still learning. It is extremely important to visit the school and watch practice, to see which coaches are teachers, which are screamers, and which relate to the players well. Both parents and athletes can also learn about the coach by talking with the players without the coach around. The coaches you want your child to play for arrange for this interaction to take place.

"Tamara, Debby and I visited two schools just before Tamara's junior season started, and it made a tremendous difference in our thinking," Stocks said. "I liked many aspects of one school, but 20 minutes of practice and we were all ready to leave. The other school was more of a secondary possibility, but after watching practice and talking with the coach and the players, we were all very impressed. We are now seriously considering them.

"The other point is to watch the team play a game before choosing a school. In person is best, but tape is not bad. By watching a game, you see what style of play the coach likes. Style of play might not be clear at a practice," he concludes.

DEB GENTILE, PROMOTING A HIGH SCHOOL ATHLETE

"Most high school players have to be sold [promoted] to college coaches," said Deb Gentile, coach of Cincinnati Wyoming High School's girls basketball team and organizer of the local AAU program. "I think it's the responsibility of a high school coach to market the athlete, and help her find the right situation." This philosophy, and a 6-foot-2 junior, small forward prospect named Megan McCabe being evaluated by most of the best women's teams in the country, took Gentile to the Information Superhighway in 1996.

"There are 60 schools following Megan, wanting to know how

she does game by game," said Gentile (pron. Jen-till-e). "We used to mail letters, then we sent faxes. But you dial 60 numbers, someone still has to pay the phone bill. So we're on the Internet, and we E-mail her stats. Many schools have it, others are getting it." And getting it faster because of McCabe.

As Gentile learned long ago, the opportunity to coach a talent like McCabe is a mixed blessing for a high school coach, responsible to win games and promote her players. In high school, McCabe dominates close to the basket. Sometimes that dominance is necessary in a close game, which may be the time a coach travels 1,000 miles to evaluate a player's ability to play in college.

"We had a close game where we kept her inside. She scored 31 points and we won, but Wichita State was disappointed because they wanted to see her outside," said Gentile.

A longtime AAU coach, Gentile sees that forum as valuable in allowing college coaches to observe players at their college positions, while also allowing early exposure.

"I think the best starting point is about age 10 or 11," she said. "As players develop, coaches can start promoting them. I was talking about Megan when she was in eighth grade. She has gotten hundreds of letters; her postman is mad at her.

"Somehow colleges have got to get the player's name. I do that for my players, through word of mouth and letters, but I've seen local players not get scholarships because their coaches didn't promote them. Parents should work with the high school coach. If that doesn't cause the coach to act, send the letters themselves. There is no need to pay hundreds of dollars to a company to send the same letter you could send for a stamp."

Gentile continues, "When letters start to come, don't think form letters mean you are being recruited. They are just the start of the process. But be sure to show interest by promptly completing and returning forms. Do it in five days, so you don't forget. If colleges don't get a reply, they might drop anyone but a blue chip from their lists."

"For coaches going through it the first time it can be overwhelming," she said. "College coaches make 20 home visits to sign three players, and they do it every year. They are experts." Unfortunately, not all show a concern for the well being of young athletes.

"One school recruited a player by bringing a school roster with her name on it, and a jersey with her name on it, to her home on their visit. The player was overwhelmed, but I asked, 'Where is she on your list? How many other players are you recruiting for her position? If she agreed tonight, are you offering her a scholarship?'

"As it turned out, there were three ahead at her position, and they never contacted her again. I called the coach several times, leaving messages that said, 'If you don't want her, tell me.' Now that coach avoids me.

"I have no problem if the college doesn't want my player, but I expect them to say so when they decide. When they string her along it hurts her feelings unnecessarily, and could keep her from another scholarship. But those are the exception. There are also some super people at colleges, very honest."

With only one loss in league play since 1991, and 317 career victories at Wyoming, she knows how to win high school games. When Megan McCabe grabbed a rebound, dribbled the length of the court and hit a 17-foot jump shot to send the game to overtime, where she scored eight more points, Deb Gentile won her first state championship in 1996.

TANYA MCCLURE, A PRODIGY LOOKS AHEAD

High school and college coaches knew about Tanya McClure before her first high school game. Dave Butcher said, "She's the second best point guard in the city." A college recruiter said, "She has an experience level and awareness beyond her years."

McClure scored 30 points in her first game. The performance led to an article in the local paper. She enjoyed the article, but would have traded it for a win for her Gahanna (Ohio) team. As for pressure, she was way past that. She was a veteran.

"I fell in love with basketball when I was five years old," she said. "My brother and I used to play full court in the basement. We made a court with chalk lines, hung hoops at each end, and used a Nurf ball. When I'd go around him he'd push me, sometimes I'd get a black eye. But I loved to play against him."

Since brother Kelly McClure was 11 when they played, and he was an outstanding Division III player when she got to high school, Tanya wasn't about to be intimidated by girls only two or three years older. Besides, there were officials; any referee had to be more impartial than an older brother.

Finally, like many athletes today, Tanya McClure's athletic development had not been confined to school teams. The summer before she had played her fourth year of AAU ball, though for her third different team.

"Like many high school coaches, I worry about AAU," said the Gahanna girls coach of 11 years, Tracey Beverly. "It's good that the players can play, and they do improve, but it is not a very well-controlled environment."

Following the athletic influence of her brother and her father, Willie, who played minor league baseball in the St. Louis Cardinals chain, McClure began playing little league basketball in third grade. That led to playing for an 11-and-under AAU team. When her friends went to another team, McClure went with them. The summer before she entered high school, the Dayton Lady Hoopsters won state AAU for the fourth straight year. They were so impressed by McClure's play that they added her to their roster for nationals, where they finished fourth of 80 teams.

"That caused the colleges to start writing letters," said Coach Beverly. "That, and her play at Blue Star camp in Chapel Hill (NC). Out of 280 players there were so many good ones she didn't make the all-star teams, but people noticed her."

The attention influenced McClure to begin thinking about college before she played in high school. "It was nice to get the letters, even though they were all about the same. They were a little like Christmas cards, only better. Except some Christmas cards have money in them," she smiles, making her look far more like a young girl than a college recruit.

Asked what she wanted to know about recruiting before she could decide which college to pick, she said, "Is it a good school? Does it have what I want? Does it have a good history of basketball? Do I like the coach and the players? Is it close to home?"

Brother Kelly said, "I don't know what I'll tell her about recruiting. Coaches tell you what you want to hear. Start with prayer. I'm glad I don't have to go through it."

For now, McClure, who played with a high school team which had no seniors, will try to have fun gaining experience with her teammates.

Beverly said what makes his young star special is her work ethic and her ability to overcome adversity.

"She works very hard at basketball, she has a love for the game which is very important. She is totally dedicated, and is liked by her teammates. She loves to play when the crowd is into the game. When they are excited, she plays better. And when her Mom passed away last year, she dealt with that by playing better, too. In track [she runs dashes] and basketball both, it was like she was playing for Mom."

For Tanya McClure, college success is far from certain. Some athletes continue to improve, some plateau. Also, the longer a player is in the national spotlight, the more time college coaches have to find shortcomings in her game. McClure will be assessed and re-assessed over the next two years while she receives hundreds of letters. Plus, she is not as tall as colleges would like at 5-foot-5. Will she grow, or be able to play effectively despite her size? As a college recruiter added, "It's harder to tell with females than males. There are the same uncertainties about projecting the future, plus a female body can change in ways that aren't advantageous to athletics."

While colleges wait to see if Tanya McClure becomes the highly-rated recruit she projects to be, they should be thankful she's not a boy. "I love Michigan football and men's basketball," she said. "I always have." If she were a boy, recruiting would be over. The only question would be who would join her in the latest "Fab Five."

JIM CHONES, A PREPARED FATHER

While Tanya McClure has a head-start in recruiting with her father's background in athletics, her brother's knowledge of college basketball and her own experience with AAU, no high school student could expect better assistance in the future than Kaayla Chones. Her father, Jim, spent a lifetime preparing to help her.

As a 6-foot-3 freshman in 1996, Kaayla might feel awkward about her height. Dad could relate.

"I remember being 6-foot-3 in the ninth grade, and walking this cute girl home from school," he said. "All the way I was trying to get the nerve to ask her the big question. Finally we got to her house and I said, 'Can I be your boy friend?' She said, 'No, you're too tall.' It just killed me.

"When Kaayla was 12 years old she was 5-foot-10. She had a knack to rebound, but she was not yet coordinated. That summer, in 1994, she came to me and said, 'Daddy, I want to play basketball and I want to be good.' Her sister, Kareeda, who is on scholarship at Marquette, didn't start to play until her junior year. I told Kaayla how difficult it would be, but she loved the game, as I had. I saw it as a ballet, with the constant motion," said Chones. "Since she loved basketball, her height was an advantage.

"In the summer, I have eight basketball camps. That summer she went to every one; the next summer she went to every one, plus a team camp, drills in the backyard and suicides on the easement at a 30-degree incline. I've been teaching her Kevin McHale moves; the more she learns, the more she wants to learn."

After she started for Ohio state champion Garfield Heights Trinity as a freshman, Kaayla transferred to Eastlake North for the

1997 school year. "We think it will be a better place for Kaayla to develop basketball skills," said her mother, Elores Chones. "Quite a few parents told us the coach is a good teacher, very patient."

The controversy was reminiscent of Jim leaving public school for his senior season, when he led St. Catherine's in Wisconsin to ranking as the best Catholic team in the country.

"How can you deny kids an opportunity to better themselves?" he asks today.

Assuming her interest holds, Kaayla may face intense recruiting pressure from colleges. Dad will be there to guide her.

"At St. Catherine's, the coach had to hire a student secretary to handle all my letters," Jim recalls. "I wanted to see UCLA, but I was afraid to fly that far. When Wisconsin recruited me, Coach John Powlus took me to lunch at the Governor's Mansion. I was a kid from a dead-end street in Racine, and didn't know what to think of a place with marble floors and maids.

"I had a good visit to Michigan State and committed there, but Coach John Bennington died of a heart attack in late June. There was no binding letter then, so I canceled.

"Marquette hadn't recruited me, so my high school coach contacted them," Chones continues. "I was embarrassed when (Coach) Al McGuire came to our house. Our vinyl floor had shredded and rolled up. He went over to the couch, slouched on it and said, 'You've got a nice place here.' There were roaches crawling on the walls. He told my dad, 'I think Jimmy can be a great player, but he has to learn to do what I tell him.' We liked him. When my father died, I began to think of Al as a father-figure. Now, he's more of a big brother.

"When Kaayla and I talk about recruiting, my advice will be to look for three things. First, a coach who is a teacher, not one who plays the best recruits all the time. Big players take time to develop. Second, a winning program over one that is being resurrected, because she needs to learn about winning for life. And, third, education for what she wants to do after basketball.

"There is a conflict between the need for schools to win games by keeping the best athletes eligible to perform, and what is best for the student," said Chones. "You get around that by designing a program based on the strengths and weaknesses of the student to meet both needs. But, realistically, the term should be 'athlete-student'. Adults talk about academics, but sports dominate."

Alabama's Bear Bryant was talking about the reality of the "athlete-student" more than two decades ago; it remains true today.

"Colleges ask children to look at recruiting from a mature perspective, but kids don't know what they are doing. They usually just look at sports. They need mature guidance," feels Chones.

When she attends college, Kaayla will have to adjust to that change. Again, Dad can help.

"The student-athlete is a very complex person. She has so much growing up to do, physically and emotionally. Her expanding perspective of who she is, where she is, that's a form of education. There is a responsibility of knowing, she has to deal with it. A student-athlete is never like a normal student," he said.

In time, Kaayla may have to think about professional basketball. Dad spent two years in the ABA and eight in the NBA as a productive rebounder and scorer, plus nearly two more overseas. He can help there too.

"My grandmother Irene, who was 6-foot-1, was the leader of our family. She helped me understand that pro sports are a job. No excuses, just results. I was not ready for that, physically or mentally. I played for the love of the game, to compete, to feed my ego. It's another conflict, with coaches and players having different goals. Irene helped me refocus during my pro career," he recalls.

Eventually, Kaayla will have to shape a life after sports. Dad took a while to do that, and will be able to help smooth his daughter's path.

"When Washington cut me before the 1983 season, I didn't know what to do except go to Europe to play. I spent a year in Florence and some time in Rome. That was like watching grass grow. My wife and the girls were living in Pepper Pike, in the home we bought in 1979 when I was with Cleveland," recalls Chones.

"One day she [Elores] called me and said, 'I'm pregnant, and the doctor said it's more than one.' I said, 'You're lying.' She said, 'At least three, maybe four.' I said, 'Maybe I'll finally get that boy.' She said, 'The odds are in your favor.' I worked out a deal to leave the team, went home and got three sons." (Kameron, Kendall and Kyle are three years younger than Kaayla, and may be featured in a sequel to this book.)

"I had no preparation for retirement. I woke up in the middle of the night, wondering what I was going to do. After a year and a half I hadn't done anything. When I finally got a job, the guy said, 'Why do you want to be a stock broker?' I said, 'Because I like the suits they wear.' That's the level I was on. But he hired me because I had name recognition, and that's a big part of selling."

While he was a broker, Chones broadcast some Division III basketball games. After nearly four years, he left the brokerage business and took a job with Cleveland Community College in minority development. He started broadcasting Cleveland Cavaliers games, liked it and has been doing that for 10 years. His camps have been open to boys and girls for seven years. In 1994, he founded the Sports Marketing Association, to produce sports marketing projects, and has a radio call-in show. Life after basketball makes sense.

"Athletes are trained to be soldiers. They can't reach the necessary level of efficiency without being consumed by the sport they play. The transition from athlete to citizen is traumatic; people have no idea how difficult it is. Those who survive do it with resiliency, and finally understanding that the same things that led to success in sport—discipline, effort and concentration—lead to success in life," he continues.

As much as Kaayla and Jim Chones have in common, he intends that they will not share a knowledge of poverty. His father went bankrupt twice. For four years the family moved from one relative to another, once being evicted by an aunt for eating a piece of sausage from the stove. "I know about homelessness," he said. When his mother was making salads and washing dishes six days a week, "for five kids who were eating faster than she could buy groceries," he left college to sign a professional basketball contract.

"I took a lot of criticism," said Chones, the second college player to leave school early for the pros. But Al McGuire, who went 25-4 without his best player and might have won a national title if Chones stayed, had no problem with the decision. "My refrigerator has meats and pastries, his is empty," said the coach in support.

Which brings to mind one more thing Jim hopes to share with his daughter, a college degree. "I went back to Marquette four summers in a row," he said, "until our second child was born. I'm still 16 hours short of a degree, but I think I'll be able to finish with correspondence courses."

STAN LEWIS, A FATHER LEARNS THE RULES

Stan Lewis, in the tiny southern Ohio town of Oak Hill, had a lot more to learn about recruiting than Jim Chones. His education began when his daughter was hardly a teenager.

"We were flying to Shreveport, Louisiana, so Jamie [a 5-foot-5 point guard with superb court awareness] could play in the national AAU tournament," Lewis remembers. "I started talking to a nice looking woman wearing a Maryland jacket. I said, 'You going to Shreveport?' She nodded. 'AAU?' She said, 'Yes.' Then she got a worried look on her face and said, 'Who's your daughter?' I said, 'Jamie Lewis' and she ran away. That had never happened to me before.

"Later I saw her sitting with a group of coaches and went up to ask her what I had done to offend her. Apparently she had told the coaches the story already because she said, 'This is Jamie Lewis' father,' and they all ran away," Lewis continues.

Coaches are not allowed to speak with athletes or their parents except on campus before the player's senior year. After that there are specific rules as to contact. But this still wasn't clear to Stan Lewis.

Before one of Jamie's games as a sophomore in 1995, he saw two Ohio State coaches in attendance. "As a funeral director I'm used to working the crowd, and our family had a nice (informal) visit at Ohio State, so I went up to say hello to them," said Lewis.

OSU assistant Melissa McFerrin said, "We can't talk to you." Head Coach Nancy Darsch looked straight ahead at the wall.

"We're out in the sticks, nobody will know," Lewis replied.

"Stan, we can't," McFerrin said.

"Don't worry. You aren't talking to me, I'm talking to you," he continued.

"Stan, we can't," McFerrin repeated.

"So, I finally got the point. Now I know it was nothing personal," smiles Lewis.

"More seriously," he adds, "the hard part is knowing whether to chance the big dream at a school like Tennessee, where they try to recruit a better player every year, or go somewhere else. And it's hard to know who to believe. Then there are the letters; we've got garbage bags full of them. They mean nothing, burn them. They don't mean the school wants you, they just mean you're on a list.

"AAU has been great for Jamie. At a small school in southern Ohio she might never have been seen except for that. The funny thing is, people say, 'Isn't it great to travel to Dallas, Orlando, Salt Lake City?' I'll tell you that an airport is an airport, a gym is a gym, a motel is a motel and food's the same everywhere. Her coach wouldn't let them go to Disney World in Orlando, he said, 'We're here play basketball.'"

Stan Lewis recommends AAU exposure to camps or one day shoot-outs.

"So much depends on who is on your team. With a gunner, Jamie gives the ball up and never sees it again. Basketball is a team game but shoot-outs often aren't. And sponsors tell you college coaches will be there, but usually they aren't. College coaches show up for AAU tournaments though," he said.

When she thinks back to her early days in basketball, Jamie Lewis remembers seeing some of her friends begin to lose interest in the game around age 14. "They still played, but I spent more time on it and they spent less. Thank goodness for boys—they always want to shoot, or work on drills."

On the subject of choosing a college, she was concerned about "liking my teammates, the girls I'm recruited with and the style of play. I like to run and gun!"

Having been through the recruiting process with her son, Jamie's mother, Sherry Lewis, placed a high priority on "finding a school which cares about the person as well as the athlete."

Then, in a preview game days before the 1996 regular season was to start, Jamie Lewis lost her junior year. "She went up to shoot a jump shot, and at the last instant decided to pass," remembers Stan Lewis. "She came down wrong and tore up her ACL.

"None of the career records now, but she's taking it well. It's helped her see there is more to life than basketball. She's way ahead of schedule. She was back for AAU in the summer," he said. "All of the schools that were recruiting her stayed very supportive. Nobody has backed off."

In July, before her senior year, Jamie Lewis announced she would accept a scholarship to Ohio State.

AAU: THE ESSENTIAL, IF UNKNOWN, ELEMENT

A dominant theme of this chapter has been the importance of AAU (Amateur Athletic Union) in receiving a scholarship to play women's basketball in college.

"AAU play is the single most important place for us to evaluate talent," said Tennessee's Pat Summitt.

"AAU was good for her because it allowed her to judge her ability," said Dr. John Smith, father of All-American Katie Smith.

"Extremely important off-season activity for a player's development," said one high school coach, while another adds, "I think the best starting point is about 10 or 11."

Penn State's Rene Portland states, "It is essential to play AAU."

In 1983, less than 8,000 girls registered to play AAU basketball in the United States; by 1995, the number had become nearly 80,000. Every year the rate of increase was at least 8 percent, most years the increase was over 20 percent.

"National AAU has done an extremely good job promoting girls basketball. It is one of the few opportunities for girls to shine in athletics. College coaches tell us national AAU tournaments are a better way to evaluate players than camps," said AAU Senior Sports Manager Eddie Clinton, justifiably proud of the growth of the girls basketball program he oversees.

In light of the 10-fold increase in participation, and the emphasis colleges already place on AAU play, it might seem strange to predict that the future is much brighter than the past. Yet it is the safest bet this side of Las Vegas.

For one thing, eventually local newspapers are going to realize that athletic development takes place in the summer as well as during the school year. Any media exposure, compared to the vacuum which now exists for AAU play, will increase participation.

Clinton is not holding his breath on that score. "We've gotten used to the lack of media coverage," he said. "People don't understand what AAU is and what it does."

A more important development regarding the eminent growth of AAU participation is the involvement of Walt Disney World Co.

The Walt Disney World Sports Complex, scheduled to open in May 1997, will accommodate competition in more than 30 sports. Facilities include a fieldhouse with six NBA-size basketball courts; six baseball fields, including one with 7,500 seats; four softball fields; 11 tennis courts; a track and field complex; four soccer fields; six beach volleyball courts and more. The complex will be located inside Walt Disney World in Orlando, Fla., extending over 183 acres.

"The complex is devoted to providing athletes, fans and all others moved by the spirit of competition an opportunity to be involved in the drama and exhilarating fun of sports every single day," said Reggie Williams, vice president of sports. "Having AAU championships at our first-class facility will increase awareness about their organization and drive enrollment and participation."

"We hope to leverage the facility to increase awareness of AAU," said Alex Vergara, Manager of Sports Marketing at Disney. "We want to increase enrollment in AAU at the grass roots level, hopefully leading to intercollegiate athletics and the Olympics."

In 1996, Disney hosted the national girls 10-and-under basketball tournament, giving it what Vergara calls "the Disney difference." The event served as a test run for 1997, when Disney will host the 10s and 13s, as well as about 40 other AAU events. By 1998, well, who can say?

"We are not sure how the Disney–AAU relationship will develop exactly, but it has huge potential," said Clinton. "It should have a big effect on the younger-aged kids, particularly in basketball and track and field."

In 1995, only 3.2 percent of the girls playing AAU basketball were age 10 or less. Could any company be more attractive to those girls than Disney? Imagine being an AAU coach and asking a 10-year old to go to Disney World. You could sell sand on a beach with that sales pitch.

Obviously the Disney–AAU alliance goes far beyond girls basketball. The appeal applies to every AAU sport, for boys as well as girls. While a young person's passion for Disney may decline a bit with age, that is only a relative condition. Disney holds a strong appeal for all ages.

Young athletes play organized sports sooner, kids of all ages enjoy Disney World and all that it represents, the AAU grows even faster . . . it's just a matter of time.

Even couch potatoes benefit. Because Disney owns ABC and three ESPN stations, all America will be seeing new forms of athletic competition in the future.

Small wonder AAU moved their national headquarters to Orlando.

WENDI HUNTLEY, WALK-ON TO CAPTAIN

Unlike Jamie Lewis, Wendi Huntley did not have to recuperate from an ACL injury before college. But unlike Katie Smith and other athletes mentioned in this chapter, Huntley did not have scholarship offers from top basketball programs before her senior year of high school. Notre Dame Academy in Toledo, Ohio, a private, college-prep Catholic academy for girls, was not exactly a sports factory.

"The only reason we played against other teams my junior year was that I spent my sophomore year convincing the nuns there was enough interest at the school," Huntley recalls. "Before that, basketball was an intra-mural sport."

As graduation approached, there was some interest from small colleges which had seen her in camps, "but you only have a short time to play intercollegiate athletics, and I wanted to try Division I. I knew I had to walk-on to play in college at that level, so I tried to find the best place to do it. I made the decision based largely on basketball," she remembers.

Huntley was able to do that because she had already taken care of her academic responsibilities. As an honor role student at a strong academic school, grades and board scores were no problem.

"I wanted to go to law school," she said. "There are a lot of good schools, so I just had to be sure I didn't get a bad one. Then I had to get good grades wherever I went, and I had to do well on the LSAT (Law School Admissions Test). In case law school did not work out, I thought about teaching English and coaching, or journalism as a way to be involved with sports."

Huntley wanted to play in the Big Ten, so she checked out nearby Michigan. The idea of paying out-of-state tuition for at least one year doomed that idea. "My other considerations were the coaches; the returning players, especially at my position of point guard; and the travel experience," she recalls. "I had been to several camps, so I knew many of the coaches at different schools. I had been to Bowling Green's camp twice. I liked their coaches, they were interested in me, they had a senior point guard and they had participated in tournaments in other states."

Huntley went to Bowling Green and only a made-for-TV movie could have a happier ending. She earned a basketball scholarship for three years, and was team captain as a senior. She graduated with a Bachelor of Science, then graduated from the Ohio State University Law School in 1991. Today she is a practicing attorney for a large law firm, where she specializes in sports law.

Though colleges were not aware of Wendi Huntley as an athlete, she found a way to prove her value, enjoy her sport and use the scholarship process to reach her other goals.

DIXIE JEFFERS, COACHING A DIVISION III POWER

If Wendi Huntley had not found a way to play Division I basketball, she probably would have ended up at a school as unique as Capital (Ohio) University.

"We don't recruit players who we don't think can play at this program, at this level," said Capital Coach Dixie Jeffers, after compiling consecutive Division III national championships and a 63-1 record in 1994 and 1995. "I'll ask a student-athlete, 'Do you think you can play here?' If she wavers, we may waver ourselves. We want a cocky attitude. We had to be selective to create the chemistry which led to the success."

That selectivity is the responsibility of the coaches and the players already in the program.

"We encourage the prospect and her parents to visit together," said Jeffers. "If the parents are divorced, they may all come. We've had eight people at once—two families, grandparents, a real gang. We schedule time for the family to meet with our players without any coaches, so they can ask frank questions and interact. Our players have various backgrounds, city and rural, but they understand hard work and discipline. In 10 years here only once did the players not want a recruit. We didn't take her. After the visit, we want the parents of the recruit to talk with the parents of our players. Parents are part of our recruiting process.

"I look at our recruits and their parents as a consumer, so I sell my product, academics, basketball, social and the quality of their future teammates. At the same time, I'm buying. We want a certain chemistry, so I read the facial expressions as parents interact with their daughter."

Coach Jeffers had some interesting thoughts on male and female athletes.

"You can put the same demands on them, but you have to allow females to do different things as well," she said. "Athletics can be 'everything' for a male, not for a female. When I see burn-out in my players, I know we need to do different things. I played for a male coach in college [at Morehead State University in Kentucky]. He didn't want us to date or to room together. We thought we were cheated out of life experiences by that. Most successful female athletes have fathers really involved in their lives, but those fathers have to realize that their daughters need balance. Females can succeed at many specific goals, more importantly everyday life, through a balanced approach.

"The father–daughter relationship is immense, and wonderful as long as it is not overdone. Fathers tell me how their relationship with their daughter has been enhanced by having something in common, like basketball. The caution is that parents not live their lives through their daughters," said Jeffers.

"Another difference between male and female athletes is, after a fight with his girlfriend, a boy can concentrate on basketball. After a fight with her boyfriend, a girl probably can't. Girls can be petty. They can gang up on one girl, fight and cry. Later they all hug, but they may waste two or three days in between," she adds.

"We don't try to keep players from having experiences, but we constantly teach them to minimize the negatives. You can't carry anger with you. We say it, talk it and drop it. I call it the 'harmony' issue. Life is simple, basketball is simple, but we are all so busy we don't take the time to communicate and get on the same page. We teach communication, respect and discipline, rolled into one. At times I say, 'What's wrong? What do we need to change?' They enjoy having input. Other times they don't have choices.

"Coaching is more complicated than it used to be," Jeffers continues. "It's not just Xs and Os. There are so many dysfunctional families and personal problems. You have to be a friend, mother, sister, psychologist and coach—five parts. Women go to college for the coach. They certainly don't come to Capital for the facilities. Parents tell me they feel comfortable with me. A coach who cares about players knows what's going on in the program. He or she may ignore it, but the coach knows."

Then she touches on the differences between D-I and D-III basketball.

"At this level, you never know who will come back. We lost two seniors (for the 1996 season). They both had two NCAA championships and bad knees, and wondered what more they had to gain. I can see their point. Yet D-I coaches tell me, 'Your players play harder than mine. We give them a scholarship, it seems like they always have their hand out for more.' I've had D-I players work my camp and say, 'This is Heaven. Players actually talk with the coach here.' I think Division I is missing the boat. There are so many restrictions on coaching, so much time spent with the media and so much emphasis on the money, they hardly have time to coach."

Jeffers incorporates the reality of scholarship opportunities into her recruiting approach.

"If they get a scholarship, I'm happy. With my D-I background, I can help them explore the possibilities, as well as address the negatives. But kids don't understand that if D-I isn't interested early, they probably won't be interested. I say, 'Hey listen, if D-I comes that's great. But why not explore my institution? If necessary, you'll have a fallback choice.' Also, they may go D-I, not be happy and may transfer back. I can build a relationship with the student-athlete while D-I schools are deciding who gets the scholarship. Some D-III schools back off when D-I schools get involved. That's a mistake."

In 1996, the Capital women lost in the NCAA tournament to a team they had defeated three times during the season. Within minutes after the end of their 23-5 season, Jeffers was planning on a return to what she considers normal.

"A year from now," she forecast, "this game will be a great lesson for our kids."

Chapter III
MEN'S BASKETBALL

*"It's a pleasure and a privilege to go through
recruiting, but it's not all good."*

Kathy Schindewolf
Mother of recruit Nate Schindewolf

Men's basketball is the perfect sport for the '90s athlete. It's easy to get to the pros, and there's so much money when you arrive. A really top-rated player might go straight to the NBA out of high school, like Kevin Garnett or Kobe Bryant. If not, play a year or two of college, then go. In baseball, you can turn professional immediately after high school, but those bus rides in the minor leagues are nasty. And if you don't go after high school, you have to wait three years, just like football. No, basketball is the answer. The closest thing available to instant gratification.

A fine analysis, except for the facts.

There are unquestionably great NBA stars who left college eligibility behind to claim NBA fame and success. Visible Fab Fivers Chris Webber, Jalen Rose and Juwan Howard; the first five selections in the 1995 draft, including four sophomores and Garnett; nine of the first 10 drafted in 1996 all made a strong impression on collegiate and professional observers. Americans notice the successful; the less successful receive less attention.

Scotty Thurman of Arkansas came out early and was not drafted. Rashard Griffith of Wisconsin was unhappy with his offer and went overseas. Roderick Rhodes of Kentucky declared for the draft, found insufficient interest, and wanted to return to college. Then he decided there was so much talent at Kentucky his playing time would be at risk there, and he transferred to Southern Cal.

So there are successes and sad stories, but most of the time things work out well, right? Let's see.

Since 1979, Brick Oettinger with the North Carolina-based newsletter *ACC area Sports Journal* has been selecting the 10 best prep prospects each year. He's told fans about Ralph Sampson, Sam Perkins, Patrick Ewing and Michael Jordan long before they chose a college, much less began to star in the NBA. His annual Top 10 is a good tool to use in comparing potential to NBA performance.

In the three-year period from 1983-85, 30 players were chosen Top 10. Since then, in a span of time long enough ago to give athletes an opportunity to work their way back to the league after a stint in the CBA or overseas, yet recent enough to include players still in the league, how did these stars—the "can't miss kids"—do in the league?

The players seem to fall into three groups. In the first group are those who had long careers in the NBA, the can't-miss guys who didn't. Most are still playing. Danny Manning has battled injuries, Rod Strickland and Danny Ferry have absorbed a healthy share of criticism, but nine of the 30 played at least five years and truly had careers.

The next group of nine superstars never played in the league, according to *The Official NBA Basketball Encyclopedia.* James Blackmon, Tom Sheehy, Antoine Joubert, Guenther Behnke, Delray Brooks, Kevin Walls, Kevin Madden, Tony Kimbro and Lowell Hamilton attended the best basketball schools, and generally had fine college careers, but they never stepped on an NBA court during a regular season game.

Last, 12 played briefly in the NBA, none of them more than three years. North Carolina's Jeff Lebo played four games, Houston's Ricky Winslow appeared in seven and Georgia's Cedric Henderson played in eight. North Carolina State's Chris Washburn, the third pick of the 1986 Draft by Golden State, played 72 games and was out of the league in two years.

To summarize, of the 30 best high school players in the three-year period from 1983-1985, only 30 percent played in the NBA for more than three years. Put another way, 17 of the 30 played less than 82 games, one full, regular season.

Were they failures? If their only goal was an NBA career, what else would you say? If they ignored all the academic, social and career opportunities which basketball provided because they "knew" they would make the NBA, they blew it. On the other hand, if they got a college degree, spent their university years with outstanding teachers and students preparing for the inevitable life after basketball, they simply entered the next stage of their life sooner than they hoped. If success is based on their life's work, it is still taking shape.

The United Negro College Fund has a theme, "A mind is a terrible thing to waste." For the athlete who single-mindedly pursues an NBA career based on high school success, the chances are high that his theme will be, "A life is a terrible thing to waste."

LES CASON, THE CAN'T-MISS PLAYER WHO DID

Each year there is one name on the lips of every college basketball recruiter, the absolutely can't-miss prospect. When it's Lew Alcindor, Patrick Ewing or Chris Webber, that's one thing. In the fall of 1970, it was Les Cason. That was another.

At East Rutherford High School in New Jersey, Cason scored 535 points as a freshman playing varsity. By senior year, an average game was 30 points and 20 rebounds. One of the few national basketball magazines of the time proclaimed "AMERICA'S #1 PLAYER—LES CASON."

There are dozens of recruiting analysts today; in 1970, there were two. Howard Garfinkel had *High School Basketball Illustrated*. The other written service, which began over 40 years ago, was *Cage Scope*, by Dave Bones of Toledo, Ohio.

Today Bones is still producing *Cage Scope*. He prepares player evaluations for his market, "primarily of college coaches, with some dedicated alumni," at a cost of $195 per year.

In addition to personal evaluation, one source of information has always been questionnaires sent to high school coaches. Bones wrote to Cason's coach and quickly received a reply. "It was a good rundown on Les Cason and a better one on himself," Bones recalls. The 31-year-old coach is now seen on ESPN and ABC. It was Dick Vitale.

Cage Scope's report on Cason read "level-headed youngster ... agility and coordination are something to see ... catlike quickness ... veteran observers rate him at least equal to Alcindor at the same stage ... grades poor due to low reading level ... coach wants maj. col. asst. job." Bones had not seen Cason play; the information came directly from Vitale.

Of course, Cason received a great deal of attention from colleges around the country. He took a paid visit to Long Beach State before the first game of his senior year. There Coach Jerry Tarkanian, who was discussing the possibility of an assistant's job with Vitale, noticed that Cason appeared to be more like 6-foot-8 than his listed 6-foot-11.

With Vitale guiding the 17-year-old through a hectic process, Les Cason announced on November 24, 1970, that he would attend Long Beach State. Vitale denied speculation that he would be hired in a package deal. Since there was no "early signing period," the decision was not final, though Cason considered it closed.

Soon after, an announcement was made that the high school would close. With an elementary school teaching certificate, Vitale was not eligible to coach at a new regional high school in the East Rutherford school system. Besides, he wanted to coach college ball.

After becoming the second-leading scorer in New Jersey high school history, Les Cason was invited to several post-season all-star games. In a time before national AAU competition and exposure camps, these games were exciting. It was the first opportunity to see several highly rated players compete with each other, and to compare their talent.

In the most prestigious game, the Dapper Dan Classic in Pittsburgh, Jerry Tarkanian saw his star play for the first time. Cason, who later said he had pneumonia, played poorly. Tarkanian, according to a friend, "wanted to puke".

As things worked out, Cason graduated "near the bottom of his high school class," according to Vitale, and did not qualify for an NCAA scholarship. Tarkanian was no longer obligated to him. The coaching position which had been mentioned "never became a reality," remembers Vitale.

Cason could have paid his way to Long Beach State, sat out his freshman year, studied and become eligible to play. In theory. In fact, that connection was ancient history. Cason ended up at San Jacinto Junior College in Texas for a year.

"He was very unhappy and called home all the time," recalls Vitale, who arranged for his former player to "enroll in a special program for minority students at Livingston College," a part of Rutgers University where Vitale had been an assistant. Not having accomplished much academically at San Jacinto, Cason entered Livingston as a freshman and sat out his transfer year.

By then, Tom Young was the head coach at Rutgers. He was hired over a disappointed Dick Vitale, who took an assistant's position at Detroit University. Vitale later became head coach at Detroit, before a brief stint with the Detroit Pistons. Cason was academically ineligible for the first semester of the 1974 season, played infrequently the second semester and in 14 games the next season. He never lettered and never played in the NBA.

In addition to *Cage Scope*, Dave Bones has also been involved in Blue Chip basketball camp in Kentucky with Rick Bolus since 1979. He learned long ago to question the opinion of an aggressive, young coach.

THE RECRUITING STRUGGLE

Ian O'Connor of the *New York Daily News* found Cason in Greenwich Village during the Final Four of 1996. Cason said he was out of work, had been arrested 60 times for selling drugs and carried the AIDS virus.

Reflecting on the matter, Dick Vitale said, "Nothing in my coaching resume pains me more than what happened to Leslie Cason. He gave me visibility and opportunity in coaching. I loved him and spent many, many hours with him. There is no doubt this put a strain on my first marriage which led to divorce.

"Unfortunately, he's one of many that happens to. We can tell players about life, but they have to make their own decisions and be accountable for those decisions. When drugs and alcohol are involved, bad things happen," Vitale adds.

"At Magic Johnson's Roundball Classic I told some of the most highly-rated players in the country to watch out for players like David Robinson, who was not heavily recruited but kept working and became the No. 1 player in college basketball. No one can get by on talent alone. Leslie's senior year I told him he wasn't as quick as he had been, that he wasn't playing with the same intensity and emotion. But he was scoring 30 points a game against small schools, leading us to an undefeated season and, therefore, didn't really believe he wasn't improving.

"I tell kids, 'Basketball is a means to an end, not the end itself.' It is a journey that ends for everybody. Even a pro career ends in your 30's; for most, the end is way before that. Use what you learn in basketball to compete, to make it in life," concludes Vitale.

The lesson for every parent and every recruit is that there is no such thing as a "Can't miss prospect." Unless a player is rated the best player in the country, he isn't considered as good as Les Cason. Cason did not succeed on the court. Of the other so-called "All-Americans" that year, none of the first five in the magazine played in the NBA. Conversely, many players who went on to exceptional pro careers, men like David Thompson, John Lucas, David Meyers, Alvin Adams and Maurice Lucas, were not chosen.

DICK DEVENZIO, DUKE GRADUATE

A few years earlier, as a *Parade* magazine high school All-American in the late 1960s, Dick DeVenzio experienced recruiting at its worst before selecting Duke over North Carolina and UCLA. But he doesn't remember it that way, because he didn't let it happen that way.

"Do you know the difference between a dilemma and an opportunity?" he asks today. "A dilemma is spending four years in one prison or another, an opportunity is choosing a college for four years. Yet every year I read about players signing early to get the pressure over. This must be taught to them, because they all say the same thing. Pressure is not having people offer you a $60,000 opportunity."

"This business of pressure and victims is a misconception. The fact is you get to meet all sorts of articulate people, and become more articulate yourself. You learn to ask questions, and process answers. When you are told that Harvard, Yale and some school you never heard of are the three best in a field, and the guy telling you this is from the school you never heard of, it's probably time to wonder," he adds.

"Having a chance to meet and talk with outstanding people in the sports industry is not a bad thing," he reasons. "Not only is it a new experience, it's a once in a lifetime opportunity. It's not like there are guns or drugs involved. If you don't want calls on Tuesday night, ask coaches to call on Wednesday. They want to please you, so that's easy.

"I think its too bad the rules have changed [reducing contact]," he said. "People have less exposure. From the player's perspective, the bigger worry is getting enough information to make an informed decision. Some high school coaches shield the athletes, but should teach them to enjoy the process. Think of the contacts they could develop. Many athletes want to get into coaching after college, so why not have contacts at several schools? It increases the chances of getting that g.a. [graduate assistant] position."

Now a motivational speaker and author, DeVenzio has opinions which are unusual in these politically correct times.

"For an athlete to have sports as a top priority is not a bad thing. How could a great player NOT be thinking about the NBA, for example? But when I talk to high school students I tell them a story to suggest they can have an education, too.

"Imagine you are going to the playground for a game with your basketball under your arm. Out of the corner of your eye you see a $20 bill up in a tree. If it's in a hazardous location you may keep walking, but if it's on a low branch you put down your ball, climb up and get the money, climb down, pick up your ball and go play. You have both," he said.

"Education is there for the taking. You can't play ball 24 hours a day. Unless you sign a pro contract, you have to study to stay eligible. No one can be one-dimensional without getting burned.

Education doesn't have to be the No. 1 priority, but you can still pick up the money [get the degree] and play the game."

He takes a pro-active stance on the recruiting process.

"If you're not being recruited, send letters. Contact the coach yourself; 98 percent of the coaches will follow up. Each coach has two concerns: Can the athlete help us? Can we recruit him or her? If the coach is contacted, half the battle is won. It is not hard to inject yourself into the recruiting process."

Moving on to the subject of choosing a college, DeVenzio remarks, "NCAA officials say 'Don't choose the coach, choose the school'. Come on. After board scores, grades and athletic ability define your choices, you don't have bad schools. Why would you choose Duke over Stanford, or the reverse? Or Louisville over Memphis? Maybe you know more about one than the other, or something about one is more important to you, but there are no bad choices.

"Some more bad advice is that you can flourish in any situation," he continues. "You need to know how you fit into the coach's plans and how the players feel. Not just the current players on the team, but past players for that coach. Get names, not one or two the coach selects but 30. If he can't get that done, he's not a person who can get you a job after graduation, or else he's hiding something."

However logical, contact by a recruit with a "representative of the institution's athletics interests" is an NCAA rules violation. The rule was adopted to protect recruits from alumni, but it hinders them from evaluating choices.

From his personal experience, DeVenzio said, "When I got a snow job from a coach, like 'We have the third best business school in the country,' I'd say 'Would you put that in writing? It will make my mother feel good.' People say things they don't want to see on paper, but if they are willing to write something down, it's probably true. Another example would be, 'We can't give you a scholarship now, but you'll probably get one later.' Say, 'Would you put that in writing? It would mean a lot to my mother.'

"True story," he adds. "Lefty Driesell was at Davidson and my English teacher didn't know anything about the school. Lefty Driesell provided voluminous information about Davidson, which truly is one of the best. Coaches are ready and willing to document the truth which supports their case.

"Dean Smith at North Carolina told me something I'd like all recruits to hear. He said, 'At Chapel Hill, some things will go wrong. Don't think you should have gone elsewhere. If you decide to go somewhere else, don't question that decision later. Make the decision work," remembers DeVenzio. "My freshman year when I had some problems I would have thought about leaving without that specific advice.

"You make choices. At Duke you can't swim in the Pacific Ocean. At UCLA my parents in Pennsylvania couldn't see me play [not many years before ESPN and SportsChannel, anyway]. A sense of regret is inevitable. While I'm not saying never transfer, I am saying persist—find ways to make the situation better. After high school, you have to start over in college academically and socially. It's a big problem for athletes, who hardly ever pick up where they left off. It's hard to start at the bottom, but most have to do it."

AL MCGUIRE, BUYING CARPET

Today sports fans see Al McGuire as a part-time color announcer for college basketball. Yet when Cason and DeVenzio were being recruited, he was one of the most unique, innovative and successful of all college coaches. From 1964-77 he directed the Marquette Warriors to 295 victories against only 80 losses. Since 30 of those defeats took place during his first two seasons, his average record for the next 11 years was 25-5. Under his guidance, Marquette won the NCAA and NIT championships.

Al McGuire is in the Basketball Hall of Fame as a coach, but he could have made it as a personality as well. When Notre Dame fans were heckling him during a game he turned and said, "If you don't behave I'm going back to Marquette to start a football program."

Asked to evaluate himself as a player, he said, "I had a great outside shot, but something happened to it when they made me play indoors."

"I recruited one player a year," recalls McGuire. "My co-coaches gave me one name, I never saw them play and I never went back to their home. I said, 'I came here because I want you, and together we can blow their sweatsocks off. But if you don't come to Marquette, we'll beat you. The best thing you can tell me is 'Yes'. The next best is 'No', because then I'll go get somebody else. Just don't tell me you're going to think about it, don't tell me 'the check is in the mail.'

"Butch Lee went to DeWitt Clinton in New York. He couldn't believe I wanted him without seeing him play. I said 'Butch, there are nine million people in New York. You were All-City two years. Why should I put on a Brooks Brothers suit and sit in a smelly gym to find out you can play?' Butch was born in Panama and almost beat the [1976] U. S. Olympic team single-handed."

This approach resulted in many future NBA players teaming with McGuire. "We were 11 of 13," remembers the man known as Chairman Al. "I lost two New York City kids. Jimmy McMillian went to Columbia and Brian Winters went to South Carolina. It was my style, come in late and close the sale."

Both McMillian and Winters played nine years in the NBA; Winters became coach of the NBA expansion Vancouver Grizzlies.

"The tightness [pressure] in coaching today is not because of the coaching or the recruiting, it's because of the extracurricular dollars. These guys make two to three times their salary with outside interests, and they think they're businessmen. They aren't. They are like pro athletes, they couldn't find a Jewish guy in the Bronx.

"The first thing I want to say about recruiting is I never wanted my son (Allie) to play for me," which he did from 1971-73. "I don't think any son or daughter should play for their parents, college, high school or grade school. The locker room is sacred, out-of-bounds. But he went to North Carolina, talked to Dean Smith, came home and said he didn't want to waste anybody else's money. He wanted to play at Marquette.

"In recruiting, the first thing for the player to decide is the right level. How good is he? The guidance has to come from someone not related to the parents or the high school coach. They are too involved to get the true level. Camps will tell everyone they're great because they want you to pay to come. That's all just stroking. The problem is to be realistic. It's like with an antique. You need an expert to tell if it's in good, very good or mint condition. It could be missing an arm and some people would think it was mint, unless it was Venus. That's pretty good. Missing an arm, Venus. I'm a pro."

Assuming the use of the word 'unique' has become clear by now, McGuire's second priority for succeeding during the recruitment process is finding a school that has "the right courses and the right world. Don't go to the Ivy League if you're not the Ivy League-type. Some of those professors at Harvard and Yale spend twice as much time getting dressed as anybody else because they don't want to look like they put any time into dressing. If you want to wear earrings, go where they wear earrings. You need to connect with the social life of the school. No school has a monopoly on education, though some schools have a monopoly on money. Go where you'll be comfortable. Like Northwestern, they beat Michigan in football this Saturday. Their students will celebrate by reading two books this week instead of one. [It was an amazing development October 7, 1995, before many people entertained the thought that the Wildcats would go to the Rose Bowl within three months.]

"The ballplayer has no ability to make this decision at that age, none, none, none. The parents have to be realistic and not live their lives through their kids. This is the second most important decision the player will make. Who you marry is the most important, who you share your life with, and that usually results from where you go to school," he said. "But every player or parent I ever asked about recruiting just stood there nodding their head, 'Yes, yes, yes.' This is a major, major decision."

McGuire concludes with some specific thoughts:

- "Don't count the letters. If you get one letter, you'll probably get 60."
- "No parent should allow their son or daughter to be put in the post exclusively in high school. It's very hard to learn to play outside if you always played inside, and the odds are you will move outside in college."
- "If you live in the suburbs, before deciding your kid is good watch them play on the blacktop." Find good competition.
- "Don't ever, ever, ever believe what an assistant coach says. You have to hear it from the head coach. 'Are you offering a scholarship? In your offense will I be tied down like Gulliver's Travels, or on strings like Charlie McCarthy?'" (It may be advantageous to frame your own questions.)
- "Recruiting is like someone who buys carpet once in a life-time from someone who sells carpet 50 weeks a year and has been doing it for 15 years. One doesn't know anything, the other knows everything. Who is going to get the best of the deal? Stop shaking your head 'Yes.'"

JOHN WOODEN, ONE-OF-A-KIND

When he was referred to as "The Wizard of Westwood" 25 years ago, it seemed appropriate. After all, his UCLA teams won 10 NCAA basketball championships in 12 years, winning 44 of 45 tournament games. Now, looking back, it seems like an understatement. John Wooden won championships while teaching that playing the game properly was more important than winning, and getting an education was far more important than either. His thundering achievements eclipsed every other coach, then and now.

"In choosing a college, education should be the first consideration, then basketball second, not the reverse as is so often the case," said the quiet man who won seven consecutive NCAA titles. "The college education is the important part, because it can be of great service throughout life. He or she will be an athlete for only a comparatively short time. The athlete must look past the immediate future to see the long term future. A limited few play after college in football or basketball, even though they all think they will.

"Although many, many students are not sure of their major when they go to college, they have about two years to decide. It is not necessary to specialize early. When they decide, it has to be with the long term in mind. The great football coach, Amos Alonzo Stagg was asked after a successful season, 'Is this your best year?' He replied, 'I won't know for 20 years.'

"Young people have difficulty thinking about the future," said Wooden, who won 19 conference championships during his 27 seasons at UCLA. "Parents can help them, but to do that, parents have to separate themselves from the thrill of being recruited. For some parents, and it is more likely in the lower income brackets, being recruited becomes more important than selecting the right school. For example, many parents asked, 'Will my son start early?' I got that far more than 'Will my son get a good education?'

"I could name players who could have played at UCLA, who went elsewhere because I wouldn't promise them they would start. Friends would tell me, 'Tell him he will start. If he's not good enough, he probably won't leave. He'll adjust.' But I'd never do that. When I was asked if he would start, I'd say, 'If I think he's good enough. I'm imperfect, but if I'm wrong, it will hurt me more than the youngster. It's my profession, my judgment.'

"Actually, the best players don't always make the best team," continues Wooden. "That's referred to as chemistry by some. I could name many times when the best player at a position was not a part of the best team. It wasn't necessarily his fault, sometimes habits are so deeply ingrained they can not be broken. I'm not sure I ever had a team when the best five players were the best team. I'm getting old at 85, so I may be forgetting one," he said with a chuckle, "but I can't think of one right now. I do remember one player who came to me and said, 'I should be starting. I know I'm better than (and he mentioned another player).' I said, 'I know you are. Isn't it too bad you are letting him beat you out?'"

When athletes and parents are concerned about finding the proper level of competition, Wooden sees that as a minor problem.

"If the coach recruits an individual [offers a scholarship, not mails a letter] he feels that individual has the talent to be productive. The coach knows better than the youngster or the parent, because of his experience judging talent for the college game. We are all imperfect; a player can fail for many reasons.

"When I recruited a player I said, 'I'm recruiting you for basketball, but that should not be your first concern. Education must be. Then basketball, because that is paying your way. Then social, and there must be some of that. However, if the social takes precedence, you will lose all three," Wooden summarizes.

Denny Crum, former UCLA player and assistant, and a Hall of Fame coach himself at Louisville, refers to Wooden as "the Man O War of coaches and the Secretariat of men." That may be an understatement.

JUD HEATHCOTE, LOOKING BACK IN RETIREMENT

When John Wooden retired at UCLA, Jud Heathcote was coaching at Montana. In 1976, Jud moved to Michigan State, where he won the NCAA with Magic Johnson in 1979 and a total of 340 games. Coach Heathcote retired after the 1995 season.

Some people remember Heathcote for his green blazers, or his head butts after a bad call or a Spartan turnover. Others will remember him for his sense of humor. When people asked what he would do during retirement, he said, "I'm going to work on my book." If anyone said, "I didn't know you were writing a book," he replied, "I'm not! I'm reading one." Then he did write one, *JUD: A Magical Journey*.

But many who knew him well remember a man of strong convictions, who said what he believed, regardless of the circumstances. In short, after 24 years as a college head coach, 19 at Michigan State, the perfect man to ask about recruiting.

"First, you need to face reality in terms of the sophistication of certain players in this day and age," Heathcote begins. "Sometimes they play games with schools. They aren't honest, they are just looking for trips, or something.

"One Detroit kid came to our office on an unofficial visit with two adult males, neither his father. My coaches and I went through our presentation, then these guys sent the player outside to talk to some of our players. Then they said, 'He is an extra-special player, who can do extra-special things on the court, and he deserves extra-special treatment from the school he decides to attend. What do you intend to do if he comes to Michigan State?'

"I said, 'At Michigan State we are going to give him the chance for an extra-special education, and we are going to be sure he gets extra-special coaching.' They said, 'What else?' and I said, 'What else do you have in mind?'

"When they left, I told my coaches, 'If I ever hear that you called him, or talked to him, or wrote him a letter, you are fired.' They said, 'Good,' and he went to another school.

"My coaches saw another player, now in the NBA, receive $500 from his AAU coach as a sophomore in high school.

"I don't know what they are saying, but college coaches are not in love with the AAU process. In most states, high school coaches are not permitted to coach AAU. That often results in guys masquerading as coaches, telling players their high school coach isn't using them properly. They may have the players' best interests at heart, or they may have their own."

Asked about the typical student-athlete, rather than the sophisticated, elite player, Heathcote said, "There are a million factors in the recruiting process, and the recruiting decision. I've seen studies where freshmen and sophomores were asked why they chose certain schools, and they didn't report accurately. I believe the three most important factors, in order of importance, are style of play and playing time, the coach, and the players.

"First, you won't play ahead of the Fab Five.

"The year after Syracuse finished second to Indiana in the NCAA [1987], Jim Boeheim told me, 'We recruited the world, but they saw they wouldn't play so we finished second with all the top players. When the media asked, we said we were recruiting juniors because we had everyone back. It was a crock, but they bought it.'

"It used to be that freshmen sat, sophomores were subs, and juniors and seniors played. Then freshmen wanted to start their first year. Now, the 't' is gone. They expect to 'star' their first year. But even superstars like Kenny Anderson [Georgia Tech for two years, then the NBA] and Allen Iverson [Georgetown two years, then NBA top selection in 1996] struggle in their first year. Many players play and are still disgruntled, as many as are sitting.

"In Division II and III you have kids who love the game; in the upper levels of Division I, players have an obsession with the NBA. If they don't make the progress they think they should on their college team, they start to blame everyone. Usually realization sets in junior year, either they have a real chance or they don't.

"Second, kids sign because of the head coach, or even the assistant coach. They want to have a playing relationship with the coach. I got knocked as a recruiter because I tried to paint as honest a picture for the kid as I could. Many coaches promise a starting position during recruiting, then when the player arrives they backtrack and try to paint a positive picture. They'll say, 'Keep working on this or that,' and hope the player doesn't leave.

"When we had Scott Skiles and Sam Vincent at guards, I tried to sell B. J. Armstrong on the idea of playing as our third guard. (Iowa Coach) George Raveling promised him a starting position at Iowa. B. J. went there; when he didn't start he almost left.

"Don't get sold a bill of goods that isn't there. Analyze the class ahead, and the rest of the class you go in with. Then hope the next class isn't better. You have to beat somebody out to play.

"Some coaches have a forward coming back who averaged 15 points, 10 rebounds but they'll tell a recruit, 'He's just not exactly what we need. You come here, you'll start, we'll have him come off the bench.' Players have to see through that. A career is four years, not four days or four months. But in all honesty, kids and parents don't want to hear that story. They want to hear their kid is better."

"Third, in high school players are together at practice and at games. In college there are meetings, travel, and study tables. Players spend much more time together. They don't all have to be friends, but they have to have mutual respect to get along.

Heathcote then discussed a very difficult part of the recruiting process—evaluation.

"I agree that sometimes players overestimate their abilities, and parents usually do. There's no question that the happiest players are the ones who are playing. But here's the other side. I've talked to dozens of guys who were successful at one level of play, and every one wondered what it would have been like to compete at a higher level.

"Coaches struggle with the same thing. I offered a high school forward, named Shawn Respert, a scholarship over the objections of two assistants because I liked his hands and thought he could convert to guard. The next year my assistants over-ruled me and we took another high school forward, 6-foot-3 Eric Snow.

"Eric struggled as a sophomore, but played because he was the best we had. As a coach I had four or five guys who just worked and worked at the game. Earvin (Magic Johnson) was one of them, but no one worked harder than Eric Snow."

Since Michigan State averaged 20 wins a year while they were in the backcourt together, Respert ended his career second in scoring in Big Ten history after a redshirt year, and Snow was fifth in Big Ten career assists, the Spartan coaches worked through their difficulty pretty well. Considering each coach was wrong half the time, that is.

Heathcote closed on what happens during a home visit.

"All coaches talk about education, graduation rates. I used to say, 'If you don't want to work to get a degree, we don't want you.' Parents love that part of the visit, because they know the importance of education and they want to be sure where the coach stands. The players take education for granted. They can't wait to hear about basketball. If 10 different coaches visited the same home, the education discussion would be very similar, the basketball talk very different.

"At Division III, it's the reverse. Players know the cost, the time sacrifices. With Division II, most players don't go there by choice, they go because the opportunities they wanted didn't work out. When I was at Montana, every good player we had didn't want to be there at first. They were there because they were passed over by the PAC 8 [before Arizona and Arizona State made it the PAC 10]."

KENTUCKY RECRUITING

Throughout the 1996 basketball season, there was speculation was that Kentucky's first string could win the national title and their second string could make the Top 10. The Wildcats appeared to be loaded with talent. By the end of the season, before the Wildcats won the NCAA title, observers contended that Coach Rick Pitino should be a candidate for coach of the year for "keeping 11 McDonald's All-Americans happy while winning games."

While Coach Pitino deserved serious consideration for coaching honors based on a national championship and a 34-2 record, wise decisions made by himself and his staff during the recruiting process put them in a position to enjoy working with all that talent. In a time of athletes with inflated egos, Pitino found a large group of young men who put team above self, victories above scoring average and a championship above everything.

From the stars to the benchwarmers, seemingly every Wildcat fit the mold.

Tony Delk scored 24 points in the title game, but his team high season's average was less than half the 38.6 points he averaged in high school. Reserve Ron Mercer had been selected the Naismith Prep Player of the Year months before contributing a career high 20 points in the final. He chose Kentucky because he wanted to win, not take all the shots. Starting forward Derek Anderson was uncomfortable as the "designated star," so he transferred from Ohio State. He only played 16 minutes, but added 11 points and defensive pressure. Anthony Epps committed to Kentucky as a walk-on, then got a scholarship when more prized recruits went elsewhere. He became the point guard and played 35 minutes in the final game. Mark Pope had been PAC-10 Freshman of the Year at Washington, but took a chance at Kentucky. He worked so hard he was elected co-captain before his first game. Antoine Walker used to be called "out of control," yet chose a coach noted for high expectations. After two years, Walker went to the NBA.

Sophomore Cameron Mills went to Kentucky as a walk-on rather than accept a scholarship from Georgia, where playing time would have been more likely. Mills did not play a key role on the court, but he did not cause any problems for the team by complaining about being 13th man, either. Like his teammates, Mills unselfishly put the team first.

Delray Brooks began his career at Kentucky as assistant strength coach when the 1996 seniors were freshmen, became an assistant coach and received the designation "lead" recruiter from Pitino in April 1995. He provides insight into the recruiting process at Kentucky, while also representing the athlete's side. As a highly publicized recruit himself, he selected Indiana, then transferred.

"I didn't consider style of play in recruiting," remembers Indiana's Mr. Basketball of 1984. "My decision to transfer from Indiana to Providence was purely a basketball decision. I was on the bench, I wanted to play more and I wanted to play a more up-tempo style, more running, pressing and shooting."

That transfer, to play for Pitino at Providence, not only influenced Brooks' coaching career, but his recruiting philosophy.

"The parents and the player have to decide what's important to the kid. I believe it has to be a basketball decision. Any school can provide a good degree if you apply yourself. If you struggle from a basketball standpoint, the rest won't matter. I thought I'd be good enough to play any style," but at the highest levels that wasn't the case. His skills simply weren't as valuable at Indiana, with a motion offense, as Providence, with a faster paced, 3-point-oriented attack.

"I still feel Indiana has the most beautiful campus in the country, and it's a good school. I still get chills when I go back there. Providence was smaller, with less facilities, but I was happier. Basketball is so important, regardless of the NBA, that if the basketball is good, the rest will be good," Brooks continues.

"Go where you can get better as a player. Whether or not they play in the NBA, did they get better? If you see freshmen outplaying juniors, players aren't getting better. On your visit, talk with the players. They'll be honest with you.

"At Kentucky, we recruit on a need basis. We only want players who can play at least a limited amount as freshmen. One role is to contend for a starting position; if not a starter, then play 20-25 minutes a game. The other role is to play 10-15 minutes a game. After arrival results take care of themselves, but that's our thinking during recruiting. Also, we want players who want to be here as much as we want to have them." Kentucky may withdraw a scholarship offer if it is not accepted immediately.

Brooks concludes with two red flags. "If you are being recruited higher than you think you should be, maybe the school is looking for role players. If the coach doesn't make your role clear, you need to ask. Also, if one school knocks the competition, ask yourself, 'Why are they doing that?' It could be lack of confidence or lack of direction in their program."

TWO PLAYERS FOR ONE SCHOLARSHIP

In terms of television coverage and shoe contracts, not many schools are on the same plane as Kentucky. But all schools which offer scholarships have to decide which player gets one. Sometimes they let the players decide.

In the summer of 1991, Ohio University Coach Larry Hunter decided the program needed to recruit a guard who could score consistently outside the 3-point line. He looked at many players, rejecting some and being rejected by others.

Hunter settled on two Ohio high school stars, Gus Johnson of Huron, the Northwest District Player of the Year three times, and Landon Hackim, who averaged 19.8 points as a freshman at Cuyahoga Falls High School and improved it every year. After deciding both would be effective players in the Mid-American Conference, Hunter offered both scholarships. That is, he offered both of them the same scholarship. He did not need two shooting guards, he only needed one.

Johnson accepted the offer and had a good career. As a freshman, he started at point guard before injuring his knee. As a sophomore, he was OU's leading 3-point shooter and played both guard positions for a 25-8 NCAA team. Junior year he played shooting guard as the team won the Preseason NIT and was ranked as high as No. 11 in the country. Yet none of that would have happened for Gus Johnson if he had waited 10 minutes longer to accept the scholarship offer. By then, Landon Hackim had called.

Hackim ended up at Miami (Ohio) University where he set the conference record for 3-point field goals. Among his other career highlights were making first team all-conference as a sophomore and beating Arizona in the NCAA tournament in 1995.

Two players, one opening, the first one to decide gets the scholarship. To recruited athletes who have been told how desirable they are, it is uncomfortable. "I'm not ready to decide . . . I don't like this pressure . . . maybe there is no other player (parents who have hesitated to buy a house or a car might suggest this one) . . . I really like being recruited and don't want it to stop . . . "

Of course, there is the other side. The coach is expected to win games. He may choose to hold a scholarship until the exceptional athlete decides, or he may take the certainty of a good player over a chance of signing a better prospect.

Any coach knows how imperfect the evaluation process is. The best coaches are teachers, and teachers think they can make students better. However, no one can teach an empty classroom. The teacher wants to fill the classroom with qualified prospects, stop recruiting and start teaching. The coach who is essentially a recruiter will concentrate on bringing in the best players, find they aren't as good as he thought, then encourage them to leave so he will have scholarships to give to other players. He has less time to teach, and less inclination.

Basketball Hall of Fame Coach Fred Taylor was an outstanding teacher. His Ohio State teams won five consecutive Big Ten titles from 1960-64, an unmatched accomplishment in the history of that conference. Indiana's Bob Knight, who played on the first three of those champions, said, "Fred Taylor did more to determine how basketball would be played in the Big Ten than any coach in any conference. Coaches changed their approach to defense and their thinking on shot selection because they couldn't beat Ohio State if they didn't."

More than 20 years after resigning, Taylor said, "I think I made a mistake by offering a player a tender, then holding it for him until he reached a final decision. Sometimes that made it too late to get another player. I'd make sure the players and their parents knew how many scholarships had been offered, but you can't stay with just one player forever, then have him go someplace else."

Purdue's Gene Keady puts it this way: "Usually, you have three players you are recruiting at each position. If you are recruiting three positions that year, whoever commits first at each position is the one you take. I don't play games and say 'you are our first recruit, second recruit or third recruit.'"

In 1995, with Johnson entering his senior year, Ohio University wanted to bring in a shooting guard to develop. The coaches particularly liked two Ohio high school seniors for that scholarship: Jason Grunkemeyer of Cincinnati Moeller and Nate Schindewolf of Manchester. After following them during the summer, Larry Hunter offered each one the scholarship. He told the players and their parents the Johnson/Hackim story so everyone understood exactly what was happening.

Grunkemeyer and Schindewolf had visited OU informally as juniors, and knew the program and coaches well. Each was leaning toward committing, but wanted to get as much information as possible before making such a crucial decision. Both scheduled early official visits, Grunkemeyer on the first weekend after Labor Day, Schindewolf, one week later. Schindewolf never got there.

With a plane ticket in hand to fly to Maryland the second weekend after Labor Day, Grunkemeyer canceled that visit and accepted the scholarship to Ohio University. He said, "a lot of it had to do with the fact OU had another player they were recruiting in case they didn't get me. I felt if I didn't commit I might lose that scholarship. I didn't want to take that chance." As for the timing of his decision, he just made it.

"Nate wanted to commit before his visit," said his mother, Kathy Schindewolf. "My words to him were, 'I'd like you to see the school and meet the players before deciding.' We were so close to going [for the visit the next day]. The night the scholarship offer was withdrawn, no one [in our family] agreed with my thinking. As a Christian, I know God answers prayers in different ways. I don't know why, but I believe He intervened and had a different plan for Nate."

It seems reasonable that a player should be able to take a visit before deciding on his school. However, certain players never get a chance to attend certain schools for a variety of reasons. Most aren't good enough, others don't have grades. Some meet both requirements, but play a position which is already well-stocked at their favorite school. In a sense, that is what happened to Nate Schindewolf. The OU shooting guard position had too many players one day before his visit.

Despite the initial disappointment, Schindewolf's future is very bright. He accepted a scholarship to Miami, where he will compete for the position Landon Hackim vacated. Life can be ironic.

As longtime high school coaches, fathers of both Jason Grunkemeyer and Nate Schindewolf have more insight to the recruiting process after going through it with their sons.

"The amount of mail is unbelievable. We must have received 2,500 pieces, and it's meaningless. The problem is, many kids think each letter is a scholarship offer," Jake Grunkemeyer said.

"In July many of the schools were inviting Jason to visit," Jake continues. "His high school coach began to ask, 'Are you offering a scholarship?' Sometimes there was a suggestion, but not a clear offer.

It would be a waste to officially visit a school without a firm offer. In July, you don't know how many visits you will need.

"We investigated the schools thoroughly. I had enough contacts, knew enough people who knew people, to find out what we needed to know. I'm thorough—if I'm raking leaves, I'll rake every leaf. You have to do your homework; college coaches do theirs.

"All coaches sound good on the phone," concludes Jake Grunkemeyer. "You need to know what they are really like. They are all salesmen. There are some quality people, there are others I would not want my son playing for."

Gene Schindewolf, Nate's father and high school coach, was initially reluctant to discuss the recruiting process. It was not completely pleasant. However, he saw the need for parents to realize what might be in store for their children.

"Coaches say things that don't come true; there are letdowns along the way and people show interest, then back off," he said.

"It isn't near as much fun as you would think," adds his wife, Kathy. "It's fun in the beginning, but then the calls would come when Nate would just be eating supper, or doing homework or going to bed. It's tough for a kid to keep up with everything."

And it's tough for parents to get a call from a program which is no longer interested in their son, even if dozens still want him for two different sports.

As a football player, Nate Schindewolf had started three years and was rated the fourth-best senior quarterback in the state by *Ohio Football Recruiting News.* But he preferred basketball. As a junior on a 20-3 team, he averaged 24 points and nearly seven assists per game, making first team all-state. In August, *Ohio Prep Roundball* rated him as the top player in his class and reported that North Carolina was recruiting him. With a 3.8 grade average and a high ACT score, Nate was a recruiter's dream. This recruiting business was going to be fun.

That was until he became a victim of the numbers game.

All colleges start out with a list of hundreds of players, every year. As soon as they get the name of a promising player, say in eighth grade, they send a letter of introduction to the boy's coach. "You always like to be the first one to contact a player," coaches agree.

From this list of several hundred to one thousand, some players don't turn out to be very good, others express no interest in the particular school. The list dwindles to several dozen, all talented, all interested. Since a school may sign three players in an average year, schools drop dozens of interested, talented players every year. Nate Schindewolf went through that.

After some schools backed off in recruiting, and the Oh University opportunity disappeared, he decided on four official vi its. All were close enough to Manchester, near Akron, to visit during football season and to attend for four years of college.

"Four straight weekends we had a football game Friday night, got up early Saturday morning to be on the road by 5 a.m., drove to a school for a visit, then drove back late Sunday night," remembers Kathy. "I'm glad it's over."

"The number one reason he chose Miami was the players," said Gene shortly after his son's decision. "Also, the academics are strong, the program has been successful, he liked the college town atmosphere and it's a four-hour drive. Many of their away games in the conference are much closer than that."

Then, months later, Miami Coach Herb Sendek left to take the coaching position at North Carolina State.

"The coaching change was not difficult for Nate," said his father. "He realized the coach could leave. He had learned it was a business. Plus, Coach [Charlie] Coles was a nice guy during Nate's recruiting. We were pleased he was promoted from assistant."

Coach Schindewolf offers suggestions for parents of a recruited athlete.

"Ask questions. Colleges deal in numbers, parents have just one time to get it right. It's your flesh and blood. When you get answers, were they true or what you wanted to hear? If you are not comfortable with one answer, ask again in another way, or to another person. Do the answers match? How does the coach stand with the administration? Does the administration support the sport? What role will your child play in the system? If the coach leaves, is it still a good choice? Most importantly, don't be pressured into deciding without an official visit. See the players, maybe a practice, get a feel for the atmosphere. It wouldn't be a sound decision without considering those things," he said.

Kathy Schindewolf concludes by saying, "It's a pleasure and a privilege to go through recruiting, but it's not all good."

BRICK OETTINGER, RECRUITING ANALYST

"Brick" Oettinger spearheads the University of North Carolina's involvement with the state prison system as Director of the Correctional Education Program. Since he initiated the position on September 1, 1974, more than 300 inmates from the state's 91 prisons have gone to an actual campus for college courses prior to or upon release. This is in addition to correspondence courses, and is important because the recidivism rate for these college students is seven percent. National studies show a recidivism rate for any other type of program, including work release, of more than 50 percent. "Since it costs $25,000 per year to incarcerate someone," said Oettinger, "we make our argument for funding by using dollars and savings. Humanitarian arguments don't work anyway." The budget has been increased 12-fold since 1977, with no increase in staff and all funds going into programs.

While this is interesting, what does it have to do with recruiting?

Atlantic Coast Conference fans have a fascination with basketball which is unmatched by any other league. While Kentucky and Indiana fans share their passion, the SEC and Big Ten are more generally football conferences. Rabid hoop fans are the rule throughout the ACC.

Years ago, those fans wanted to know where the nation's best high school seniors were going to college; now they want to know where the best freshmen and sophomores are leaning. Since 1977, in his other life as recruiting analyst for the *ACC area Sports Journal,* Brick Oettinger has been telling them.

"I became interested in recruiting in the late 1950s when I was playing high school ball," Oettinger remembers. "I was a stringer for writers, a source, and built-up a network of contacts. I went to the first Capital Classic in 1974 and have been to every one since. And I coached in a prison league for 12 years and got to know the high school officials who worked there. As ACC writers got more and more into recruiting, so did I."

With the perspective of two such different vocations, Oettinger looks at recruiting as something more than "How good is he?" and "What are the chances that he'll go to my alma mater?"

"People who know they won't be playing ball after their early 30's have a big advantage in making their college choice," he said. "They look for a school with something to offer in their major field of study, try to decide where they'll be happy socially and begin to plan a career. When they visit the campus they use their 48 hours wisely. They get to know the players and have fun, and also meet key professors, see the whole campus and ask probing questions. I got to know Steve Wojciechowski during his camp summer [before senior year in high school]. He had good board scores, good grades and knew what he was looking for. He probably would have gone to Duke without basketball. But not many recruits are like him.

Most of them have been taken care of grade wise and had their rear-ends kissed.

"I like the tougher NCAA restrictions. North Carolina turns down 80 percent of its applicants every year. It is limited to 24,000 students by the legislature. Higher test scores and grades narrow the gap between athletes and regular students.

"The money is ridiculous—it reflects on the values of our society—but it's there. Still, the players can't be sure who will get it. Remember Earl Jones of Mt. Hope, West Virginia?" said Oettinger. "There are two or three wash-outs from the Top 10 every year." Jones was regarded by all the experts as the best player in his class, ended up at The University of District of Columbia and played 14 games in the NBA, scoring 13 points.

"Another example is Randy Livingston. Every year the New Orleans AAU team won the national tournament, every year he was MVP. He was amazing. Then he tore his ACL as a camp counselor before he went to LSU, and then he suffered a broken knee cap," Oettinger said. After three years of injuries, Livingston entered the NBA Draft in 1996. He was taken in the second round by Houston, based on his potential if fully healthy.

"I don't like everything about Dean Smith because I know him too well, but he cares about his players going to the NBA when they are ready and he cares about them graduating," Oettinger continues. "[James] Worthy, [J. R.] Reid and [Michael] Jordan all came back two summers after their junior year and all graduated one year behind their class. Dean encouraged them, and had them negotiate contract bonuses they got when they did graduate. It's very hard to graduate if the player leaves after two years, particularly if they weren't on track.

"If players take academics seriously, they can use basketball for business contacts later," said Oettinger. "Steve Previs played in the backcourt with George Karl [Seattle Sonic coach] on the Bob McAdoo, Bobby Jones 1972 North Carolina team. The next year he played [32 games] for the ABA Carolina Cougars, owned by Tedd Munchak. Munchak owned a variety of businesses, was impressed by Steve as a person and hired him as a management trainee when he was cut the next year. Previs shot up the organization. That's the way sports should be used by all athletes. Instead, they often look only at what they can get right now, and wind up not impressing others who could help them later."

HOWARD KEENE,
FATHER OF A TOP 10 RECRUIT REFLECTS

As a consensus Top 10 player in the 1992 recruiting class, 6-foot-5 guard Richard Keene from Collinsville, Ill., had his choice of high-profile programs. That meant he had to eliminate all but one. Fortunately, he had a great deal of support.

"We had a two-parent household which was familiar with sports," explains his father, Howard, the Chief Operating Officer at Rawlings Sporting Goods. "I played college basketball, and so did his high school coach, so he had a lot of input. And it was unusual because the interest was there on the part of the colleges. After NIKE camp we told him, 'Narrow the list to a reasonable working number.' To be included on the list, which was about 10, a school had to commit a scholarship to him. Then we unofficially visited Illinois, Duke, Kansas and Indiana. The only official visit he took was to Duke."

Yet he did not go there.

"Illinois was on probation at the time and couldn't offer official visits. But it came down to Duke and Illinois, which both told him he was their No. 1 shooting guard recruit," said Keene.

"We emphasized that he be comfortable with the environment, since he would be there four or five years. He wanted to play early, which both schools seemed to offer. [Keene became a four year starter for the Illini.] Academically he wasn't sure what he wanted, so flexibility was important. He started in Liberal Arts and Sciences at Illinois. After his sophomore year he went into their new Sports Management program, which allows several business courses. And I talked to him about going away to college. If you go away, sometimes it is not easy to run home when you want to, even though your friends might be able to do it. He was just over two hours from home, which made it easy for my wife and me to get to games."

Howard Keene went from high school in southern Illinois to Louisiana State University, then transferred back to Southern Illinois University at Carbondale for his senior year, which probably did not help Duke's chances.

"For us it was a positive experience," concludes Keene. "The toughest thing for a kid to understand is that colleges recruit so many players. One school told us they start with 100 players, watch them and keep narrowing the list. Another school was recruiting two kids at Richard's position, and planned to take the first to commit. I don't have a problem with that, except he wasn't honest about it until I confronted him. He said, 'That's part of the process.' I didn't feel comfortable with him after that."

JEFF COLLIER, FATHER OF MR. OHIO BASKETBALL

When Jeff Collier decided on a basketball scholarship to Georgia Tech over Nebraska in 1972, the world was very different. "At Tech I went to Coach 'Whack' Hyder's home," he remembers. "When my son was recruited, we had dinner at Bob Knight's home and Bobby Cremins' home. Those are mansions. Things have changed: the money, the pressure, everything."

As a 7-footer with agility and a 3-point shot, Jeff's son, Jason, was one of the top recruits in the nation entering his senior year at Springfield (Ohio) Catholic Central. Through a dual perspective of father and former athlete, Jeff remembers the recruiting process.

"Jason was unique in that he was used to the pressure," said Jeff Collier. "He swam from age seven to 13, and was ranked nationally in the breast stroke. When he got more interested in basketball, he had been through pressure already."

He was also unusual in that he didn't play much AAU ball.

"He had a lot of opportunities, but every time he got involved, the team wouldn't go anywhere. It was difficult finding good coaching. His high school coach wasn't too hot on the idea, because some AAU coaches think they have possession of the kid. With 30-40 games, and the competitive camps, it is easy to get burned out during a summer. Not playing worked out well for him," said Collier.

"Jason got his list down to 10 schools, and we arranged home visits with them. It seemed like every day in September was scheduled. He was worried about saying no to anyone. Then the Xavier coach helped us when he said, 'The second best thing you can tell me is no. That way I don't waste my time.' Jason called five of the schools, and Indiana, Georgia Tech, Duke, North Carolina and Notre Dame were left. They came to our home, and he went to visit their campuses.

"During the visits and the trips, Jason started to get tired. I thought he should see each one before he decided, and told him, 'You feel tired now, but I'm 41 years old and I look back on it as one of the best experiences of my life.' I also told him, looking at schools of this quality, there is only one way you could make a mistake. That would be to go to Indiana and not be able to handle Bobby Knight's disposition,'" Collier smiles.

"Some schools were excellent, but they just didn't feel right. It came down to Indiana and Georgia Tech, and he decided on Indiana. Coach Knight told Jason, 'Brian Evans graduates and you could step into that role if you work hard. If you don't play it will be because you didn't work hard enough.' All coaches said he would have the opportunity to play as a freshman.

"In selecting a college it is important to know what you want. Jason wanted a school which is a contender for the national championship, a winning coach and a place where he would get better as a player. Like everyone his age, he hopes to play after college. He positioned himself with good schools," said Collier.

"One thing he did which I thought was good was go to some open gyms and play with the guys at the school. You can do that [except during official visits] if coaches aren't around, and it lets you know if you are competitive or over your head."

"As far as parents, the coaches will try to recruit you," adds Collier. "We just said, 'We're along for the ride, it's his decision.' And I would say, if anyone tells you they will give you something improper, they would also be the first to take it away. We didn't have a hint of anything like that, but it can happen."

Jason Collier completed his senior year by being named Mr. Ohio Basketball and leading his high school team to the state championship.

For the Collier family, the future will hold 3 ½ hour drives to Bloomington, trips to the store to buy IU clothing and memories of a unique experience. Jeff Collier will always remember seeing his mother-in-law walk over to Bob Knight, put her hand to his lips and say, "Such a nice mouth. Why do all those nasty words come out of it?"

DICK REYNOLDS AND DAMON GOODWIN, DIVISION III

In the Ohio Athletic Conference, the third oldest conference in college athletics, Dick Reynolds of Otterbein and Damon Goodwin of Capital compete as equals. Due to the location of the schools, less than 20 miles apart, they often recruit the same players. As Division III coaches, they do not offer athletic scholarships. National recruiting observers do not rank their incoming classes.

The big difference between the two men is experience. As the 1996 season began, Reynolds held the all-time OAC record with 415 coaching victories, Goodwin had 14 in his one year as head coach.

"I don't like the term 'recruiting,'" said Coach Reynolds. "It sounds like you're selling something. I try to present the school, let you decide if Otterbein fits into your interests, budget and other needs at this time. I tell recruits our priorities are one, family; two, education; and I'd like basketball to be third. I don't focus on basketball, the ego side. I want the kid to choose Otterbein for Otterbein. I don't know what players will make it in our program.

"Nobody knows who fits where. The marketing of kids through exposure camps and shoot-outs is so out of hand that the reality of D-I, D-II and D-III is very clouded. This year I called a player I thought would be a good OAC player and Virginia was visiting him.

"Given the cost of schools, I don't have a problem with a kid playing as high as he can. But here's the choice most have to face: is it better to not play or play sparingly for free, or go to a smaller school, get a more personalized education and play ball for four years? If the NBA is not a realistic factor, get a good degree and enjoy life," said Reynolds. "Television and the press have put grandiose illusions in some kids' heads. D-III is the realization area.

"My wife tells parents, 'It's hard to have my husband yell at your son when you have to pay for it.' But to win at this level you can't have a sometime athlete. My philosophy is to get the best one, two or three D-III players in a 50 mile radius of campus, and establish contact with one or two D-I players who may transfer back later. To compete in D-III at the national level you must have at least one player who could have been D-I with the right fit."

Reynolds has led 11 teams into NCAA tournament play, two to the Final Four. In 1981 the school's all-time leading scorer Ron Stewart was a third team All-America; in 1991 Ohio State transfer James Bradley made first team All-America. They were the cornerstones those top D-III teams needed.

"What's funny is when you hear a Division I president say, 'We can't hire a Division III coach here because they haven't proven they can recruit.' When we recruit, four things can happen: the family doesn't have the necessary money, the player gets a scholarship, he comes to our school or he goes to another D-III school," said Reynolds, citing two more variables than D-I coaches face.

"Division III is a lifestyle, very different from Division I. My shoe contract is to go in the store and buy a pair. But it's nice to know that no one in your conference is cheating. For a conference away game we leave in the afternoon, play the game and return that night. Worst case is we are gone from 2:30 to 12:30. With less recruiting and less media demand, I have time for basketball and time for the players.

"In our conference I can't go to the school or the home to meet with a recruit," he continues. "The only contact I can have is on our campus. In this day and age, kids like to know you are interested in them, so we go see our favorites play often. When they get here, if kids don't go to class, they don't play, whether they are first string or third. I tell parents, 'I'm going to give you back your son as a young man.'"

The lifestyle fits Reynolds, who remembers hearing former NBA coach Hubie Brown speak several years ago. "He said, 'Show me 10 coaches at a major college level who have been somewhere 10 years who don't have a drinking problem, a divorce, been fired or some other major problem. Are you sure you want that?'"

While Damon Goodwin has yet to match Dick Reynolds' coaching accomplishments, he was a recruited athlete out of high school and started on two NCAA teams at the University of Dayton, where he served as graduate assistant for a year. While an assistant at Wittenberg, the team won five conference titles, went to the NCAA tournament four times and won two NCAA titles. In his first year at Capital he was 9-9 in conference play, 14-11 overall.

"We brought in 11 players in our first recruiting class," said Goodwin. "It was a transition type of thing. When we get settled we'll bring in four or five players a year. Some of the Division III powers like Wittenberg bring in 10-12 every year."

Like Otterbein, Capital mails to about 300 prospects before the season, then narrows down the list. "In Ohio every year there are three or four players who end up in Division III who could have been Division I," said Goodwin. "We need to get players like that to be where we want to be. We don't guarantee a spot to anyone, or say, 'If you come we'll stop recruiting someone else. A D-III coach can never tell a good player not to come to school. Then, even if the player qualifies for Division I, he may not get into Capital. The worst high school grade point among our freshmen is 2.7.

"Some of the kids you talk to end up Division I. From our list of the top 15 prospects at the end of the year, six got scholarships. But generally kids have to understand that 95 percent of the time they won't get that scholarship. That's tough for the parents and the kids to accept. The college coach won't be the one to tell them. I have to build a relationship so that when they realize they have to go another direction, they look to me as an alternative," said Goodwin.

"Academically I could tell you how good Capital is, but it wouldn't mean a whole lot. Players and parents have to do research on their own. The question is, 'Where do you want to be five years from now? We sell the business program here. Last year a player walked into a $35,000 a year job," he adds.

After determining that they want a player and that he's likely to qualify, Capital schedules a visit. Unlike the big boys, expenses are not paid.

"During the week he and his parents would arrive around 9 or 10 and stay until about 4:00. I would meet with them briefly, then they would go to Admissions to learn that process. Before lunch they would tour the campus. Two players would take the recruit to lunch, so he could talk openly; I would eat with Mom and Dad so they could be candid. After that they would have time for any special interest the recruit might have. The concluding session is a meeting between the recruit, the parents and me. But all this takes place after a relationship has been established. We get into some personal hopes and dreams, and money is a difficult topic.

"A coach hopes the cost is similar to sending the kid to a state school," said Goodwin. "Then you can discuss the benefits. Sometimes it just doesn't make sense for the player to come to Capital."

In the 1996 season, Otterbein went 12-13. Capital had an 18-7 record, and Damon Goodwin was voted OAC men's basketball coach of the year.

MAX GOOD, PREP SCHOOL COACH

Prep school, that's where kids go to get their grades up to qualify for athletic scholarships, right? Could be. Or, it could be where kids go to be seen by colleges. Maybe the coaches overlooked a player, or maybe the kid matured late and became a college prospect, or maybe the player was in a system which didn't showcase his talent properly. Maybe no one decided a player was worthy of a scholarship, but he hasn't decided to give up the dream. Whether the backboards of basketball or the blackboards of education need work, a prep school like Maine Central Institute addresses both.

"We've had 90 kids here since I came as coach," said Max Good, after six years on the job. "Of the 42 who needed test scores, 38 made them. The others came for exposure. We've won 178 games and lost 12, playing prep schools, junior colleges and Canadian four-year colleges, mostly on the road. We've sent 48 kids to Division I colleges in that time, several more to D-II scholarships, and we send them with the study skills to succeed in the classroom."

In his seventh year, 1996, MCI went 27-4.

Good is a Maine native who attended MCI. After eight years as head coach at Eastern Kentucky, he returned in 1989.

"I take care of basketball in two hours a day, the rest of the time I spend monitoring their social and academic progress. Many people who come here have very high self-esteem athletically and very low self-esteem academically. That can be a dangerous combination. We try to lower one, and raise the other."

On the court Good emphasizes pressure defense and rebounding. He plays up-tempo on offense too. "You don't have to pass the ball 12 times to get a good shot," he believes.

All out athleticism, the game of the '90s. Players love it, but MCI doesn't bring them in unless the student-athlete will benefit.

"We've turned down great athletes we couldn't serve," said Good. "Division I requires a core of 2.0, and won't count our grades in the average. So we can't help the D-I athlete without the core. D-II schools will recognize another year in calculating that core grade. We can help with the test score, if the player wants to work. We don't keep the ones who don't."

The help comes at a school of 500 students located in rural Pittsfield, Maine, pop. 4,500. Hunting, hiking, skiing, fishing, skating and snowmobiling are the primary interests of the residents. Basketball players "try to get that 700, win some basketball games and try not to freeze," according to 6-foot-10 Etdrick Bohannon when he played there in 1992. At that time, 700 was the necessary test score.

One thing they spend a great deal of time doing is getting used to Good, who said, "after me they won't have any problem adjusting to Bob Knight at Indiana or John Chaney at Temple. I tell them to take their scrapbooks and letter jackets and video tapes and trophies and put them where the sun doesn't shine. They had to be good to get here, but once here their past doesn't matter. We're in a rap video, MTV, Beavis and Butt-head age. Kids are a product of that. Young people are screaming for discipline, coaches may be the last bastion of hope for them. Everything we do is in the best interests of the kid, though a casual observer might think we are abusive. It may not be what they want, but it's what they need."

Study tables are mandatory for two hours in the evening. If grades are not acceptable, two hours in the afternoon are added. For some players this is the first supervised studying they have ever done, and it's the easy part.

"If I don't like something that goes on, we have 5 a.m. practice—17 last year," said Good. "Andy Bedard was here in 1995, then he went to Boston College. One of the assistants told him they were going to lift weights at 6:30 a.m. and asked, 'Are you ready for this?' He said 'After playing for Coach Good, I'm ready for Idi Amin.' I don't enjoy my players while they are here, I enjoy their success afterwards. Players call and say it is easier in college than it was here. I want to make sure when players leave here they will be low maintenance, self-reliant. The behavior they learn here has to be internalized, not something they do because we expect it.

"One college coach said, 'I like the idea that with an MCI player you get a college sophomore with four years of eligibility.' The first year away from home is very difficult. We absorb that, eliminate most of the problems at college."

MCI and Good have produced a number of success stories so far. Sam Cassell of the Houston Rockets went from MCI to NBA titles. Purdue had three MCI players in 1996. Alumni Johnny Rhodes of Maryland, Miles Tarver at Minnesota and Kellili Taylor at Pittsburgh showed up on ESPN.

While James Stocks did not play on television, he's an MCI success story too.

Stocks didn't particularly like basketball growing up, quitting the school team twice. Following a growth spurt he became a 6-foot-4 starting guard for the varsity, a classic late bloomer out of sync with the recruiting cycle. Scholarship decisions had been made long ago.

He went to MCI for exposure.

"James called after the first open gym and said, 'Dad, these guys are phenomenal,'" remembers his father, James. "Out of 15, I'm either 14th or 15th. Since 11 travel, I said, 'You know what you have to do.'"

"The open gym exposure was remarkable; he had D-II offers before he played a game for MCI. Though they played against older, stronger players, MCI had a lot of blow-outs. James played then, but it was in practice where he improved the most. And it helped him to be around city kids and see how hungry they were. They would play, or even go lift, when they had time for fun. He got so big and strong I hardly recognized him when he came home. And now he's on scholarship at University of Massachusetts-Lowell (D-II), near Boston," said Stocks.

After one year, James Stocks decided to transfer to the University of Cincinnati, where he planned to join the basketball team as a walk-on. "He wanted a more up-tempo style of play," said his father.

MIKE PRICE,
NO CONFLICT BETWEEN HIGH SCHOOL AND AAU

While Max Good has an unusual place in the recruiting process as a prep school coach, Mike Price has two roles which are common to almost every recruiting situation in college basketball. He is both a high school coach and AAU coach, having decided to keep both roles rather than become a college assistant coach.

"I thought it over," said Price about the positions he was offered in the summer of 1995, "and decided that what I like to do is coach basketball. NCAA coaches have time restrictions about working with their players. Here I can work much more with our players, and also spend time working with other players on the AAU team."

The man liked coaching basketball too much to be a college basketball coach.

Varsity coach at Oak Hills High School in Cincinnati, where he also serves as athletic director, Price started the AAU program for Cincinnati boys eight years ago "for selfish reasons. I wanted our players to have a place to play in the summer.

"The girls AAU program is way ahead of the boys in Cincinnati and throughout Ohio," he continues. Still, there were 13 traveling teams from age 11 to age 17 playing in 1995. The 13-and-under team finished 33-10, with four tournament titles; the 15-and-under team was 40-4, and five championships; while the 17-and-under team was 46-9, with three tournament titles and fifth place at the AAU Nationals. Price coached the 17s.

The cohesiveness of the Cincinnati team was apparent when they won the adidas Summer Shootout in July. After a spring and summer traveling and competing together, they played with passion, winning the tournament despite the fact that one player had a form of pneumonia. Doctors said it was caused by playing in air-conditioned gyms, then going outside to 90 degree heat.

In addition to coaching, Price also spent a great deal of time discussing his players with college coaches. The coaches were anxious to find out about these players who didn't seem to lose games, or to improve their position with players they were already recruiting. Coaches were prohibited from talking to the players or their parents by NCAA rules.

"Many of the coaches wanted to discuss the need for Dave Esterkamp or Chad Kamstra to be more athletic in order to play at the Division I level," Price shrugs. "I kept telling them Esterkamp is an outstanding baseball player, and Kamstra was an excellent wide-receiver before dropping football for basketball."

Esterkamp earned a scholarship to Bowling Green, while Kamstra signed with Toledo. For the next four years those AAU teammates will battle in the Mid-American Conference just like they did in the Greater Catholic League during high school.

Another AAU teammate and GCL opponent, Mike Marshall of St. Xavier, never left any question about his athleticism, but surprised everyone by his choice of college scholarships.

Discussing a shoulder separation, Marshall said, "My first

thought when it happened was, 'I might lose basketball.' Then I noticed how much it hurt." He was considered one of the top linebackers in the country, and actually playing football when he suffered the injury. Yet his first thought was about basketball, which college coaches felt he played pretty well for a football player.

Football always came first for the soft-spoken Marshall, until he was hurt as a freshman. "I played on the freshman team in basketball and started to take it seriously," he remembers.

After a summer of AAU basketball, Marshall switched to football in August. Halfway through his sophomore year he was starting and coming to the attention of college coaches. He remembers thinking, "This doesn't compare to basketball."

Basketball Coach Dick Berning moved Marshall to varsity in the middle of that sophomore year. He was doing well, for a football player. Then, during his second summer of AAU basketball, Marshall began to seriously question which sport was for him.

"All during football season [junior year], basketball was in the back of my mind," said Marshall. "My teammates knew what I was going through."

College football coaches knew this kid could play linebacker for them. At 6-foot-3, 225-pounds with 4.5 speed in the 40-yard dash, he was labeled "can't miss." *BLUECHIP ILLUSTRATED* rated him among the 10 best linebackers in the nation. Penn State, Illinois and Michigan State wanted him to visit. However, Marshall was looking forward to basketball season, where he would average 14 points and eight rebounds as a junior.

The spring of his junior year, he went to Oak Hills High School for some basketball drills with Price. "When his father picked him up, I complemented Mike on his work and improvement," remembers Price. "Then I added, 'Especially since you are so much better in football.' Both father and son turned and gave me a 'if looks could kill' glance. That's when I began to suspect something unusual was going on."

That summer Marshall played an undersized power forward on the AAU team which finished fifth nationally. "I played well against players listed as the best in the country, and decided I could play at that level," Marshall recalls.

Price told basketball recruiters Marshall might take a basketball scholarship despite his football ability. Bowling Green, Davidson, North Carolina-Wilmington and Butler made offers.

While Marshall has a near-perfect football body, that was not so in basketball. Because of his leaping ability, he played inside in high school. In college he will be too short for power forward, so he will have to move out on the floor. Some players can't make that adjustment. But now Marshall knew that several programs would allow him to try.

As a senior co-captain, he spent a month with the football team in August. He asked an assistant coach who had played college football what that was like, and was told, "It's a business in college." Marshall enjoyed the Friday night games, but not the thought of 10 more weeks of practice. On August 23, he dropped off the football team.

"My teammates understood," said Marshall.

Football Coach Steve Rasso said, "He could have gone anywhere he wanted. I've never had a better one."

People who didn't know him couldn't believe it. When they asked why he gave up football fame and a likely NFL career, the wise-beyond-his-years teenager simply said, "It's a decision I made and I'll have to live with it."

Marshall decided Butler was the place for him. "They want me to swing between the forward positions at first, then eventually move to 2-guard as my skills develop," he said. "I'll major in marketing."

A lot of hard work stands between him and success as a college guard. Some would see that as a problem, but for Marshall it is an opportunity. "I love to play basketball, and I love to practice it," he said. "It's like a release for me; it gives me a chance to express myself."

Butler's football program is Division I-AA. Marshall did not speak with the coach before signing the basketball letter of intent. So the most heavily recruited football player in the school can be found on the basketball court, doing what he loves. Did he make a mistake? How many adults can say they love what they do?

Without AAU, Mike Marshall may not have decided he preferred basketball to football. Without AAU, colleges may not have believed he could help their teams. Yet, only the most devoted basketball fans are aware of the importance of AAU play.

"The media doesn't follow anything we do," said Price.

Because NCAA rules restrict the number of times coaches can watch high school games, talent evaluation takes place primarily in July, at competition camps and AAU tournaments. For great athletes who jump higher and dribble better than others, camps may be fine. But for players who excel at team-defense or moving without the ball, AAU is a much better showcase. On the right team, of course. Some AAU teams look like camp games that never stop. The Cincinnati team was an example of a situation where good players playing unselfishly beat more publicized players. College coaches noticed the team first, then the players who made up the team. The result was increased scholarship offers.

Given the importance of finding a good AAU situation, Price provided thoughts about choosing a team.

- "Check on the experience and skill of the people doing the coaching. Make sure the coach has the best interests of the players at heart. The best way to determine that is to talk with current and former players.
- "Make sure AAU doesn't dominate a player's time. Do the AAU coaches coordinate with local coaches? It should not overshadow high school.
- "Decide if the AAU team provide the right level of exposure for your child.
- "Parents should be involved like they should at school activities. Go to practices. If possible, take vacation and travel with the team. And investigate the finances. How is money made and spent?"

He then discussed the general issue of costs.

"AAU charges $10 for an individual to join, which covers all sports. For our traveling teams, players are responsible for hotels and meals, while the team covers entry fees and travel expenses. In 1994, Cincinnati AAU had eight traveling teams, and four of them went to AAU Nationals. We spent $31,000 that year," he sighs.

Around the country, AAU teams raise money by holding tournaments and organizing spring leagues, fall leagues and "shootouts," which college coaches are supposed to attend. Cincinnati AAU holds a tournament but not the other activities due to conflict with high school activities.

Another question which comes up about AAU programs is recruiting. Not by colleges, but high school coaches who recruit their AAU players to transfer high schools.

"It's a concern, and it happens," said Price. "If kids were to transfer to Oak Hills, it could ruin the AAU program, and would definitely affect friendships I have with local coaches."

During the 1996 season, Price took Oak Hills to 20 victories. Along the way, he met several players from the AAU program. Dave Esterkamp and Cincinnati LaSalle defeated Oak Hills in the regional finals, on the way to LaSalle's first state championship. Esterkamp said, "Coach Price showed me so much about basketball that I didn't know. It helped me a lot to play for him last summer."

According to Ohio University assistant Mike Ehlfers, "Mike's in it for the kids. Whether they are his players or somebody else's doesn't matter to him."

Not surprisingly, Price takes an active role in promoting players to colleges. Each year he sends a letter to nearly 400 colleges. It includes information on each player on his high school and AAU teams, plus names of other "Cincinnati players to watch".

He recommends parents actively participate in their children's recruitment.

"Go any place close, see what they have to offer," Price said. "Parents can help by doing research on the academics of schools, especially through independent sources like *U.S.NEWS & WORLD REPORT* and high school guidance counselors. And definitely get phone numbers of other parents. Ask about the experiences of their children. Some comments won't be valid, you'll hear positive and negative, but expect that.

"Most important, parents need to realize the decision belongs to the student-athlete. The way they react, directly or indirectly, can affect the decision. Then, after the decision, show support, not displeasure. It makes me think of when my mother used to buy me these outlandish clothes, two sizes too big. Horrible. 'I love this,' she'd say. I'd say, 'Then you wear it.'"

The child will be "wearing" that college for a lifetime.

BOBBY KORTSEN, *USA TODAY*

"The guy's a Juwan Howard clone . . . if he gets his stuff together he'll be the best in the class . . . you can't win with that guy . . . great player but nothing but problems . . . those guys think if money does not touch their hands they aren't involved."

With his background in high school, junior college, college, AAU, and professional basketball as a player, coach, evaluator, organizer and administrator, Bobby Kortsen could be having this conversation with almost anyone in the game. On August 21,1995 it was an NBA scout. No matter who he's talking to, Kortsen, who works with Dave Krider for *USA TODAY* and *Street & Smith*, and serves as co-director of the Dave Krider Basketball Camp, doesn't pull any punches.

"Ninety percent of Division I coaches don't know what they're doing. That's why they get fired. Look at the schools with all the resources you could ask for who can't win," he said.

"The player has to ask, 'What do I want from the game of basketball? Pro career? Playing time?' If its education, go to the Ivy League or Northwestern or Stanford. If there is no hope of the NBA, be honest with yourself. Of course, few kids are," he said.

"It takes time to develop most college players. College coaches should look three years down the road—redshirt year, two more years to develop. Often they don't, often players don't. Brigham Young [where Kortsen went to college] has a pretty good idea. The Mormons redshirt, go on a two year mission, then have four years of eligibility. Their players are bald because they're 25 years old, but they are mature, play smart and stay out of trouble.

"When it comes to choosing a college, if you want to make a living in the game, go someplace where you can play. You find a 6-foot-8 white kid with good grades, 90 percent of them go too high and sit [on the bench]. That's because their parents make the decision and they want to go as high as possible. Gary Trent [11th choice in the 1995 NBA Draft] made a great choice. If he goes to Kentucky, he doesn't get drafted. He went to Ohio University and put up numbers that forced the pro guys to watch him."

Kortsen stresses getting seen in trying to play after high school as well.

"Good AAU teams can give the best exposure for basketball skills. Winning gets you noticed. Exposure camps are best for showing athletic skills; coaches come to see who can run and jump."

"It's very important when players develop. You see a fully developed freshman you see the end result. Younger bodies will blow past him. Some of today's best high school players may be as good as they are going to get," he feels.

"Look at the McDonald's All-America team. Neither of the top two picks in the NBA Draft, Joe Smith or Antonio McDyess, made that team, but Joey Beard did [after attending Duke, Beard transferred to Boston University]. There's a lot of politics in the selection of those teams, and too much praise can cause a player to think how good he is rather than how to get better. Not just coaches but players have to project their future. But at that age, a kid is not mature enough to understand. There's a lot of flattery in recruiting, it's the nature of the business. The only hope is to find adults who care about the players, who will tell them the truth," said Kortsen.

"But high school players should know that nobody will advise them out of the goodness of their heart. They have to know that going in. They [adults] have a motive or they wouldn't be around. When people ask me about the coaches I know I'm positive, but I say, 'Here's what you're getting in for ...'"

Despite his contacts and the various interests of his Columbus Basketball Club, which offers competitive leagues and sponsors AAU teams and tournaments, Kortsen is careful not to recruit for colleges. "I'd make one guy happy and 300 mad."

"The way the whole system has evolved, you have to be a strong person to get through it," he concludes. "The cards are stacked in the school's favor in recruiting, not the player's. Sometimes a school will back out of an early commitment if the kid doesn't keep improving. Choosing a school is like choosing a new family. The recruit has to find out what the coach is really like, not just the image that's presented. And look at the time the recruit will be spending with the players. He won't be happy if he doesn't like the people."

JOE PETROCELLI, 566 VICTORIES AND 42 SCHOLARSHIPS

Joe Petrocelli began coaching at Kettering Alter, located in suburban Dayton, when it opened in 1964-65. After the 1996 season ended, the school had gone to the state semi-finals for the third year in the last four and Petrocelli had 566 career victories. His friends calculate that around 2004 he will set the Ohio high school record for coaching victories, 697 by Paul Walker of Middletown.

"My views have changed so much over the years," said the man who has seen 42 Alter grads receive college scholarships. "As a young coach I was conservative. I treated it like someone was invading my players. All the mail and phone calls came through me. Now I believe a coach has to evaluate the situation based on the background and maturity level of the player.

"As I got on, I am less involved. I give them the mail, let them know how interested I think a college coach is, and explain how to set up a visit if they decide to take one.

"As a coach, recruiting is such a learning experience," adds the man everyone calls 'Petro'. "The first time you have a kid who is heavily recruited, you usually get caught up in the process. I probably did, too.

"John Paxson [who graduated from Alter in 1979] narrowed his list to Notre Dame, North Carolina and Duke. We had a coach from each school at practice once a week, men like Danny Nee [now head coach at Nebraska] or Scott Thompson [head coach at Cornell] from Notre Dame, Bill Guthridge [still assisting at UNC] or Roy Williams [Kansas head man] from North Carolina. As a coach it was a thrill to have Dean Smith of North Carolina or Digger Phelps of Notre Dame at a scrimmage," he recalls.

"Today everything is so limited I think it is even more important for a player to go to Five-Star or a camp like that to be seen," said the man who has coached, taught and administered at Howard

Garfinkel's camp for 20 years. "Colleges do so much evaluating in the summer.

"AAU is viable for kids to be seen, too. The objection by high school coaches, if the high school coach is not involved, is that there are unscrupulous people who may take advantage of the kid for their own profit. The other problem AAU causes is, there are so many trips to places like Las Vegas that there may not be much of a thrill for your player to go to Centerville," shrugs Petro. "It can be tough to keep their interest up."

Then, thinking as the athletic director he has been for three years, he adds, "Because girls' basketball camps are not as high profile or as numerous as boys', it is much more critical for girls to play AAU. Women's coaches evaluate in the summer, and girls have to be seen if they are going to be evaluated."

With Nike sponsoring its first competition camp for girls in 1996, that opinion may change with time.

Generalizing to recruiting in all sports, Petrocelli said, "Everybody says, 'Let the kid make up his own mind', and to a certain extent you do. But parents and coaches can channel the thinking. I think the coach has an obligation to raise potential concerns, and make recommendations based on the player he knows, not just from games but practices and classes.

"The coach should help the player decide what is important, then help him develop questions in those areas. If engineering is important, spend time with those teachers. If playing time is important, you have to ferret out that information for yourself. What players are there? Who is coming? What is the system? For some players I have them develop columns of advantages and disadvantages for each school.

"As an example, a lot of our players have gone to the University of Dayton to play," he adds. "The plus is, they plan to live here and work in Dayton, so playing there helps them make a name for themselves. The downside is, if they don't play, there is much more pressure on the player and the coach who recruited him.

"The majority of our kids come from strong families and get guidance from their parents. But the coach still has to talk about where the boy or girl can realistically play. Parents view their children with a prejudiced eye, and are not good at evaluating. That is difficult for anyone to do accurately and consistently.

"In evaluating players, out of lots of mistakes, my two biggest were Jay Burson, who I thought was not strong enough for the Big Ten but had a fine career at Ohio State, and Scott Skiles," Petro concludes. "When Skiles was at Five-Star he couldn't get his shot off. I couldn't see him as a major college player. Maybe he just had a bad week, because when Michigan State played at Dayton in the NCAA I was happy to pay to see him play."

Jimmy Salmon, The Young Veteran High School Coach

He looks younger than his 29 years, but fifth year Paterson Catholic (N.J.) High School basketball Coach Jimmy Salmon has been around the game long enough to take care of himself and his players just fine. Whether it is coaching against the best in the high school game, or counseling his players as they consider some of the best college opportunities available, Salmon has experience and insight which belie an angelic face.

"I went to Five-Star as a camper twelve years ago," he recalls. "My playing career was nothing to write down, but I convinced them to let me come back as a counselor. I've probably worked over 30 weeks since then." And picked the brains of some of the top coaches in the country.

With 1996 seniors Timmy Thomas and Kevin Freeman, Salmon sat across the table from college coaches like Rick Pitino and John Calipari. But that was never a problem; they coached Five-Star camps together for years. In fact, when Kentucky and Massachusetts played in the Meadowlands in 1994, both practiced at the Paterson Catholic gym, the better to make an early impression on Thomas. Salmon was able to escape the understandable awe which many coaches face and concentrate on what his players wanted.

"Timmy decided he wanted to sign late," said Thomas' coach and cousin. "When you are ranked as one of the best players in the country, you have the luxury of waiting. The way college basketball changes, you get a cleaner picture of the make-up of the team in the spring. You know if the coach will be there, if anyone is transferring or going early to the NBA. Once Timmy decided that's what he wanted, I just told coaches that anyone who tried to talk him out of that would be eliminated. We had no problem.

"It never got to be a circus around here, because we limited media attention until this year, and told the schools when to call and when not to call. I asked Timmy for a list of 20 schools by July 1, 15 a couple of months later, then 10 and now five. He's got it to Kentucky, North Carolina, Villanova, Rutgers and Seton Hall," said Salmon in mid-January 1996.

After averaging 28.7 points and 11.8 rebounds per game,

Thomas committed to Villanova in May. He mentioned he would declare for the NBA after his freshman year if he would be among the first five to be drafted.

Coach Salmon supports signing late for some players, but not necessarily others.

"Last year we had guys sign early with Austin Peay and Marist. Those were good decisions for them. I tell players, 'If you know what you want and it presents itself early, take it.' This year Kevin Freeman may have made a mistake by not signing early. UMass offered him, but told him he had to decide early or they were going to take someone else. He liked it, but wanted to take other visits before deciding. He is originally from Massachusetts, I thought the academics, social and athletics were ideal, but he wanted to take other visits. We'll see how that turns out in the spring." Freeman will attend Connecticut, so it turned out well.

Like many high school coaches, Salmon is concerned about access AAU coaches have to high school players. He has found some solutions to the potential problem.

"I've been accused of being overly protective, but there are street agents out there looking to move in on your players. With AAU they take them all over the country, put them into hotels, eat with them and build up a rapport. If you are a three month coach, and your players are with these guys for nine months, well, now days kids transfer schools all the time. Some change states. A high school coach reports to the principal, the athletic director and the board of education, but the AAU coach has no accountability. And the NCAA rules are ridiculous, too. College coaches can only see a kid two times in high school, but they watch him all summer.

"Our kids play AAU as a team, but in New Jersey I'm not allowed to coach them. So my brother and my best friend coach them. We've got a shoe sponsorship with adidas, so the AAU guy can't offer them anything we can't." Jim Salmon hoped that would be enough.

HOWARD GARFINKEL, TOM KONCHALSKI AND FIVE-STAR CAMP

From Joe Petrocelli to Jimmy Salmon, Five-Star comes up in many discussions of basketball development. Before NCAA rules brought AAU competition and exposure camps to such prominence, colleges visited teaching camps to evaluate high school players. Five-Star was one of the first teaching camps, instituting station drills (at the suggestion of then Army Coach Bob Knight) and emphasizing lectures, while providing competition as well. It continues to serve high school players today.

A New Yorker named Howard Garfinkel had spent most of the first 35 years of his life trying to find his place in the world of basketball. The highlight was probably when he helped North Carolina State assistant coach Vic Bubas identify local talent in the mid-1950's. By 1964, his latest idea was a magazine called *High School Basketball Illustrated (HSBI)*. It would cover high school basketball talent in the New York City area, and be quickly adopted by fans like himself.

The timing was good, with the main article on Lew Alcindor, who was leading Power Memorial to 71 straight victories. The kid would turn out to have an NBA career as Kareem Abdul-Jabbar. However, the high school market "Garf" anticipated did not develop and there were not many fans who shared his interest.

As Garf prepared to drop his magazine, a college assistant coach suggested a change in the marketing approach. It should be expanded, and made into a scouting service for colleges. When eight colleges quickly purchased $50 subscriptions, Garf had working capital, not only for the magazine but also a camp idea which he had been trying to get off the ground. The two projects grew together. In fact, the name Five-Star came from his method of evaluating players: a big-time talent, who could contribute to a Top 20 team, got five stars, while lesser prospects received fewer.

The quickest way to summarize the impact Garf had on the sport of basketball is to say that the NCAA passed two rules designed to limit that impact. The NCAA normally only paid that kind of attention to a Bill Russell (eliminating offensive goal tending) or Lew Alcindor (prohibiting dunking).

First, the NCAA ruled that college coaches could not work, which included coaching and lecturing, at a camp run by anyone with a recruiting or scouting service. So, Garf sold *HSBI* to then-partner Tom Konchalski. Later came the ruling that college coaches could not work away from their own institution.

Today, Five-Star remains highly regarded as a teaching camp. Tom Konchalski is in his second decade producing *HSBI*, which has not been illustrated for many years. Both Garf and Konchalski have insights to offer athletes on the recruiting process.

Howard Garfinkel still refers to his Ten Commandments of Recruiting, written some 20 years ago.

- Honor thy father, mother, coach or keeper, but make thine own decision.

- Thou shalt know thyself and thy level of play, and seek a college one notch below what you think you are and two notches below what your father thinks you are.
- Thou shalt not bear false witness about thy grades.
- Thou shalt be realistic about thy grades and seek advice from thy guidance counselor.
- Thou shalt not accept a paid visit without a prior commitment of a scholarship unless it is thy dream school.
- Thou shalt speak to both starters and bench-warmers on thy paid and unpaid visits.
- Thou shalt seek a college compatible with thy personality and lifestyle.
- Thou shalt covet a team and coach compatible with thy style of play.
- Thou shalt not accept an illegal offer.
- Thou shalt forsake (position) conversations.

With all the rules changes in 20 years, those commandments hold up well.

Konchalski is more subdued than his former partner, but he is also an astute judge of talent. Having watched athletes succeed and fail for a variety of reasons over the years, his observations are also valuable.

He emphasizes that academics cannot be avoided.

"They need the 13 core units, and can't put them off until their senior year. Grades and test score are requirements which can't be avoided. Athletes need to know their academic requirements and take care of them," he said.

"Regardless what is said, most players make a basketball decision in choosing a college," he adds. "High-profile programs and conferences are the keys for them. So often they say, 'It's always been a dream of mine to play Division I.' To me, it is a sign of maturity to change your dreams as the facts change. Why sit on the bench for a poor D-I team with a marginal academic school? Go to a good Division II team with strong academics and play! The shear joy of playing the sport can be lost in the ego trip of prestige conferences.

"Another common mistake is committing to schools before taking their visit," he continues. "They don't know enough to decide without seeing the school.

"A pet peeve of mine is players who visit when their sport is out of season. For basketball, the team can't practice before October 15. Wait until then, and watch the interaction between coaches and players. In fact, I would only take two or three visits during the early signing period unless absolutely sure I was going to commit in the fall. Players who take all five have no way to check other places which might become interesting.

"While players can't control their high school schedule, they can control their basketball activity out of season," concludes Konchalski. "They should pick activities to showcase themselves selectively, and not make the mistake of burning out from over-activity. Some good AAU teams which are well-coached help athletes look better, other AAU teams are thrown together. Some exposure camps are more structured than others, and some camps spend more time teaching than the rest."

In the words of William Shakespeare, "To thine own self be true."

Chapter IV

NON-REVENUE SPORTS

"I enjoy the entire recruiting process except

determining the extent of the scholarship offer ...

Parents are always surprised at how little

scholarship money is available."

Anson Dorrance
Head Coach, North Carolina Women's Soccer

College baseball is not like college football or basketball. Baseball coaches face problems which would send their peers in search of antacid tablets.

In football a player can go to the pros after three years. That can happen in baseball too, but a large number go right out of high school as well. Kids sign a college letter of intent before their senior year in high school, get drafted seven months later, take three months to evaluate their alternatives and go to the minor leagues instead of college. Not only is the player lost, there is practically no way for a coach to get anyone to take his place.

With players going to the NBA from high school, such a trend may be starting in basketball, though on a smaller scale.

On top of the roster uncertainty is the numbers problem. With 85 scholarships for, say, 24 positions, football coaches are able to be nearly four-deep at each spot. In basketball, men have 13 scholarships for seven to eight guys who actually get critical playing time, so most key figures have a back-up. If anyone can play more than one position, numerical depth is not a problem. Women, with 15 scholarships, have more flexibility.

On the other hand, baseball has ten positions. But with back-to-back doubleheaders, four starting pitchers and one reliever would be an unrealistic minimum. To fill 13 positions, baseball coaches are allowed 11.7 scholarships. Unlike D-I football and basketball coaches

ive the flexibility to give partial scholarships; obviously, they
o do that to recruit a team. But this "flexibility" causes more
ms. Which position gets .5 and which .7? Is a great player at a
 ition worth .5?

"The uncertainty we go through every year is unnerving," said
Ohio State Coach Bob Todd. "You just don't know what you'll
have."

With five straight Big Ten championships from 1991-95, Todd
has figured out a way to thrive in a difficult situation. Other college
coaches in non-revenue sports face similar problems. It is difficult.

"Parents can spend a lot of money sending their kids around
the country to tournaments, but they figure they'll get it back with a
scholarship," said Ohio State golf Coach Jim Brown. "Then they find
out there are only so many scholarships at the top schools. I tell them
not to make the decision based on money."

All non-revenue sport coaches interviewed concurred, "Don't
think about the money." They said it because the most difficult part
of their job is deciding how to divide not enough portions among just
enough people. But to some parents and athletes, money is very
important. They don't have enough of it either. A large scholarship to
a good school might be a necessary choice over a small scholarship
to a dream school.

So most non-revenue sports include a new layer of disappointment in the scholarship process called "equivalency limits." That
refers to the latitude equivalency sports have to divide scholarships
among players.

Because so much of the media is concentrated on football and
basketball, the concept of equivalency is not well-known to most college sports fans. Football and basketball (women's and men's), as
well as three women's sports: gymnastics, tennis and volleyball, are
"headcount" sports. Each athlete on scholarship counts toward the
headcount limit, eliminating partial scholarships. All other sports are
equivalency sports in Division I. All sports, including basketball and
football, are equivalency in D-II.

Despite the equivalency problem, if a D-I university offered
every scholarship available in every sport approved by the NCAA,
about 75 percent of the available opportunities would be for sports
other than football or women's and men's basketball. These are
opportunities in what some call "minor" sports. On the other hand,
schools do not offer every scholarship in every sport. Just because a
sport is approved doesn't mean it is offered, just because it is offered
doesn't mean the maximum number of scholarships are given. More
questions to ask during recruiting.

So much for the bad news. The good news is that an outstanding group of college coaches of non-revenue sports, and a remarkable high school coach, have provided their insight into recruiting in their sports.

ANSON DORRANCE, NORTH CAROLINA WOMEN'S SOCCER

Considering what Coach Anson Dorrance's North Carolina team has done to the sport of women's soccer, Webster would have spelled his name DOMINANCE.

Their record included nine straight NCAA championships before a 1-0 loss to Notre Dame in the semi-finals ended the 1995 season after 25 straight victories. For the last 10 years their regular season record was 231-2-8. Before the win streak began, the Tar Heels lost in the championship game in 1985 after winning three straight NCAA titles. In 1981, the year before NCAA championships were held in women's soccer, UNC won the AIAW national title.

Bud Wilkinson's 47 straight football victories at Oklahoma and John Wooden's 10 national basketball championships in 12 years at UCLA are two of the greatest achievements in the history of college athletics. In comparison, the Tar Heels won 82 straight soccer matches from 1990 to 1994, and 13 national championships in 15 years.

North Carolina recruits players from three specific areas.

"The highest levels of the Olympic Development Program, when we see them at national tournaments; youth tournaments, primarily WAGS (Washington Area Girls Soccer League), the Junior Orange Bowl in Miami, and the Dallas Cup; and our residential soccer camp. Most of our kids do all three," said Dorrance.

"The earliest we can contact someone is September of their junior year. By then we may have 5-15 names. We send periodic information in the form of a newsletter, adding names as we see players. By senior year we have at least 30 names, and modify the list as recruits sign.

"Other than goalkeeper, a quality player can play anywhere," continues Coach Dorrance. "We always recruit great players, regardless of position. We may be interested in athletic ability—quickness, speed, agility—even if the skill level is not outstanding. Or, we may be attracted to a player with an extraordinary quality in a physical, technical, tactical or psychological area. For example, she may have great vision, or be a great passer or shooter. We recruit hard psychological dimensions—the player who won't give up, who plays with pain, who has deep character. And we recruit leadership personalities, 'forces of fortune'."

"Forces of fortune?" A new soccer term? No, it is the center piece of a quote from George Bernard Shaw, 20th century playwright and essayist, and winner of the Noble Prize for literature. Shaw challenged people to "Be a force of fortune instead of a feverish selfish little clod of ailments and grievances, complaining that the world will not devote itself to making you happy."

Dorrance explains: "We recruit 'forces of fortune,' we hate whiners. I think whiners are the most destructive force in team building. North Carolina is not for everyone and we understand that. We have an elite crew with an elite mentality. Our 'forces of fortune' are athletic, they are required to train at an intensity level which is uncomfortable and they must meet rigorous academic standards at the school. If they whine, we'll help them find another school where they will be welcomed with open arms.

"Everyone puts their best foot forward during the recruiting process, which makes it difficult to identify the 'forces of fortune' from the rest," said Dorrance. Then he directs his attention to helping parents and their children navigate the tricky waters of recruiting.

"I enjoy the entire recruiting process except determining the extent of the scholarship offer," he said. "Soccer plays 16, has 22-30 on the roster and has 11 full scholarships. Parents are always surprised at how little scholarship money is available.

"I'm saving money for my daughters to go to college. If they get scholarships it will be a bonus. My advice to parents is not to make scholarship money an issue, to help the child decide where she will be happy academically, socially and athletically. But many parents view money they spend on athletics as an investment, for which they want a return in scholarship money. I'd suggest they view it as a way to develop the child, helping her focus her time on something positive and away from drugs and alcohol. Decisions made based on money often do not result in happiness."

In cases where money is a critical consideration, Dorrance suggests that the earlier the player commits, the more money is likely to be available. Also, a school hoping to build a program is more likely to make more money available than a proven power.

"Our standard offer, to a player we think will start as a freshman, is a full tuition grant," he said. "That is about .6 scholarship. That can be increased by All-America selection, making the national team and time in the program," said the coach who recruited 1996 Olympic standout Mia Hamm, leading goal scorer in D-I history, and six of her gold medal teammates.

But, how do athletes select the proper level for college play?

"It's almost impossible," he replies directly. "Players and their parents are predisposed to delusions of grandeur since their daughter totally dominates the high school scene. Parents, and the future collegian, must accept the fact that when she enters college she will be challenged by players with similar high school credentials who are older and have college experience. Research is helpful. Where did the best player in the area last year go? The year before? How do you compare to them? Are they starting for a top 25 team? A reserve on a top five team? Having an impact at their school?

"Another way is to ask the coach at your summer camp. We recruit the ones we think can play here, but we'll try to help any camper determine her best level of play. Talent evaluation is not a perfect science. I never expected Rye Johnson (a walk-on) to play one minute for us and now she plays every game.

"See the team play and try to imagine your role on that team. Definitely figure out a way for the coach at your favorite school to see you play," he adds.

"Don't be swayed by graduation losses. Every coach plans for players to graduate, and is preparing players for those spots from his reserves," concludes Dorrance. It is a comment he may have made to many recruits, as UNC returned 10 starters and several key reserves in 1996, yet attracted a highly regarded freshman class.

Susie Green "never played select soccer, didn't envision college success and didn't decide to go to the North Carolina camp until the last minute," remembers her mother, Susan. It was the summer before Susie's senior year in high school, and she caught the eye of the coaching staff.

"She was a very unselfish player, a hard worker," said Bob Sheehan, her coach at St. Ursula High School in Cincinnati. The powerful St. Ursula program, ranked in the USA TODAY Top 25 from 1991-95, didn't need her to score. Surprised that she did not have the normal all-star credentials, Carolina remained interested. They wanted coachability, speed and potential, which Susie could offer. She lettered four years, during a time UNC only lost one regular season game and won four NCAA titles. She graduated in 1995.

One of Green's teammates, Paulette Angilecchia, led St. Ursula to the state championship in 1991 as a junior and an undefeated regular season in 1992. She picked the University of Cincinnati because, "I wanted to stay close to my family and friends. They liked coming to the games and I liked having them there.

"It's a big step to college," Angilecchia said. "Players are bigger, stronger, faster and more experienced. You have to pick everything up a notch, and have the desire to work hard in practice. I think, 'I'm only going to be here two hours,' and try to have a mind set to excel. You have to push hard in practice to prepare for the game, to not be embarrassed."

JOE MACHNIK,
UNIVERSITY OF NEW HAVEN D-II WOMEN'S SOCCER

Anson Dorrance is in no way a typical college soccer coach. "Most coaches in the country would be happy to accept the players he rejects," said University of New Haven Coach Joe Machnik, who is not typical either.

In 1995, the third year UNH had a women's soccer team, Machnik led them to Top 20 ranking in Division II. Before the last three years, his only experience working with women was at his No.1 Goalkeeper & Striker Camps, held at over 25 sites throughout the summer and named the top soccer camp in the nation in 1996 by *Sports Illustrated For Kids*. Most of his accomplishments had been as UNH head men's soccer coach (110-55-21 from 1969-1980); commissioner of the American Indoor Soccer Association; roles in the Major Indoor Soccer League, from head coach to Referee-in-Chief; and various positions with the United States Soccer Federation.

Clearly, Machnik did not struggle with the change from coaching men to coaching women. "Soccer is still soccer," he said. "The game is a little slower paced, but, except for a difference in strength and power, the game is the same.

"Girl's soccer in America is really a middle-class sport," he continues. "Athletes have a wide variety of choices since women's soccer has developed after Title IX. In recruiting, I find athletes who are serious about their studies, have fantastic SAT scores and usually have their families involved. They want a good education, a good quality of life on campus and high quality coaching. They are interested in the manner (or style) of coaching. As a coach, it seems that women are more open to teaching than men, have smaller egos, perhaps."

SHARON TAYLOR,
LOCK HAVEN UNIVERSITY D-II FIELD HOCKEY

When Sharon Taylor decided to step down as Lock Haven University field hockey coach to concentrate on her other full-time job as athletic director, she wanted to find the right time for the announcement.

"I decided to retire after the 1995 season because of the two big milestones we had this year," Taylor said. "There was the 50-year anniversary of field hockey at Lock Haven, and the 20-year anniversary of the national field hockey championship. After I told the kids, they gave me an undefeated season and a national championship."

Lock Haven is a state-owned institution in central Pennsylvania, Division II in every sport except wrestling (D-I).

Taylor played field hockey there on unbeaten (7-0) teams in 1965 and 1966, and was named head coach in 1973. Under her leadership the Lady Eagles won six national championships in 23 years, made at least the final four the last seven years and had an overall record of 331-96-27. Athletic director since 1987, she looks at field hockey recruiting with three decades of experience as an administrator, coach and player.

"The sport of field hockey is unique," Taylor said. "Tactics and conditioning are similar to soccer, but the skills are not natural, like catching and kicking. You are dealing with an appendage which is not your own—that stick. There is a discipline which must be developed, and a level of frustration which must be overcome. Then there is the physical aspect of the sport. It's not for wimps. And players don't get a lot of feedback from spectators, so there has to be an internal satisfaction. Because field hockey has never been a men's sport in the United States, and most administrators are men, it doesn't enjoy the acceptance that soccer does. Soccer is more comfortable to men."

While there are 11 scholarships for field hockey at Division I schools, Division II is different. "I think we used three scholarship equivalencies last year," said Taylor. "Every player on varsity gets some assistance but money is not a big issue. I think we spent $25,000 on [field hockey] scholarships all together."

Taylor refers to herself as a "cheap date" for recruiting, doing almost all the work by phone or by mail. "Any name we got received a letter and a packet of information, but fewer than 10 times did I ever see an athlete play. One of the few exceptions was Melanie Helm [junior three-time All-American]. I found out about her after field hockey season had ended, and went to see her play basketball. I've never been to a kid's house on a home visit."

For evaluation of prospects, Taylor relied on film, coaching friends and Lock Haven alumni, who knew what would be required in the program.

When asked to advise parents and players about the recruiting process, Taylor said, "Apart from athletics, first generation college parents are very nervous about academic issues. They feel uncertain because they didn't attend college themselves.

"Regarding the sport, parents are often naive. They need a realistic view of the three divisions. Many think Division I is better than Division II, which is better than Division III. I've told parents, 'If your daughter could play for [Division III powers] William Smith or Trenton or Cortland, she could certainly play for us, and probably for most Division I schools.' The categories are not clearly defined."

For athletes themselves, Taylor had some priorities to suggest.

"First, find a school with your major. When players tell me they want to be an athletic trainer, that's good to hear because Lock Haven is strong there. Then sometimes they mention considering other schools which don't even offer that major. That doesn't make sense.

"Second, how does the campus fit? That means different things to different people. We are in a rural area in the middle of Pennsylvania with 3,500 students. Does that fit you? Field hockey is a small part of the college experience. 'Fit' could be facilities, friendliness, physical appearance—lots of things. Since some students change their major two or three times, 'fit' could be more important than finding the right major," she explains.

"Spend time at the school," concludes Taylor. "Talk with the players, especially when the coach isn't around. Find out what the school and the program are going to be like before you go there."

NANCY FOWLKES, HIGH SCHOOL FIELD HOCKEY

Imagine winning a state championship. What an achievement. Some high schools even win consecutive state championships.

Frank W. Cox High School of Virginia Beach won the Virginia Class AAA (largest school) field hockey championship in 1995, breaking its own national record for consecutive state field hockey championships with seven. It was the school's tenth since 1981 under Coach Nancy Fowlkes.

After her playing career at Longwood College in Virginia, "I knew I wanted to coach," Fowlkes remembers. "I enjoyed the goal setting, the competition.

"Emilie Tilley retired as coach at Cox and went into administration. Her record was 98-2-7, so the program was very well established," said Fowlkes. The state titles might have started under Coach Tilley, but such a thing didn't exist then for girls.

"People grow with experience. I think at first what I tried to do was be her. I was fairly successful at impersonating her personality, then spent about three years in the late '70s developing my own. At clinics I've heard coaches say they were always in it for the kids. Early on, I was in it to win. When I started to become more interested in the kids, it became more fun," said Fowlkes, candidly.

As someone who has been so successful coaching her sport, who learned the importance of the player in the sport, and who has seen dozens of athletes go on to compete in college at all levels, Fowlkes is well qualified to discuss recruiting from the perspective of a high school coach.

"The whole recruiting process starts with goal setting," she said. "Field hockey players select schools for a variety of reasons; they won't be playing professional field hockey. Athletes from good programs should be familiar with goal setting, both team and personal goals. We start each year with the state title in mind, and expect each player to improve her strength, endurance and skills. Then we talk about how these goals will be accomplished."

"I talk about a number of different things with a player in recruiting. First is academics. It's silly to go to a school that doesn't offer the right major. That goes along with future goals and objectives. Some schools have great reputations for academics, others just want to keep athletes eligible. The way to tell the difference is to talk with the girls. What are their majors, their interests beyond field hockey? Talk with students outside the program. If you are interested in biology, talk with teachers and students in that area. Unofficial visits are a good time to ask questions, so see the school more than once.

"Second is the athletic program. Do you have rapport with the head coach and assistants? Do you want to play on grass or turf? How demanding is the program? Do you want to have fun, or prepare for the Olympics? I try to be honest with them about their level of play, and may have to say, 'I don't think you're a Division I athlete.' They can learn about their ability by playing with team members, if it is out of season and coaches are not present," under current NCAA rules.

"Third are the people and the actual campus," Fowlkes continues. "How do you fit in, with teammates and students? What size school is best? How far from home? Do you want a strong men's basketball team, or football team? Does your academic ability match the college?

"Fourth is scholarship money. How much is the school offering, how much is left to pay and how will you pay it?

"We talk about being ethical in recruiting, about being honest, about not taking visits if you have committed. I have to be honest with college coaches in assessing my player's ability, so they will trust my judgment for future athletes. Unfortunately, I have had problems with misrepresentations from some colleges, particularly in the areas of playing time and scholarship money. In the future, we may start asking for some things in writing," she said.

"Once players begin to know what they want, they have to make themselves known to colleges. We write letters to colleges no later than the summer before senior year. Camps are a very good way to be seen. If a player is interested in a school, I usually suggest she go to their camp. It can be expensive, but it's less than paying for college. It's also a good way to see the campus and get to know the coaches. Normally current and former players work the camp, so you develop a good sense of the program. At the end of camp, ask 'What are the two or three things I need to work on most to play in your program?'

"Players need to choose camps wisely," concludes Fowlkes. "To learn the game, go where you will receive the best coaching. For a scholarship opportunity, select a school where your athletic and academic abilities have a good fit. If you just want a fun week, that's a different question. Different camps for different goals."

GREG MARSDEN, UTAH WOMEN'S GYMNASTICS

Utah won the Division I women's gymnastics championship in 1995, their tenth in Coach Greg Marsden's 20 years leading the program. Utah's worst finish in those 20 years was tenth place. One reason for such superlative success has been effective recruiting, which Marsden believes must result in a satisfactory outcome for both the athlete and the school.

"We make initial contact around January of the athlete's junior year, with the idea of signing them in November [of their senior year, ten months later]. The first mailing goes to athletes who are well known, or who have made their interest known by contacting us," said Marsden. "We collect information, scores and video tape from January through May. We try to add names to our list by attending invitationals in winter and spring, Junior Olympic nationals, and Elite Classics and Championships. By the end of June, our evaluation has to be completed, because July 1 we begin home visits. During the home visit we hope to interest athletes in visiting the campus in September and October.

"How many we recruit depends on how many scholarships we have." Marsden and his D-I counterparts have 10 available for the entire team, so an average year would be two or three. As a "head count " sport, there are no partial scholarships.

"Evaluation is an imperfect process," he cautions. "I look for three things: her athletic talent, academic success and personality. By personality I mean enthusiasm, work ethic and ability to fit in to the program. Most coaches prefer gymnasts with a strong all-around, which all competitors at the private club level must perform. After that we look for specific strengths by event, because not everyone has to perform all-around in college.

"We recruit the best athletes, and find we have to be involved with two or three for each one we sign. I don't rank them, I just try to determine if she can help us be competitive. If there are 10 people who can help us in a year that we have only two scholarships, I'll try to eliminate four and concentrate on six. If necessary, we would then expand the list later.

"We don't ask for a commitment before the visit. If they visit, we are pretty sure we want them. If we offer and they don't decide, someone else might take that scholarship. We realize not everyone we recruit will choose us, but if someone we want chooses us, we can't wait. That's why it is important for the athlete to know what things are important to her, before recruiting starts if possible. Take charge of the process," Marsden urges.

In addition to eliminating many schools quickly and easily, before friendships are formed with coaches whose schools don't meet the athlete's needs, Marsden recommends going after the schools which appear to have what the student-athlete wants.

"I'd aggressively contact schools," he said. "You could wait, but time is lost and you might even be overlooked. Provide scores and tapes, initiate contact and ask questions. The coach will be glad to obtain information about the school, or explain how you can get it. Informal visits can be good if location permits. The more contact you have, the more likely you are to make an informed decision."

JEFF MOORE, TEXAS WOMEN'S TENNIS

"With plenty of scholarships available, good players know they are in great demand. They feel pressure to make the best choice, while coaches feel pressure knowing players have a lot of good choices," said Jeff Moore, coach of the 1995 NCAA Division I women's tennis champion Texas Lady Longhorns.

Moore has clearly thrived under this pressure, with two national championships and 10 Southwest Conference titles in his first 13 years at Texas. Sixteen of his student-athletes made All-America.

At Texas, recruiting begins early in the high school student's junior year with a mailing. "We send a letter, an information packet, campus brochures, a media guide and a questionnaire to the top high school juniors in the country," said Moore. "They are selected from the USTA [United States Tennis Association] Girl's 16's and 18's national rankings. We arrange to see students play that spring and summer from the group that returns our questionnaire.

"We go strictly on USTA rankings, and want to see recruits play at national junior events. In high school the talent range is too great. Texas high school tennis is very strong on a relative basis, but one player from Texas makes the top 75 every two years or so. Colleges are recruiting internationally to find players. In America the level of play among juniors is improving, but the talent pool is not deep."

When evaluation begins, rankings are far less important to Moore and his staff than projected success in college.

"A top ranked player may have reached a plateau with her game," said Moore. "We have taken highly ranked players, but for us the ones from the 15-30 group have been most successful. Once we took a player ranked 34 instead of one ranked 15. They have to have a deep desire to get better, regardless of rank.

"In addition to work ethic and tennis ability, we look for athleticism and desire to play on a winning team. For an individual sport, the team concept is particularly important in college tennis. With matches taking place on six adjacent courts simultaneously, we have sort of a Davis Cup atmosphere. When the crowd reacts at one court, it can have a huge impact on the others, causing large momentum shifts," he said.

After deciding who they want to sign, and think they can sign, Texas coaches arrange for official visits. Unlike other sports, athletes do not often check out tennis programs by attending summer camps or taking unofficial visits.

"Players receive such specialized attention at tennis academies that camps don't work. We have them, they are successful, the community enjoys them, but camps have a stronger impact on general admissions than on recruiting in our sport," said Moore. "The top ranked players know they will receive paid visits from good programs, so they don't visit on their own.

"My home visit usually comes after the prospect's visit to Texas," he continues. It gives him a chance to meet the parents, who rarely visit campus with their daughter.

"In a way that's good," he adds. "When the parents are involved, the girl is less able to see campus through her own eyes."

The family may live far from campus, and the daughter has

been traveling on her own to tournaments for years. "Tennis recruits are more sophisticated than most high school seniors," said Moore, "though not necessarily more mature."

In women's tennis, schools have eight full scholarships. "Top recruits know they will get a full scholarship from a top school," Moore said. Men's tennis is an equilvalency sport, with 4 ½ scholarships.

Asked to move to the other side of the recruiting table, to offer advice to athletes and their parents, Moore said, "I'd identify the schools you are interested in and promote yourself to them. Write a letter of inquiry, send your tennis record and an unofficial school transcript, and request information. The athlete can request information anytime, so there is no need to wait to receive something. An unofficial visit is not a bad idea if it is feasible. Then stay in contact with those schools for which you retain an interest.

"It is important not to narrow your list prematurely. You need to compare others to your early leader," he said.

"Talk with current players, and not just during the visit. You are allowed to phone them. They can't call you—that's a recruiting violation—but you can stay informed about the program by calling them. It's rarely done, but it's a good idea," he concludes.

JIM STONE, OHIO STATE WOMEN'S VOLLEYBALL

In the last seven years, Ohio State has been one of the top women's volleyball teams in the country. Jim Stone, voted Big Ten Coach of the Year three times in that period, has led his team to national ranking and the NCAA Tournament all seven years.

"The recruiting process is not that much different in football, basketball, soccer or volleyball," he said. "Coaches can't live in the gym, they are restricted in their ability to see kids play, so the playing field is leveled. The kids who have the most successful experience in the recruiting process know what they want, so their decision is based on logic, not emotion. A minority do that—most don't even know what they want academically.

"Players seldom get great guidance in terms of athletic ability. Parents get their egos involved. Coaches say 'D-I player' but there are 212 D-I volleyball schools," said Stone. "Playing ability ranges greatly from the top to the bottom. High school or club coaches sometimes have an agenda, sometimes are knowledgeable and impartial.

"Outside evaluators are the best sources of information, particularly when the kids don't have to pay. If they pay, they expect to be promoted. It depends on the skill of the evaluator. For my purposes, the recommendations give me a chance to go evaluate myself. Of course, I have my own biases," Stone shrugs.

"Lisa Vitali (Moore), captain of our first Big Ten championship team in 1989, probably had the best approach to recruiting I have seen," he said. "Her father was a football coach and her brother was recruited to Purdue as a quarterback, so her parents knew what they were doing. They set up guidelines and kept her on task. They only permitted calls Sunday evening from 7 to 9 p.m., and she had to be home to answer the phone, talk and evaluate.

"Home visits were scheduled Tuesday or Thursday evening, so both her parents could be there. The Vitalis left the decision to her, made her tell coaches she wasn't interested, but gave her support and structure during the process. Coaches are glad to abide by reasonable requests. If they don't, you know something about the coach."

"Most [athletes] don't know what they want," states Stone. "If that's the case you can end up on the prettiest campus, or like whatever story you heard last. We've had girls tell us what they want to major in, then go to a school that doesn't offer it."

He is concerned about the prominence of club volleyball. Like AAU basketball, it is eroding the role of the high school coach in the life of the athlete.

"Because the seasons coincide, it is difficult for me to see many high school games," Stone said. "Most of my evaluation takes place from January to June, when there are tournaments every weekend. The players spend more time with their club teammates, and have closer ties to their club coach. The problem is, when the sport is taken outside the educational environment there are no rules, no oversight and no ethical controls. On the other hand, NCAA and state high school federations have so many rules, coaches [college and high school] are hamstrung.

"Here's an example," he continues. "High school coaches can't have access to team members for two weeks after the season. A Cleveland coach was not allowed to bring his team to Columbus for an Ohio State volleyball event. Would it have been better for the players to go in separate cars, without adults?"

"The [numerous] rules result in throwing the baby out with the bath water," Stone frowns. "Because 2 percent of the coaches cause problems, 98 percent are unnecessarily restricted. The players go into the club environment, where coaches are not necessarily better, and are not controlled at all."

Stone is also concerned about the various pressures on female athletes. "There's gender equity at the collegiate level, but that needs

to begin much earlier. Our players tell me they had to apologiz
being athletic when they were younger. It's too late for a 60 : 40
of scholarships in college because so many young women lost i
est in sports as girls."

The opportunity for a scholarship also creates pressure.

"Girls are forced to make the decision to try for a scholarship at
an early age," said Stone. "That's unfortunate. They play high school,
play club and train because they have to, not because they want to. I
see some girls playing club in February without any passion. They
are doing it because they are supposed to be there, to get that $50,000
scholarship. Playing a sport just to play it, or to enjoy getting better
for the fun of it, aren't bad things. But I've seen studies that show
boys enjoy sports outside a structured background much more than
girls. That's due to background in our culture."

SHARRON BACKUS, UCLA SOFTBALL

As impressive as a "three-peat" is, imagine doing it twice!

UCLA softball Coach Sharron Backus had an unprecedented
three consecutive NCAA championships from 1988 through 1990,
among the nine national championships her Bruins have won. She
has also "three-peated" in Halls of Fame: the Amateur Softball
Association in 1985, the National Softball Coaches Association in
1992 and the Women's Sports Foundation in 1993.

One Hall of Fame she has not entered (yet) is the UCLA Athletic
Hall of Fame. Until Backus retires, Co-Head Coach Sue Enquist, the
school's all-time leading batting average leader with a .401 mark
from 1975-78, is one-up on her coach.

"After nine years as my assistant," said Backus, "she was ready
for more responsibility. It makes a good contrast. There is a difference
of a little over 10 years in our ages, so we see some things differently. It's nice to bounce ideas around with someone. Since she played
for me, you could probably say I have 51 percent of the voting stock."

In their first seven seasons as co-head coaches, UCLA won four
national championships. They were named Pac-10 Conference
Coaches of the Year in 1995, an NCAA title season. It is very difficult
to argue with the results to date.

Like all schools with equivalency scholarships, UCLA has to
decide how to spread aid among athletes. "It's the saddest thing in
recruiting," said Backus. "During summer ball the coach tells the
player, 'You are worth a full ride.' Players immediately attach a mon-
etary value to their self-worth, which can only hurt them."

It doesn't help the school, either. "You can't attract the best with a partial scholarship, and we only recruit the 'supers'. Some schools recruit two players for a position and take the first to sign. We decide who we want, then take the back-up if the best player goes elsewhere," she adds.

Yet colleges must field a team of about 14 regulars, and develop players for the future, with 12 scholarships (increased from 11 in 1996).

"I would like to see need-based aid," said Backus. "That way athletes wouldn't see themselves in terms of dollars."

Returning from the desirable to the actual, she said, "We are fortunate at UCLA because the whole country recruits southern California softball players. That usually helps us, being close to many good athletes. But some kids have an agenda and want to go away to college. We don't get them.

"With summer travel ball, 99 percent of kids are thinking about college long before their last year in high school. I didn't think about it until senior year. Because of that change, most are ready to sign early, which we think is usually good for everyone. Once they visit a college, whether they like it or not, they are ready to decide," she said.

"No situation is perfect. At UCLA, we don't have recreation or physical education degrees. If a student wants to teach and coach, she has to take a fifth year for a teaching credential. The trade-off is the athletic experience and the name recognition of the school after graduation when she looks for a job," she concludes.

BOB TODD, OHIO STATE BASEBALL

"We want the baseball player capable of playing at a high D-I or professional level, and we also look for good grades," said Ohio State Coach Bob Todd.

"We emphasize grades for two reasons. First, a good student has a better chance of surviving the rigors of college academics. Second, usually a good student has had academics stressed at home. If pro baseball wants him, he is still likely to see the benefit of college before signing. The player who is not academically oriented normally goes straight to pro ball. If a quality prospect comes to college, he usually views it as a three year experience. After nine years here, 22 juniors have been drafted, one player returned to college."

With the NFL a factor after three years, football coaches are now less likely to redshirt top prospects. According to Todd, that is not necessarily the case in baseball.

"In the northern part of the country we need to develop players. They haven't played enough baseball because of the weather, particularly the two or three sport athlete who never settled on one sport. We may lose a player who develops quickly, but the flip side is it gives the college athlete more flexibility. If he doesn't like the [professional] team or the offer, he returns to school. It expands his opportunity."

Todd would love to sign the "can't miss" kid in the early signing period. Typically, however, he would prefer to watch the development of most recruits and decide in the spring. Other D-I programs see a kid Todd considers a good prospect as a gem, and are able to make an offer earlier. This speeds up Todd's decision-making process. Of course, that "can't miss" kid is the one who is most likely to be drafted next summer as well.

Then there is the issue of limited and partial scholarship aid. How much aid do you offer to a prospect, and what happens if the guy isn't very good?

"I don't believe in taking money away for athletic ability. My commitment to the family revolves around education. Parents are devastated when money is taken away," said Todd.

The other school of thought has to be, "Give the kid a shot, if he doesn't work out we'll get somebody else." There is a thin line between a player wanting to transfer and a coach wanting to get a scholarship back. Coaches asked about on this matter may avoid direct questions and say, "Things have a way of working out". Coaches who "recycle" scholarships can bring in more players, give more to each one and increase their chances of finding good ones. The arithmetic is compelling. "It happens," said Todd

When asked how to spot a program which runs off players, Todd said, "Check their recruiting classes against their rosters. If they bring in 18 players every year and have 27 on their roster, there is a problem. Get records from sports information, talk to the players about guys who are no longer there. Pick a school based on where you want to go and will be happiest. Don't be bought or the college experience won't be what it should be."

Yet for many athletes, the choice of going to college or pro ball is as difficult as choosing a college.

"For an athlete who wants to play major league baseball, is a college education a goal? If it is, he should go straight to college," said Todd. "At one time less than four percent of those who signed [major league contracts] out of high school ever got their college degree. Plus, the college experience is different one course at a time than for the full-time student.

"Some scouts and organizations prefer college players, they see college as a feeder system. Others prefer to mold a young player to their system. But, with free agency, people come and go in an organization. Besides, maturity which comes through three years in college can help a natural hitter develop other skills, or a pitcher with an 82 mph fastball get to 88-90.

"The main issue is, how much does it cost the parents for their son to play in college and is it worth it to them?" Todd said.

Cost to the parents is a big reason why the Buckeyes primarily recruit Ohio kids. The parents of a recruited athlete will probably have expenses and in-state fees are less than out-of-state. No baseball players were on full scholarship at Ohio State in 1996.

"Plus, Ohio high school and summer league coaches do a good job developing baseball players," Todd adds. "If we get the best five or six Ohio kids every year, we'll be competitive."

Also, players in warmer climates good enough to help Ohio State are heavily recruited in their area. Mark Chonko from suburban Kansas City, one of the few out-of-state players on OSU's 1996 roster, is the son of Arnie, the school's last two sport All-American (football and baseball) in 1964. Without a close tie like that, the athlete will probably stay closer to home.

ROY SIMMONS, JR., SYRACUSE MEN'S LACROSSE

When Syracuse won the national championship in lacrosse in 1995, it was their sixth title since 1983; a trip to the semi-finals in 1996 was the 14th straight time the Orangemen advanced at least that far.

Roy Simmons, Jr., coached his alma mater during that time, after an undergraduate career which included playing with possibly the greatest lacrosse player of all-time, Jim Brown. In 1957 Brown and Simmons led the Orangemen to an unbeaten season, but there wasn't a play-off format then. Johns Hopkins won the national championship based on strength of schedule. Brown went on to earn acclaim as the greatest running back in professional football and, in 1970, Simmons succeeded his father as Syracuse coach. In 1992, he joined his father as a member of the Lacrosse Hall of Fame.

The winningest active coach in college lacrosse with 257 career victories, with a list-topping .749 winning percentage entering the 1996 season, Simmons is well qualified to discuss his sport.

"It's the oldest sport in America, Native-American in origin. The Jesuits went to Canada and saw the Indians playing it. They thought the stick looked like a Bishop's crook, hence the French

name, lacrosse. Harvard, Princeton, Yale and Dartmouth pick
on it, so the prep schools followed after that. It's a preppy
more in private schools than public. Jim Brown's mother work
Manhassett, Long Island, so he picked it up there. Not only wa⟩ ⁿᵉ a
great athlete, he was a polished player by the age of 10. He played
lacrosse before he played football, and he was bigger, stronger and
faster than anyone else," said Simmons.

"In public schools, the emphasis is on football, basketball and
baseball, because kids are looking for a way out by becoming a professional athlete. Not unlike rugby, lacrosse is regional in nature, sort
of tied to the 'good-old-boy network.' It has never taken off in America
because it hasn't gotten into the living room through television."

The NCAA allows Division I schools 12.6 scholarships. Like
most schools, Syracuse does not authorize the full amount. Since
Simmons plays 25-30 men in a game, the team travels with 32 and the
roster includes 48 players, he is always in a numbers crunch.

"We have to cut up scholarships," he said. "Very rarely is there
a full ride. Kids love to say they have a 'lacrosse scholarship;' coaches have to figure out how to skin the cat, to do the job. The reality is
not seen by the kids at first. That reality is loans, second jobs for parents, re-mortgaging the house, maybe the mother working for the
first time. I've had kids make a commitment to me, then graduate
$40,000 in debt.

"We had twins here, the best lacrosse players in the world,
Gary and Paul Gait from Canada. Their lockers were right next to
Derrick Coleman, the basketball player who signed a $30 million
contract," adds Simmons.

There was nothing like that for the Gait's, despite being three-
time first team All-Americans, honors Coleman did not match.

Ivy League schools that do not offer scholarships provide not
only athletic and academic, but financial competition for Syracuse.

"They have quite a bit of need-based aid," said Simmons.
"When it comes to the FAF form, we don't offer 100 percent aid, we
don't have that kind of endowment, but some of the Ivy League
schools do. Canadians can't get need-based aid, because foreigners
are not eligible. By splitting scholarships into equivalencies we miss
some players. Some we get threaten to leave after they have some
success, others have a change in their family economic situation and
have to leave. The Xs and Os of the game are minor compared to the
financial, to needs and wants, and to emotions as we try to keep a
team together. It's a sophisticated collage."

As with any sport, an athlete has to be seen to receive a scholarship.

"I won't give aid based on press clippings, the boy has to find a stage. That is unless he's from one of those magic areas, like Baltimore or Long Island, those few places where you see kids dragging a lacrosse stick instead of a baseball bat," he adds.

One way to be seen is by attending camps patterned after the Nike basketball camp. "The original idea was to gather the best 200 or so players together for one week," said Simmons. "The stands are full of coaches and it's a real meat market, at $450 a camper. All colleges have camps as well. Most emphasize teaching like ours does, others are just a chance to be seen."

The other aspect of recruiting is the evaluation process.

"The coach at Dartmouth, Tim Nelson, went to North Carolina State. I didn't recruit him out of high school, but he called when they discontinued the sport. He was what we needed at the time, a feeder, like a quarterback in football, and he decided to come here. He graduated in 1985 as a three-time All-American, and three-time Turnbull Award winner [as Outstanding Attackman in Division I]. He didn't get that much better, he just had the stage to meet his goals. Now he's the youngest coach in Division I."

Simmons emphasizes the need for the athlete to know what he wants:

"Some kids want the stage in college, the competition. Others want low profile, less pressure. Williams, Trinity and Amherst are examples of great small schools with great camaraderie, but they don't have a great stage. Athletes need to go for a visit, and when they go they should know what they want.

"At Syracuse, we tell players we are more than a sport. We offer the stage and the education, but also tutoring, help finding a job, help finishing the degree, study table. We try to be all-encompassing. Any sport should be," said Simmons. "We want players to bring their families back, to be proud where they came from and what they participated in while they were getting a great education. The real question is, what will four years of lacrosse do for you in the big game, life after college? I had one player, about to graduate, who said, 'What do I do next month, Coach, when there is no practice at 3:30?'"

Great question, regardless of the sport.

Chapter V

MULTI-SPORT EXPERIENCES

"There is no guarantee how long a coach or assistant coach will stay at that school, so try to pick an environment that you think you will be most comfortable in."

Pat Fickell
Father of college athletes Luke (football), Leah (softball) and Mike (wrestling)

Sometimes the recruiting issue is not confined to a single sport. Pat Fickell's three children are involved in different sports. Carl Love coaches boys high school basketball; while his daughter likes hoops, his son is a football player. Every child of a coach considers what it would be like to play for Dad, or Mom. Jim Larranaga and Bill Mallory saw their sons make different decisions on that issue. For some athletes, sports can provide a free education through service in the military. And, with the possible exception of full ride scholarships, money is a significant issue for every family, in every sport.

PAT FICKELL, SPORTS FATHER

At Columbus DeSales High School, Luke Fickell was a football All-American and Ohio Lineman of the Year. But "football didn't know who Luke was until after his junior year in wrestling," remembers Pat Fickell, Luke's father. "That's when the letters really started, after he won the second undefeated state heavyweight wrestling championship. Guys Luke's size are a dime a dozen in football (a 6-foot-4, 260-pound nose guard) but you can't measure heart. That's what wrestling gave Luke, heart. It taught him about goals and hard work."

Pat may be biased. He might have preferred that Luke focus on wrestling. "He could have gone anywhere. But it had to be Luke's decision," believes Pat. "It's his life."

After Luke's senior season in football, he went undefeated for the third time wrestling and kept his grades in the 4.0 area. While fielding phone calls, reading letters and evaluating scholarship offers, he decided he wanted a football scholarship from a school that would allow him to wrestle.

"He only made two visits," said Pat. "He also had a visit to Notre Dame tentatively set-up, but his recruiter took a head job. He called, said someone else would call but no one ever did. Luke was busy wrestling and did not want to take time off for other visits."

"I remember sitting in my office with coaches from seven schools," said Bob Jacoby, Luke's high school coach, "like Ohio State, Tennessee and Notre Dame. I just sat back and told them how much I liked Luke. That was fun."

Luke's first visit was to Ohio State.

"During an official visit, [Coach] John Cooper told Luke, 'We've got a scholarship for you.' Pretty soon, 24 of the 25 available were gone. Luke got the last one. I didn't know if they would have held it. When they want you enough they can do things like that, but you never know how much they want you," said Pat.

"Luke's other visit was to Michigan. I've got all the respect in the world for [former Coach] Gary Moeller. He said, 'If you want to live and work in Ohio, you ought to go to Ohio State. I have you here to convince you Michigan is better.' Then he presented what Michigan had to offer. Luke's a homebody, plans to work in Ohio and liked the players, so he decided on Ohio State," Pat said.

Luke Fickell suffered a torn cartilage after playing the first football game of his freshman year, and was redshirted.

"He said it was like he was suddenly invisible to the coaches," remembers his mother, Sharon. "We told him they had to get ready to play the next game. He couldn't wait to get back on the field."

Entering his senior year in 1996 Luke had started every game, making Academic All-Big Ten three times while majoring in optometry. While academics and football have worked out well, wrestling did not go as he hoped.

"He came out late two years after football," said Pat. "The first year he was not in the line-up. The second year was after the Holiday Bowl and the wrestling season was half over. He was too big, not in wrestling shape. Wrestling is such a mental game. After being away from wrestling competition all that time, he just knew that wasn't the way to do it. When he stopped wrestling it took a big weight off his shoulders."

But Luke is not the only college athlete in the Fickell family. Daughter Leah was a junior on softball scholarship at Shawnee State, an NAIA school in Portsmouth, Ohio in 1995-96.

"I like her coach, Ralph Cole, a real disciplinarian. He'll push you. Most kids need to be pushed," said Pat. "He told her, 'Winners breed winners.' She works on softball all year long, though some of her teammates view it as four or five month thing. She gets tuition and books, not room and board. It's a good size school for her."

The youngest Fickell is an athlete as well. Mike was a starting offensive guard for a Columbus DeSales football team which made the state play-offs, but unlike his brother, Mike's primary interest was wrestling. He went to the state finals as a junior in the 171-pound class, and the semi-finals of the 189-pound class as a senior. "But, colleges really want the ones who win state," said Pat.

"Luke was a good student, but Mike is third in his class. He takes so many advanced courses his average is well over 4.0. He decided on the business school at Pennsylvania, the Wharton School, over Virginia and Brown. The Ivy League doesn't have athletic scholarships, but with the grant-in-aid, it's about the same as Virginia with a partial scholarship. He'll wrestle for sure, maybe play football later."

Regardless of the sport, Pat Fickell knows about the recruiting process. Beyond the primary consideration that the athlete make the decision, he adds two cautions.

"There is no guarantee how long a coach or assistant coach will stay at that school, so try to pick an environment that you think you will be most comfortable in," Pat believes. "Remember, coaches are like salesmen, and they have to sell you on their school, so naturally they will be very nice."

CARL LOVE, TEXAS HIGH SCHOOL COACH AND FATHER

Carl Love has averaged more than 20 wins a year as boys basketball coach of the John Tyler Lions of Tyler, Texas. He has helped many players with recruiting during that time, but had his most intense experience through his son, a football player for the school which sent Earl Campbell to the NFL Hall of Fame.

"My son was an all-state football player, and Vanderbilt was recruiting him real hard," remembers Love. "The recruiter was a guest in our home and I said, 'Are you offering Cameron a scholarship?' He answered, 'Yes, we are.'

"On Friday before the national signing day the following Wednesday, his football coach asked Cameron, 'Are you serious about going to Vanderbilt?' In my heart I was against it because I thought it was too far away. I tell kids you don't get an education by stepping on campus, you get it by working hard. If you do that, you can get an education a lot of places. Well, he wanted to go to Vanderbilt, so we called the coach to accept the scholarship.

"They were in a meeting, but the secretary said they would call back. When he was being recruited they always called back in five minutes, but they didn't call back Friday. We didn't think much of it, and called back Monday. Again he was in a meeting. We called back later, and he had gone to lunch. We made two or three more calls and never reached him," said Love.

"Late Monday night he called. He said, 'We have it down to Cameron and a boy in Colorado. The coach is in Colorado now to see him. If something goes wrong, we'll offer Cameron.'

"The next day I started making phone calls. One was to Stephen F. Austin, a I-AA school just over an hour away from Tyler. We had a [basketball] game close to there that night, so we arranged for the coach to talk with Cameron and give him some brochures. The next morning Cameron signed with Stephen F. Austin, where he led the team in tackles and was all-conference as a redshirt sophomore."

Surprisingly, Love is not bitter about the experience.

"In football, each coach fights for scholarships. The head coach decides how many go to the different positions, then things change in the final days when kids start changing their minds. I believe the coach who talked to us was sincere, he just got shut out. There is no way to protect a kid in a situation like that. They say 'Great player' all the time, but it's a canned speech. It's a cold, cruel business," said the one-time junior college coach.

When Love talks with his players about recruiting, he says, "You are not being recruited until somebody walks down your sidewalk, sits in your living room and starts showing you shiny brochures and video tapes."

In 1996, one of his best basketball players was one of the best junior football players in the nation. Miami, Florida State and Notre Dame were among the many colleges interested in 6-foot-5 high school pivot, college linebacker, David Warren.

"They really want him," said Love. "He's the exception. Most of the kids I have to chase scholarships for. I mail stats, videos, make phone calls, generally make a pest of myself."

Like after the 1995 season, when he found a scholarship for his sixth man.

"Our system doesn't lend itself to impressive statistics, but he could play. This junior college wanted to bring two of our players in to work them out [permitted for junior colleges, not NCAA schools]. I told them they could bring in three almost as cheaply," Love said. "The next Monday they called and said they wanted the guy I convinced them to add on. That fall I got a nice card from the coach about what a good kid he is; now he's starting and leading them in scoring. If you're a high school coach, scholarships don't happen by sitting and waiting.

"In the whole order of things, these basketball games don't mean anything. What matters is what you learn that serves you later on—discipline, team work, effort," Love said. "Vince Lombardi said, 'All good men want discipline.' Our kids have trouble in school, they don't play. In recruiting I tell them to be nice to everybody, to tell them what they want to hear, until you know you have a scholarship. Be nice even if it's the last place you want to go, because it may be the only place you can go. When they do decide, I try to get them to call the other coaches and thank them for the opportunity."

While he continues to work with his basketball players and their recruiting issues, Love has one more family member to help. Daughter Azure was on the girl's varsity basketball team as a freshman, made all-district as a sophomore, but broke her leg playing AAU ball. "She's struggling as a junior," he said.

But it would be a mistake to bet he won't find a way to get her to college.

JIM LARRANAGA AND BILL MALLORY, TO COACH YOUR CHILD OR NOT?

The high school athlete with a parent who is a college coach certainly benefits from early instruction, but faces an especially difficult question in the recruiting process—do I want to play for my parent in college?

"That decision is separate," said Bowling Green basketball Coach Jim Larranaga, "and takes precedence over selecting the school."

At Toledo St. John's High School, where he was a four-year starter on teams with a combined 84-19 record, Jay Larranaga was ranked among the top five Ohioans in his class and top 100 in the country. When recruiting began it was "not as heavy as those rankings would suggest," said his father. "Coaches assumed he would play for me."

Coach Larranaga did some research, talking with basketball coaches like Jim Harrick, then at Pepperdine, now UCLA; Tom Penders of Texas; Dick Bennett, then Wisconsin-Green Bay, now Wisconsin; and Ralph Willard, then Western Kentucky, now Pittsburgh. All had coached their sons in college. Coach Larranaga also spoke with Joey Meyer, who played for father Ray at DePaul, where Joey is now coach, as well as men who did not coach their sons in college. Then he discused their comments with Jay.

"Dick Bennett talked about how important it was for [his son] Tony to understand that the players didn't love his dad, that they needed space to talk. Dick recommended Tony stay on the court for 15 minutes after practice to let them talk in the locker room," recalls Larranaga.

"Jim Harrick said, 'Well before the son plays for the father they must talk about the relationship at home, the kidding, the playing around, compared to the relationship on the court. The coaches whose sons went elsewhere talked about how they missed seeing them play.

"Jay and I had always been very close. He grew up in the gym, watching teams play which I was coaching. We lived within a mile or two of the gym, so he'd walk over or ride his bike. I spent a great deal of time working with him on his game; I was his personal tutor," Larranaga said. "Ultimately Jay emphasized the importance of our past conversations, and how important it is to fit in. He had spent so much time in the [Bowling Green] gym, was comfortable with the players. 'Who would I have more faith in than my father?' he decided. Jay made the decision based on three areas of life: academics, basketball and social.

"One thing which stood out was the number of calls which went to me. Usually calls go to the player. The exception was Kevin O'Neill at Marquette [now coach at Tennessee]. He called direct and recruited direct. We liked that. When he asked to visit in the home, Jay decided not to go through that," Larranaga recalls.

After three years at Bowling Green, Jay Larranaga had an A-grade point average as a business major. Having started for three years, his decision looked very good. But for Coach Jim Larranaga, the same decision was looming again. Son Jon started as a sophomore for a team which finished second in the state high school tournament.

Indiana University football Coach Bill Mallory faced a similar situation, three times.

"I talked to several coaches who had their son or daughter play for them," he recalls. "Sometimes it didn't work, seemed like it did most of the time." Mallory went through the recruiting process with three of his sons, twice when he was at Northern Illinois and later at Indiana. All three sons went to Michigan where they lettered as red-shirt freshmen and played in the Rose Bowl.

"[Choice of college] is definitely one of the most important decisions a student-athlete makes. It is a decision for the individual. The parents can help direct the process and be a sounding board, but when the parents are too forceful in the decision it blows up in their faces," said Mallory.

Mallory's first son, Mike, was heavily recruited by the biggest Division I-A schools. "I recruited him and wanted him [for NIU], but didn't pressure him. I told him it was his decision—I tattooed that baby on his chest. It came down to Michigan as the school for Mike. He felt he could play Big Ten football and wanted the challenge. I thought Mike would be a solid program player, and Bo [Schembechler, then coach at U. of M.] likes those kinds of people. I said, 'Be patient. There is keen competition, it's one of the best programs in the country.' I didn't want him to expect to play too soon. Most players take work and development."

A four-year letterman, Mike was co-captain and twice first team All-Big Ten at inside linebacker. As a senior he was Michigan's MVP. After serving as graduate assistant to his father at Indiana and coaching at Kent and Eastern Illinois, Mike became defensive coordinator at Rhode Island.

"When Doug came along two years later," Mallory remembers, "I told him the same thing as Mike. He and Mike were close, and Doug wanted to get away and try things on his own. He was a program player at Michigan also. He saw Mike work his way into playing after a redshirt year, and he worked his way through the same way." Also a four-year letterman, Doug was co-captain as a senior, when he made second-team All-Big Ten as a strong safety. He is defensive backs coach at Indiana.

"Curt was a bit different. He went through four years after Doug," recalls Mallory. "By then I was at Indiana. After a career as a four-year starter at Bloomington South High School with extensive team and individual recognition, Curt really wanted the Big Ten. It came down to us and Michigan. He had a tough decision. I tried to talk to him to explain it was his decision. He was going back and forth. He seemed to prefer Michigan, but felt obligated here. Plus the fans here wanted him to go to IU.

"I think the answer came when he told my wife, 'I know Dad will get on my case. I can handle that, he's done it often enough before. But I don't know if I could handle it when he gets on my teammates.' She told me that and I said, 'I think he's made his decision.'"

Curt lettered as a redshirt freshman at Michigan, played in the Rose Bowl like his brothers, but sustained a neck injury and became a student coach. After two years as a graduate assistant at Indiana he became linebackers coach in 1995.

"The parents really have to be open-minded. They have to put the student-athlete ahead of selfishness," said the man who had done that three times. "Sometimes the worst part of recruiting is dealing with the parents. They are living their lives through the athlete. Still, the parent should be involved in the process. They can help their son evaluate the coach, look for a sense of honesty, consider his promises, cross check what he says with players and alumni."

Two different answers to the same question. Both answers seem to be correct, in their specific situations. Maybe the answer is not as important as the process, and the opportunity for the child to make the decision he or she will have to live with for a lifetime.

NAVAL ACADEMY COACH DON DEVOE, THE MILITARY OPTION

The Navy basketball program is pretty proud of the career of a certain David Robinson. A four year record of 106-25; three trips to the NCAA Tournament; the first player in D-I history to score more than 2,500 points, grab 1,300 rebounds and shoot above 60 percent from the field; twice All-American, and once Player of the Year, no wonder. But Navy hovered around .500 most of the time before Robinson bloomed as a great player his sophomore year. Sometimes .500 would have been a welcome sight. In the five years after he graduated, the team won 37 games and lost 104. David Robinson is an outstanding representative of Navy basketball, but not typical in any way.

Of course, at the Naval Academy producing NBA All-Stars is not exactly part of its Mission Statement. Developing men and women, physically and mentally, to be sailors and winning wars rate considerably higher. But would it serve their primary purposes to win a few more games along the way?

Believing that it would, Navy hired Don DeVoe, who had been involved in college basketball since setting screens so teammate Gary Bradds could be Player of the Year in 1964. More importantly, Bradds and DeVoe led Ohio State to two Big Ten championships after Jerry Lucas and John Havlicek graduated.

To learn more about winning within the rules at the college level, DeVoe served as assistant at Army for five years, then returned to Ohio State for one. After that, he won the National Invitational Tournament and went to the NCAA at Virginia Tech, took Tennessee to six NCAAs and also coached at Wyoming and Florida. A man of proven ability and high principles, he seemed like a good fit for Navy.

DeVoe's first year the Midshipmen improved from 6-22 to 8-19, his second year they finished 17-13 and went to the NCAA Tournament. He became the 12th coach in history to guide three different schools to the championship playoffs, joining men like Frank McGuire, Lefty Driesell and Rick Pitino. In DeVoe's third year Navy ended 20-9, the first Academy team without Robinson to win more than 18 games.

Navy's five year commitment after graduation presents an insurmountable obstacle in recruiting certain players. "It's difficult to get a kid with other scholarship offers," understates DeVoe. Coaches of both sexes at other service academies battle a similar situation.

But, for some athletes, playing their sport at a service academy makes sense. Not for an NBA candidate, not for someone worried about passing the SAT, not for someone weak in math and science, but for a small, special group.

"For me, the key is that this is a leadership institution," DeVoe said. "A part of the incredible education is a college life designed to create the opportunity to be a leader, a life which first teaches you to follow, then to lead.

"A Naval Academy education is three-fold: academic, military and athletic. The physical mission of the Academy takes place from 3:30 to 6:30 p.m., with your team in season. Including summer training, the education has been valued at $175,000 to $200,000. That does not count the guaranteed job for five years, with an immediate assignment of a leadership position. After the first duty station of 18 to 24 months, graduate school is an option. The government pays for that, so you get out with a resume full of experience and no bills."

DeVoe has told the story before, believes it and knows it appeals more to adults than teenagers.

"We are the 'hard right,'" he said. "Our situation requires a visionary person. He must realize plebe summer lasts 6½ weeks. He must see around plebe year and restrictions on undergraduates. The astute young person can see the total value, but usually parents see it better than young people. Many young people focus on missed social opportunities, when, in fact, they have so much in common with their peers at the Academy. The Naval Academy is not the easiest choice, but for some it is the best."

Attending a service academy is only in small part an athletic decision. To a much greater extent, it is a life-shaping decision. But 90 percent of Academy graduates won high school letters, and those who are capable have the opportunity to compete in college.

SOMETIMES THE SCHOLARSHIP DOESN'T COVER EVERYTHING

Throughout most of the country Division III colleges are private institutions and very expensive.

However, some states, such as New York and Wisconsin, have many D-III state schools. In fact, New York University, a Final Four team in the 1960 NCAA men's basketball championship, is now a D-III school. Combining the opportunity to participate in athletics at the cost of a state school offers great value for athletes in those states.

Capital University is located in Bexley, a suburb of Columbus, Ohio. Financial data is based on expenses there, being fairly representative of college costs for private schools on the D-III level. It is intended to serve as a starting place for reviewing the financial requirements at D-I schools, such as those in the Ivy League and the Patriot League, which do not have athletic scholarships, as well as the very common situation where only a partial scholarship is offered.

"In the last seven years, the median family income has increased 30 percent while college costs have gone up 80 percent," states Beth Heiser, director of the Admissions Office at Capital. "Schools have to provide financial aid, and develop policies to attract the type of students they want." In this instance, type means test score, class rank, and grade point rather than wide receiver or small forward. It is difficult to question the term "student-athlete" on the D-III level.

Financial need remains a major factor in obtaining aid, but academic achievement will generate assistance independent of need. "Parents expect to see a reward for good grades," Heiser said. "They feel the students have earned it."

All colleges use a government form called Free Application for Federal Student Aid to determine what a family can afford to pay for a student's education. High income, high assets with low number of dependents equals major ability to pay; low income, low assets, many dependents equals less ability to pay. The figure gen-

erated through the use of the FAFSA form is called the "famil
tribution".

Employees of the Financial Aid Office subtract the famil
tribution from the cost of room, board and tuition at the s
which leaves a number identified as "need". The challenge is to find
as much grant, loan and work study money as possible to reduce the
need figure. Because the government is convinced it knows how
much the parents can afford to pay, the family contribution figure is
not reduced regardless of how much aid can be found. In reality, the
school is seldom able to eliminate the "need" figure.

The D-III coach hopes the total cost of an education at a private
school will approximate the cost of nearby state schools. Then the
coach is able to promote the value of small classes and athletic competition at little cost. If the differential is significant, the coach almost
always loses the player because the family has little or no financial
latitude. More importantly, the athlete loses the chance to compete in
college sports.

Composition of the financial package is very important to the
family. To illustrate, School A could cost $18,000 minus a $5,000 family contribution, and provide a $13,000 aid package for a net cost of
$5,000. Meanwhile, School B could cost $17,000, minus a $5,000 fam-
ily contribution, have only an $11,000 aid package for a net cost of
$6,000, but be a better deal. Here are some points to consider in com-
paring financial aid packages:

- Grants are direct reductions to cost but loans must be repaid
  with interest. A package heavy in grant money is far superior
  to one based mainly on loans.
- All loans are not created equal. On a subsidized loan the government pays the interest while the student is in school, with
  responsibility transferring to the student six months after graduation (or withdrawal). With an unsubsidized loan the student
  pays (or compounds) interest immediately. The unsubsidized
  loan will always be more expensive. Before taking out any
  loans, give serious thought to how they will be repaid, by
  whom, when, and at what total cost (principal plus interest).
- If work study is a part of the aid package, the student benefits by sharing financial responsibility for the education and
  may develop marketable skills as well. However the student-
  athlete does not have much time for work, class, study, practice and games. "It is difficult for an athlete to earn anything
  over $1,500 in work study," said Heiser. Talk with coaches
  and players before including an extensive work-study program. What are the policies about missing practice to work?

Who else on the team works? How much? What problems have surfaced? How were they resolved?

- After understanding every penny involved in the calculation of aid for every college your child is considering, remember that money is only a part of the issue of selecting a school. While an extra few dollars is pretty important when it is beyond what you can afford, this is the college with which your child will be associated for a lifetime. How much better would the academic experience be? The athletic experience? What about the people, from the students to the teachers and coaches? Where would better summer and full-time job prospects be? Not easy questions to answer, but too important not to consider. If there is real value at extra cost, maybe there is a way to make it work. Of course if the difference is slight, or there are no other options to raise more money, that may be the determining factor.

- Finally, even if Division I and II schools are expressing potential interest, only elite recruits can afford to ignore the possibility that D-III may be an option. Regardless of letters, phone calls and evaluations, there is no scholarship until one is extended. Unless the student is deliberating over firm offers, it makes sense to submit an FAFSA form to at least one school. If a scholarship develops, little time and money is lost. If not, a great deal of time would be saved and the stress of uncertainty reduced.

Now that a wide range of experts have offered their thoughts on the recruiting process, a few athletes and parents will discuss exactly what they encountered during and after their selection of a college athletic scholarship.

Chapter VI

ACTUAL CASE STUDIES

"It's not about raising kids to be recruited, it's about

raising kids to be people."

Mac Bledsoe
Father of NFL quarterback Drew and Colorado recruit Adam

Harvard Business School pioneered the "case study" method of teaching as a way to test student's understanding of classroom concepts. Teachers would provide the facts of an actual situation, or one created by the instructor, and the students were required to analyze what was happening, then present a logical solution. Grades reflected depth of understanding and logic.

My introduction to the case study method of teaching came through Manley Howe Jones, Ph.D., who challenged his students to "get into the skins of the people" presented in the cases he created, to feel what they felt and see life as they did. As managers, students would be making decisions which changed these people's lives. If the people rejected the proposed solution, a sound answer on paper would fail on implementation. Good decisions had to be acceptable to people who would embrace them and want them to work.

In this chapter, you will read true case studies of athletes and parents. By "getting into their skins," you will find much to learn from them. Scott Weakley and Mike Stumpf are college teammates whose sons grew up together, but had very different recruiting experiences. The family of A. J. Granger went through recruiting in the summer of 1995, and share their experience and insights in detail. Steve Smith was a highly acclaimed high school basketball player who looks back on the recruiting process after more than a decade, now with a wife and two children. Mac Bledsoe, a former recruit himself, decided to teach his sons how to handle life, including recruiting, themselves.

In reading these stories, ask questions like, "I wonder if he thought about life after athletics when he did that? Was that an academic or athletic choice? Did he investigate enough alternatives? Am I looking for the same thing in a coach he did? Would I want to stay that close to home?"

The goal is to learn from the experience of others.

A STORY OF TWO FRIENDS AND THEIR SONS

In 1969, Mike Stumpf and Scott Weakley enrolled at Division III Capital University to play basketball and get college degrees. Through the next four years they did just that. With Stumpf in the paint and Weakley at the point, the Crusaders never lost more than five games, or won less than 20. The teammates graduated with a total record of 83-17. Stumpf was all-conference three times, Weakley twice; Stumpf was All-American once. Stumpf is still first in school history in scoring; Weakley ranks fourth.

The two are friends today. Their sons, Mike's second and Scott's first, virtually grew up together. In the fall of 1995, those two young men left for college, but in very different directions.

Aaron Stumpf, 6-foot-4, attended Toledo on a Division I basketball scholarship. Toledo Rocket Coach Larry Gipson saw Aaron in the state regionals his junior year and said, "I don't need to see you make another basket to offer you a scholarship." The Rockets ran the recruiting race as the frontrunner.

"You've got to forget pride during the recruiting process," remembers Aaron. "I wished the Big Ten schools wanted me, but they didn't. You have to go on."

Mike Stumpf, initially overwhelmed by the entire process, began to look at it as a businessman. Now president of Riverstone Construction, which does major home remodeling and custom new homes, he states, "You have to see it as a buying process. Determine what you want and figure where you can get it. You want a place where they really want you. We decided it was important to find a coach who wasn't overly likely to move up and not overly likely to be fired. That's not easy. When we went to Toledo to play in the regionals Aaron's senior year we saw an article in the newspaper that read 'Gipson has to win or else.'"

Aaron adds, "Signing early was a priority, so my teammates knew I wasn't worried about college ball in high school, and I wanted a program that wasn't rebuilding."

The process actually started in eighth grade after Aaron played in an AAU tournament. "You've got to get out of your bailiwick to see how good you are," said Mike. "Go outside your comfort zone. If you're good enough, exposure helps."

As a result of that first tournament, Aaron was invited to join the All-Ohio AAU program in Columbus. There he played against nationally recruited players like Samaki Walker, who went to Louisville and left after his sophomore year to be a lottery pick in the 1996 NBA Draft.

"I had to adjust and find my role," said Aaron of the on-court experience which helped prepare him for the pressure of recruiting.

"You've got to grow up," Aaron emphasizes. "When you talk with coaches they are very friendly, your buddies. You've got to ask, 'Are you ready to offer me a scholarship?' It's like making a cut, or not making it."

Mike adds, "It's hard work to go on unofficial visits, but you learn a lot and kids need direction. Parents have to make time to do that."

Most parents go through the recruiting process and gain a skill which they never use again. Maybe someone asks their opinion and they can share their knowledge, maybe not. But for Mike Stumpf, the lessons learned will be valuable soon enough.

"It's starting all over with Carey," he smiles. His daughter earned recognition as one of the top 25 freshman girls in Ohio as a varsity basketball player during Aaron's senior year, and also plays volleyball.

Things were different for Kevin Weakley, Scott's 5-foot-9 son. Aaron and Kevin played in the same AAU leagues, but taller and more athletic guards played on the traveling team ahead of Kevin. Despite leading his Worthington Christian team to the state high school tournament final game as a junior, D-I colleges decided they needed a bigger point guard. Kevin turned down NAIA scholarship offers to attend D-III Otterbein.

"Everyone told me Division I schools were interested," said Kevin, "but none ever called. I thought, as a player, if I was good enough people would see me. I led the fall [AAU] league in scoring."

Scott Weakley coached his alma mater Capital for five years. The last two, Mike Stumpf's oldest son Ryan was on the team. Weakley resigned in 1994 to go into private business and watch his three sons grow up. When he talked, he expressed the thoughts of an involved parent and as well as an experienced coach.

"Division I coaches could do a better job of evaluating heart and attitude. Their major criteria is athletic ability," he said. "Division III coaches have to measure heart, because they seldom get great talent. Attitude, teachability, coachability, and leadership are essential.

"In a way, the NCAA has created the recruiting chaos that exists today. Division I coaches don't have time to get to know people before they sign them. Everybody knows about the top 50 players, the most talented, but there are maybe 500 other good players in the country. Some have great attitudes. They can become great players, but coaches can't spend enough time evaluating to recognize them," said Scott.

"At D-I they invest $40,000 to $60,000 in players they may have only seen two or three times. At D-III the player invests as much for the chance to play, but his coach has checked with the janitor to see what kind of kid he is. In the business world you'd go bankrupt not evaluating your investment better than that.

"The recruiting process has moved from the college coach, the high school coach and the parents to AAU coaches and camp organizers. When I was coaching at Capital we'd rent the gym out for those exposure shoot-outs. Those things, and the camps, make a lot of money. It's good business for the people that run them, but do the kids benefit?" Weakley wondered, remembering several instances when a coach came in the gym, said hello to one player and left, though hundreds of players spent $65 to be seen.

"I know balancing athletics with all the facets of higher education is a challenge, but sometimes I wonder if university administrators are a little hypocritical in the recruiting process," he said, based on many hours of NCAA meetings.

"In October [of Kevin's senior year] we knew things might be frustrating. We decided to give it to the Lord and not let it be that way," said Weakley.

The former coach never took an active role in promoting his son to colleges. "It's not my job as a parent. When I was coach I got letters and tapes from parents, and didn't pay much attention to them. I was too busy doing my job."

Kevin adds, "I believe the Lord will take care of me if I do my best—work hard, play hard, have fun.

As if on cue, Scott adds, "Have fun. Work hard. Do everything you can within the rules to be successful. That's fun. Worrying about getting a big scholarship can cause you to care more about personal performance than winning. Go to a place where the coach is committed to you. Otterbein saw Kevin play every game his senior year. That coach will help you through the tough times. Go to school where you expect to live after college. Make a name for yourself. I tried to sell that as a coach, I believe it as a father."

As the sons left for freshman year, both fathers and both sons seemed content with the result. Then, their experiences as college basketball players were just as different as their recruiting had been.

At Otterbein, Kevin Weakley started every game, led the team in assists, was second in steals and third in field goal attempts.

Aaron Stumpf played a total of 36 minutes in 11 games for Toledo, where Larry Gipson resigned to become interim assistant athletic director.

A. J. GRANGER'S FAMILY GOES THROUGH RECRUITING

When A. J. Granger committed to Michigan State University October 5, 1995, the casual Spartan fan may have shrugged his shoulders. What's the big deal about a kid from a small Ohio high school who averaged 13 points and eight rebounds a game as a junior? He may have thought, "How are we going to beat Michigan?"

In fact, first year MSU Coach Tom Izzo won an intense recruiting battle with some of the best programs in the country for a very highly regarded player. Who was it that said, "There are lies, damn lies and statistics"?

A. J. Granger's high school numbers did not adequately represent his basketball ability. He took less than nine shots a game on a 27-0 state championship team which had an average score of 74-43, with all starters averaging close to double figures despite playing little in the second half. Knowledgeable coaches saw his skill level immediately in AAU competition.

Granger's high school coach at Liberty Benton, Steve Williman, said, "Our kids are unselfish. A. J. has no ego—coaches appreciate that. As for college, he is the type of player who has unlimited potential. He has to play inside in high school because of his size (6-foot-9), but he'll be able to move outside in college. He has all the tools to score inside and on the perimeter."

Williman, a former college graduate assistant coach, brought insights to the Grangers during recruiting. At the same time, he was impressed by their research. "The Grangers did their homework in analyzing different programs," said the coach.

The story of A. J. Granger's recruitment, discussed candidly by his parents Dawn and Joe, reveals much about the process of receiving an athletic scholarship.

"It all started in fifth grade, when Jim Clay called," begins Dawn Granger, a secretarial superintendent at Liberty-Benton. "We were lucky, because he was a good person who found quality kids and took them around Ohio to different tournaments. He is very good teaching young kids.

"From sixth grade on, every summer but one our family vacation was based on A. J.'s basketball," she remembers. "With the travel, meals, hotels, extra shoes, extra sweat suits and everything it was

$4,000 to $5,000 a summer," part vacation, part investment. "He was growing and maturing emotionally through playing, and it helped him for the high school team," said Dawn.

"People say, 'You have a chance to be seen, which was a plus, but the teaching was always most important," said her husband Joe, who used most of his four week vacation from Cooper Tire traveling and watching basketball each summer.

"He was hitting the weights for track and basketball," Joe continues. "Around eighth or ninth grade he started getting stronger, more able to push back. At certain points you could see the mental progression as well."

AAU ball was soon supplemented with summer camps. "Before sophomore year I went to the Krider Camp in Cincinnati," recalls A.J. "Never touched the ball. There were three guys on the team being recruited by Iowa and schools like that, and they shot all the time."

Though not the type of player to excel in the run-and-gun summer camp setting, A. J. Granger needed to get the attention of college coaches. After a sophomore year when the Liberty-Benton team went 22-2 and he averaged double figures, "Coach Williman told us A. J. needed to be in a big-time AAU program, that he wasn't getting enough exposure in high school," remembers Dawn.

The Grangers selected an AAU program, but it wasn't the right one. "They used him as a center, and all the colleges wanted to see him play forward," said Joe Granger. "He is a versatile player, can play '3' or '4' and can see the floor; he needed to show that." Especially since he had to play center in high school. "And we found out there wasn't very much teaching there," adds Dawn.

When Bobby Kortsen called about his Columbus Basketball Club, the Grangers asked about the teaching, if they had a center ("It was OK for A. J. to play there some, just not all the time," said Joe.) and what the other players were like. Then they agreed to go to a couple of practices before making a commitment to the team.

Matt Cooper, 6-foot-10 and eventually a Dayton signee, was on-hand for center, and coach Jon Daup "turned out to be another Jim Clay," according to Dawn. The logical team change was made, and touched off more problems than recruiting ever did.

"The other coach threatened us, he said, 'Your son will never play at a good school if he leaves my program.' Coaches called Coach Williman asking if A. J. was quitting basketball, and he called others just to make sure there was no misunderstanding. It was difficult," remembers Dawn.

That summer the two teams played in a tournament.

"That coach screamed at A. J. the whole game," said Dawn.

"Tyler, our other son, five years younger than A. J., was sick so he and I went out to the car. I could hear the coach yelling out there."

Joe remembers thinking, "Away games in college can't be much worse than this."

That tournament was only a small part of the busy schedule A.J. kept between his junior and senior year in high school.

The first weekend in June was Ohio's state track meet. "He got almost as many letters for track as for basketball," said Dawn. "He was third in our division in the discus at the state meet, but the distance was farther than anyone from the larger schools. In some ways track might have made more sense, but he just loves basketball."

AAU practice dominated the second week in June, followed by an AAU tournament in Cincinnati that weekend. For the next two weeks, A. J. worked at the Liberty-Benton basketball camp, traveling to Columbus for AAU practice Tuesday and Thursday evenings and playing in a high school team league on Wednesday nights. The third weekend was a high school team camp in Cincinnati, the fourth the AAU tournament in Zanesville. The weekend of June 30 was another team camp.

Then things got hectic.

July 1 is the first day college coaches can call a recruit in his home. "We got 130 phone calls that weekend," said Dawn, giving the impression it was a number she would remember for a long time. "We asked coaches to call only on Tuesday and Thursday nights, and only from 8 p.m. to 11 p.m. Even though they only are allowed to call once a week, we have call waiting, they would call back, calls would stack up and it was usually after midnight before he was off the phone."

In the fall of A. J.'s junior year, the Grangers had begun to make unofficial visits to nearby schools which had shown early interest.

"If parents are financially able to afford to do it," said Joe, "they should take unofficial visits before the official visits begin. Summer visits are not as good, go when school is in session. Coaches will help schedule time with people you want to see."

Unofficial visits may increase the attractiveness of a school, or remove it from serious consideration. Either way, the time is well spent. In early July, the Grangers took three days to visit four schools, including Ohio State for the fourth time.

Ohio State was always the leader. "You grow up in Ohio, how can you think about leaving?" said Joe, a Buckeye fan for decades. "But sitting in Mr. [Coach Randy] Ayers' office we knew the dream was dead," recalls Dawn. "It was hard to go to those other schools because we were so disappointed about Ohio State."

The Grangers did not wish to be quoted on the reasons their dream was dead. They were anxious to help athletes and parents with the recruiting process, but reluctant to be critical. However, Ohio State had lost 16 of 18 Big Ten games the previous season, and was 16-38 in conference games in the previous three years. Ohio State had lost several players due to transfers, expulsions, academic problems, NCAA violations and other reasons. Many of the new recruits had been rejected by other schools and none of the top players in Granger's class were considering Ohio State.

Ohio State lost 15 of 18 conference games during A. J.'s senior year. When four more players left the program, the Grangers had no reason to second guess their decision.

July 6, A. J. left for the adidas ABCD Camp at Fairleigh Dickinson University in Teaneck, N. J., where veteran evaluator Tom Konchalski reported an "astronomical number of players present." It wasn't A. J.'s best showcase, but he played well.

On July 14, the Columbus Basketball Club left Columbus by bus for Las Vegas, where they would play in the 64-team Big Time Tournament.

"A. J. and Joe flew one day later," recalls Dawn. "He needed rest and we thought, at his height, the bus ride would cause problems with his knees. The bus broke down in the mountains, and the team arrived a day after A. J. and Joe got there."

The tournament ended July 23. After a few days of relaxing, playing in open gyms and taking lots of phone calls, the Grangers left for an AAU tournament in Columbus July 27-30. There a college assistant coach remarked that Granger had one of the best summers he'd seen a kid have, saying it reminded him of an NCAA tournament run where everything goes right.

August meant open gyms, a heavy dose of weight training and unofficial visits to two schools which were in A. J.'s top five, Notre Dame and Indiana.

"At Indiana, A. J. was offered a scholarship. They thought he would accept immediately," said Dawn. "He said he was interested, but not ready to decide. He wanted to go on his official visits and get as much information as possible before deciding. I'm afraid he offended them. They recruit a lot of Indiana kids who grow up loving the school and would do anything to go there, so they expected him to know right away."

A. J. Granger narrowed the list to four schools, asking Pittsburgh, Notre Dame, Michigan State and Cincinnati to make home visits in September.

But before September arrived, the Granger family got another lesson in recruiting.

"Xavier had offered a scholarship when we visited informally in July," said Joe. "They called and withdrew it. One of their players had unexpectedly regained his eligibility and they needed the scholarship for him. It was a reality check for us."

In fact, an offer can be withdrawn at any time if it is not accepted. "One of the reasons A. J. announced his decision October 5 was to be sure it wasn't withdrawn," adds Joe.

After four home visits, A. J. decided to narrow his list to three schools for official visits. "I had been to Cincinnati for team camp every summer, and decided it was a little more of an urban setting than I wanted," he remembers.

The Grangers visited Michigan State the second weekend in September, Notre Dame the third and Pittsburgh the fourth. But after Michigan State, they knew.

"I grew up following the Big Ten," said A. J. "I didn't know as much about the Big East. But it was really the coaches, the players, the location and the academics."

"Early on he didn't know how important distance was," said Dawn. "We had to let him experience it. Stanford and Duke were involved early, but his only visit beyond three hours was Pittsburgh. We're glad he'll be close, because he may need to get home some weekend. The coaches told us freshmen hit at least four walls that first year."

"The coaches wives and I got to be good friends," said Dawn, looking back. "We'd talk about shopping, they'd send me notes—I really clicked with some of them. And on those home visits, the coaches would sit at our dining room table and pour their hearts out to you. Then the official visits, when they'd feed you great meals and put you in nice hotels," she shook her head.

"For a while, we wanted to take the best from each situation," said Joe. "We would wish that Larry Hunter were coaching at a bigger school than Ohio University, or Herb Sendek [at a bigger school than Miami], or Pittsburgh were closer. As adults, we worried about hurting other people's feelings. But, like many coaches told us, its a business."

The last two weeks of September were hectic. As the list narrowed from five to three, the phone calls seemed to increase. When A. J. got back from one visit, another coach would call and try to erase the memory. Still, one thing that impressed them was seeing Coach Izzo or Coach Willard joking and interacting with the players.

"There is still some child left in these big boys. There needs to be some parenting going on," Dawn states.

Unfortunately, not every memory of the recruiting process is positive. There was the time the Grangers sat in a head coach's office and his assistant fell asleep. Three times. There was the time they asked a head coach about one of his player's publicized problems with the law and were told, "he doesn't have a problem."

There was also the time A. J. asked the question he always asked—"What can I do to make your team better?" and a head coach did not have a good answer. "It was clear this coach doesn't do much coaching. He must leave everything to his assistants," Joe said.

Now, during trips to Columbus to take their younger son Tyler to Kortsen's AAU program, the Grangers find themselves thinking about the possibility of their seventh grader going through recruiting. "He's a different person, we'll have to handle it differently," thought Joe.

Asked for some specific recommendations they would pass on to an athlete being recruited, Joe mentions, "Get someone involved with you. If your high school coach is not knowledgeable, he can call other high school coaches for advice. We were fortunate that Coach Williman was experienced enough to give us good questions to ask, yet willing to call other coaches for ideas."

"That is crucial," adds Dawn. "Having help might be the difference between getting a scholarship and not getting one. For correspondence or typing, ask the Guidance Counselor at school, who would be the primary contact for evaluating academics as well."

Both parents agreed to the importance of being tested in AAU competition. "College coaches said, 'AAU is not great, but it's necessary,'" said Joe.

As for evaluating colleges, "Go on Friday and go to some classes. The player misses high school football games, but that is the best way to see the college," Dawn mentions.

"We asked about support systems, tutors for every subject, computer access and found all schools pretty much the same. The big thing on an official visit is to spend time with a mix of players, especially the younger ones who will be there when you are. The colleges give you a host to show you around, someone they think you'll like. Talk to as many different players as you can," Joe adds.

When A. J. Granger was young, his parents said, "You've got a gift, use it." He has, and the dream of a college scholarship has been realized. It is too soon to know if he will be successful in basketball at Michigan State, because there is so much hard work ahead. Luck is involved as well. He could be hurt, or have better players arrive on campus.

Twelve years earlier, another Ohio kid made a college choice and experienced some of that uncertainty. Today it is interesting to see how Steve Smith remembers that choice.

STEVE SMITH, A 30-YEAR-OLD LOOKS BACK AT HIS "HOOP DREAM"

The movie *Hoop Dreams* captured the hearts of America with its story of two inner-city Chicago kids who went to a suburban parochial high school to reach their college and NBA goals. As so often happens, the NBA did not work out.

Steve Smith followed the same path a decade earlier, but no one had a video camera to record it. Though more heavily recruited than either William Gates or Arthur Agee in the movie, Smith's professional hopes never materialized either. Now 30, married with two sons, Smith has an experienced perspective for student-athletes, which blends successes with disappointments.

A seventh grader when his single-parent mother died suddenly of a liver ailment, he left Columbus, Ohio to live with his aunt and uncle in Dayton, about 80 miles away. While dealing with his grief he let his once excellent grades drop, but did develop an identity as a basketball player.

As a ninth grader he was too good to play on the reserve team, but not good enough to start on the varsity. The Dayton Roth Falcons won the state championship in 1981, led by three seniors who received D-I scholarships. Smith played against them everyday in practice and learned about winning.

With all five starters gone, not much was expected from Roth in 1982. After Smith scored 32 points in the first game, expectations began to change. Roth went 15-4 in the regular season, then won nine straight tournament games for another state title. Smith made the all-tournament team, but most impressive was the all-city team he did not make.

"He asked me not to nominate him for first team," Coach Mike Haley, now winner of four Ohio high school state titles, recalls. "He was afraid Dayton Public League coaches wouldn't vote two Roth players first team, and he didn't want a split vote to hurt senior Michael Carton." Averaging 20 points, eight rebounds, four assists and three steals a game, Smith was a unanimous second team choice.

Roth was one of five Dayton public schools closed that year. The seniors, including current Miami Dolphin Keith Byars, were off to college. Haley was named coach at Dayton Dunbar, where rising seniors could join him because of open enrollment. As a junior, Smith was directed to go to Belmont, like it or not. Then the Belmont coach, without talking with him, told the press there was no decision to be made, it was out of Smith's hands.

"I felt I was being dictated to, and discriminated against due to the way the boundaries were drawn," Smith remembers.

When a private school began to recruit him, he saw an option. He inquired about another private school, Kettering Alter, with a rich basketball tradition and a history of sending players to college. Fans throughout America knew of Alter grads Jim Paxson of the Portland Trailblazers and his brother John Paxson of Notre Dame, and later the NBA champion Chicago Bulls. Alter's college prep curriculum did not concern Smith.

"I knew I had not applied myself at Roth," he said. "The school system was not as good as Columbus, and I was sliding through. I knew I could do the work at Alter if I applied myself. When I got there I found the environment motivating. Most of the people were working hard and it rubbed off on me."

The change in racial composition wasn't an issue for him either. Roth's enrollment was at least 90 percent African-American, like himself, while Alter was less than five percent. Nor did the change from Roth's full court pressure, fast-breaking style to Alter's more patient attack cause concern.

While there were adjustments, on balance the change was a complete success. Alter was 21-5, then 23-3. Both years they lost in the regional finals, one game short of the state AAA semi-finals in Columbus. Smith was All-Ohio and *Street & Smith's* All-America.

He was heavily recruited. Ohio State selected him and four other Ohioans to offer scholarships the spring before the early signing period, then an innovative idea. Michigan told Smith he was their "top recruit in the country," though a scholarship was never offered. When Smith visited the University of Southern California, he met Henry Winkler, a huge star as "The Fonz" on the television hit, *Happy Days*.

And a trip to Marquette ended regrettably.

Several recruits stayed in the same hotel, abused room service charges, drank alcohol and made excessive noise. Marquette Coach Rick Majerus, now at Utah, withdrew scholarship offers from all the athletes involved, including Smith. What might have been his best choice of college was no longer available. Smith eventually chose the

University of Dayton, which would win three games in the NCAA Tournament that year.

His hope of being a hometown hero got off to a slow start as a freshman when the returning small forward, Damon Goodwin, was moved to guard. Coach Don Donoher seldom substituted and was a disciplinarian on shot-selection, not Smith's strongest point.

"I told them with Steve you have to accept a bad shot as part of the package at times," remembers Alter Coach Joe Petrocelli. "I felt the good far outweighed the bad, but they didn't see it that way."

Sophomore year, Smith came off the bench to score a team high 20 points in a 64-59 victory over Fordham, but went back to the bench. When the steady Goodwin graduated, that starting position opened up. Now more disciplined, Smith intended to grab it.

"When I started the first exhibition game as a junior, I thought it would be the beginning of a ritual," he recalls. "At that time I still thought the NBA would be a reality. But then came the favoritism and politics of college basketball."

When star point guard Negele Knight was ruled out for the entire season after surgery to both ankles, Donoher changed his priorities. He decided to emphasize the development of a five man freshman class for the future. A freshman got the big guard position and Smith played irregularly. After 12 points and six rebounds in an upset of Ohio State, he played briefly in five of the next 11 games, sitting out the others.

The sports editor of the student paper graded each player on the season and gave Smith a D-. Then the remaining point guard suffered a knee injury. Steve Smith, never having played the position in his life, started at point in the next game against Cincinnati. With Oscar Robertson, one of the greatest guards in NBA history, courtside to announce the game for his alma mater, Smith played brilliantly. Not having made a field goal in over six weeks, he scored 18 points and added eight assists. He was an easy choice as game MVP in Dayton's comeback victory.

Donoher reflected on his decision by saying, "Steve's played a lot of ball. He's got a point to prove, right? He's competitive. He's got to say, 'I'll show my coach I can play.' He was the picture of composure."

Stories about Steve Smith filled the papers. One article talked of his relationship with Little Brother Larry Davis, and challenged Dayton adults to participate in The Big Brothers—Big Sisters Association if a student-athlete could find the time to do it.

In the next game, Smith directed the Flyers to a victory over Butler, scoring 14 points. He led the team in scoring in a loss to 28-3

DePaul, and had nine against Bradley. Then the point guard returned and Smith was back on the bench. After averaging over 15 points in three successive starts, he didn't even play in two of the final five games of the season. The Flyers finished 13-15.

As a senior co-captain, Smith again played sporadically. He graduated in four years with a bachelors degree in Communication Management.

"You can be happy socially even when your sport doesn't work out," he believes. "That got me through, knowing people, being comfortable with the college and the city. For me it was good to stay near home."

Asked what he would say to a recruited athlete trying to select a college, Smith said, "I'd ask, 'What are you looking for in a college? How are the dynamics between the coach and the team? Is the social situation good, meaning both on the team and in the student body away from the team? If you are happy socially, you can grow as a person and in the classroom. How disciplined are you? There is increased independence, more peer pressure and male/female relationships are never easy."

He feels strongly about one other matter, the one which kept him from playing for Majerus at Marquette, who believed Smith could develop from a "great athlete and a good player into a very good college player."

"Alcohol is a big problem—in high school and college, among blacks and whites, athletes and non-athletes," Smith said. "It's a poison that effects your body chemistry. Beer caused me to gain weight, which didn't help my game. Those athletes who didn't drink had an advantage. More importantly, alcohol has had a devastating effect on the entire African-American community, causing undue hardships, physically and mentally.

"Each person has to be individually responsible, but alcohol is pushed so much by the media it's acceptable. Athletes aren't the only ones; you read about coaches with drinking problems, too."

Now Smith calls himself a "homebody." He is a child welfare specialist, a social worker for Catholic Charities in Chicago, a subcontractor of the Illinois Department of Social and Family Services. He works with African-American children living with foster parents, mostly teenagers and 90 percent male. He figures, "I get paid to help people," and he doesn't drink.

After a high school career with 94 victories and only 13 losses, two state championships and many individual awards, the NBA dream ended about ten years ago. A life of raising a family and helping people remains. The NCAA idea of a student-athlete can work, amid bumps and bruises.

MAC BLEDSOE, AN UNUSUAL FOOTBALL FATHER

"It's not about raising kids to be recruited, it's about raising kids to be people," said Mac Bledsoe, thinking back to the recruiting experiences of his sons Drew, in 1990, and Adam, in 1996.

"First, you need to know how (wife) Barbara and I raised our kids. Our model was that children were on loan to us for 18 years. By the time they were age nine, they should be making half of the big decisions. By the time they were 16, they were as close to being adults as a two-year-old was to being born. Therefore, a 16-year-old ought to have as much authority over his life as we had over the life of a two-year-old."

Coincidentally, Drew first tried downhill skiing at the age of two. Twenty-some years later, in 1994, he set NFL records for pass attempts in a season and single-game marks in attempts and completions with the New England Patriots.

In the spring of 1996, Mac was in the process of organizing The Drew Bledsoe Foundation, a charitable foundation to better children's lives through parenting which son Drew initiated with a $1 million contribution. Mac would be leaving his career as a high school English and speech teacher and assistant football coach to expand the network he had established as a nationally known lecturer on family relationships and children's self-esteem.

"My mother, now in her early 70s, helped both the boys deal with recruiting," said Mac. "She sat them down in a rather matriarchal way and said, 'Everybody will tell you this will be a very tough decision [deciding on a college]. You don't have a tough decision, this is an easy decision. If you are worried, look at the 12 or 20 schools recruiting you. You can't make a bad decision from these topnotch universities which are great football schools with reputable men as coaches. You have already made the tough decisions when you decided to lift weights, decided to stay drug and alcohol free, decided to keep up your studies, got high SAT scores. If you had not done those things, you might have a bad reputation and low grades. There might be four schools recruiting you, two you didn't like and two you couldn't get into. Then you would have a tough decision.' I think for both boys it was extremely quieting.

"When Drew went through recruiting, it was a time of self-discovery for my wife and me," Mac continues. "Though I had been a coach for 18 years, we had to feel our way as we went. Now there are fewer scholarships [85 from 95], the coaches are more selective, it is a little more competitive. Coaches do their homework earlier and offer scholarships earlier. Drew had to blaze his own trail. Word about him hadn't gone as far, not as many coaches had seen film. Adam was more of a known quantity, more coaches saw film of him. No one committed a scholarship to Drew before his senior year, while Adam had three offers before his.

"Because they had been raised to make their own decisions, college was truly their choice to make. They both had the same process. They wrote down their values, what was important in their lives. After visiting the schools they listed the strengths and weaknesses of each school and compared them to those personal values.

"The decision became clear as they looked at their values and compared the plusses and minuses," he said. "The selection process was a great educational process as they learned to deal with highly motivated coaches and to hold to their ideals under pressure. The fact that I was a team captain at Washington in 1968 was discussed by others, but had no effect on their decision. Why should it? The times are different; the people are different; and my kids are different from me.

"With Drew", said his father, "each time he took a trip he came home pumped-up about the positives they had shown him. As time passed, he began to compare each to his values. After Washington and the University of Miami, he talked about national championships and national TV. Then he thought, 'these are not even on my list of values. I can go to school in a small community and still play against the best teams in big stadiums.'

"Also, with Mike Price at Washington State, there was never any pressure. We wondered about the coaches who applied pressure; what would they be like on 4th and goal? As it turned out, Drew had the judgment of someone much older and more mature. When Mike Price started Drew as a freshman there was heavy criticism, but Coach Price never turned that pressure back on Drew, he never said anything like, 'I stuck my neck out for you, you better come through.'

"Mike took the exact same approach with Adam," said Mac. "Adam really liked him, but he found a coach and situation he liked even better. Coach Neuheisel said, 'We want you as our quarterback. If not you, we probably won't take another quarterback this year.' When Adam announced for Colorado, Mike called immediately to congratulate him.

"With both boys it really came down to the coach," said Mac. "My personal opinion is that the coach you play for will probably be the major influence over your college experience."

Between the decisions the coach makes which directly affect each player, the coaches he hires and the atmosphere he establishes, there is little room for discussion. But if the coach is so important, what about the likelihood that a high-profile coach like Neuheisel may go to another school?

"We asked, and he answered that to Adam's satisfaction," said Mac. "Coach Neuheisel talked about the other jobs which he might consider, and his plans for Colorado."

Any final guidelines to be followed during recruiting?

"We thought it was important that it be the kid's decision," reiterates Mac. "We decided not to make the trips, so they could be perceived as what they were, young people making their own decision. At the same time, when the decision was made and communicated we thought it was important that there be adults in the room, to support them and make sure there were no misunderstandings. Both were recruited in an above-board, ethical fashion."

What about advice for a friend with a child being recruited?

"First, teach the child to make decisions, to form personal values. That process begins at birth. Second, teach them to be well rounded. Prepare them to be people. If football disappeared, if the money disappeared [from his NFL contract with the New England Patriots], Drew could teach school and be happy," said Mac.

"More specifically, I think it's a real mistake to allow college coaches to do all the recruiting. It can be important for the athlete and the family to recruit the college. There is an impression that colleges know about all the players, but there is talent the colleges do not see. Elite schools miss some players, schools with smaller budgets are more likely to miss them. The young person with a dream about a certain college, or college in general, could put together a personal resume with letters of recommendation, vital statistics, weight lifting data, SAT scores and a transcript. I'd also suggest a video tape, with one complete game, a highlight tape and a close-up video of drill work. In the years I was coaching, there must have been 15 kids who might not have had a chance if they didn't recruit schools, from upper level D-I on down."

Having heard the experiences and opinions of a wide variety of experts in the first part of the book, it is time to begin to apply those thoughts to specific issues an athlete must face in deciding on a college. Goals must be developed and NCAA rules must be followed. Then, consideration of pertinent facts and an informed, logical conclusion remain. Those topics will be covered in the next section.

SECTION 2

APPLYING THE INSIGHTS

Chapter VII
GOAL SETTING AND ACHIEVEMENT

"Although they only give gold medals in the field of athletics, I encourage everyone to look inside themselves and find their own personal dream, whatever it may be—sports, medicine, law, business, music, writing, whatever. The same principles apply. Turn your dreams into a goal, and decide how to attack that goal systematically. Break it into bite-size chunks that seem possible—and don't give up. Just keep plugging away."

John Naber
Four-time Olympic gold medalist

When people work out, they can have a variety of goals; such as making the athletic team, losing weight, toning, pumping up, and showing off their achievements.

But what about the heavy-set guy in the short white shorts with the black argyles? He took off his Docksiders, got on the stationary bike, then set the effort for 1 and the course for 1. Every two minutes he "burned off" five calories. Why was he there? At that rate, he wouldn't accomplish much. Plus, he quit after three minutes. Since he apparently didn't have any real concern about self-improvement, maybe his goal was to say, "Yeah, just got back from the gym. Had a good work-out. I'm beginning to see some progress. No pain, no gain."

People have different goals. Carla McGhee is another example. After her freshman year at Tennessee in 1987, when she played for a national championship basketball team, McGhee was in a four-car accident.

"I had a head injury, a broken chin, a hole in my forehead, and broke nearly every bone in my face," she said. Combined with multiple fractures of her hip, doctors hoped she would be able to walk again. Basketball seemed out of the realm of possibility.

McGhee set goals and got busy. She left her black socks and street shoes behind, because she had serious work to do.

"I had to learn to sit-up, to stand, to chew," she recalls. "At times I felt like a child, a little toddler. I cried, I had all these different emotions. Some days I felt like, 'I'm tired, I can't do this.'"

McGhee missed a year of competition. When she returned, Tennessee won another NCAA title in 1989. After playing professionally in Europe, she joined the USA Basketball Women's National Team for the 1996 season. She hoped to win a gold medal in the Olympics, so she could put it on display at her hometown community center. She wanted inner-city youth to have a reminder that no matter what your circumstances, you can achieve your goals.

Sports teach athletes about goals, whether the goal is to make a team, to earn more playing time, or to win a championship.

Hopefully athletes already use goals in other parts of life. Academic goals can begin with avoiding trouble and passing courses, include high school graduation, and extend to honors along the way. Social goals may be making new friends, or getting a date with a special friend. Other goals might have to do with writing for the school paper, joining a service organization, or organizing a church group. The more experience an athlete has with goal-setting, the easier recruiting should be, because the first step to being recruited is identifying what time in college should produce.

Baseball Hall of Famer Yogi Berra said, "You got to be very careful if you don't know where you are going, because you might not get there." It was probably one of his relatives who said, "It's more difficult to reach a goal you do not have than it is to come back from a place you have never been."

When the late Norman Vincent Peale talked about goals he was more direct, saying, "If you can conceive it, and believe it, you can achieve it."

They all said goals begin in your mind. The "calorie-challenged" guy in the gym had not decided to lose weight, or else his work-out would have had purpose.

Carla McGhee decided to return as a basketball player long before she accomplished it. In fact, she decided to return long before doctors gave her permission to begin working-out. Then, when she was able to workout, she never settled for the minimum. She conceived something the doctors did not, and believed when they did not. After that, she worked to achieve a goal she had set.

If anyone ever looked like a natural athlete, Michael Jordan looks like a natural basketball player. Quick, fast, smooth, he has it all—now, he does. He did not have it all as a high school sophomore, when he was cut from the school team. He started working and made himself better than anyone could have imagined. It started with a goal to make the varsity team.

INFLUENCING THE FUTURE

Some people use the excuse, "I don't make goals because I don't know what the future holds." That is exactly the reason to make goals, to influence the future. If Jordan had let the future develop for itself, he might never have played college basketball, much less become a remarkable pro. If McGhee had not set "impossible" goals, she would not have played in the 1996 Olympics.

The challenge for a teenager setting life goals as the basis for making a college choice is to imagine being 50 years old. It may not seem possible, but 30-some years from now every teenager will be that old. That's the future, just like homework, first dates, first jobs and driver's licenses were at one time. The only ones who won't be 50 in the future are those among the dearly departed. Compared to that, 50 doesn't sound so bad.

What is life like at 50? Thinking might begin with parents—are there some parts of their lives to duplicate? It's OK to think about friends' parents, or coaches, as long as the teenager remembers to return to thinking about what he or she wants. Marriage? Kids? Earning a living? Playing the sport which provided the scholarship? Other sports? Involved in sports at all? Coaching, as a vocation or a hobby? Travel? Living in what part of the country? Since parents are older, who is caring for their needs? If kids were a priority, is there enough money for college?

Some of these questions are very important, others seem trivial. Which questions should be added? This is how goals begin to form, by thinking about the future.

A teacher, age 50, would think back on college, appropriate

course work, graduation, student-teaching, and early experiences in the classroom. Someone who wanted to be a teacher would benefit from talking with teachers. Would their experiences be tolerable? Enjoyable? A goal is not real until it is made with an awareness of the sacrifices required to achieve it. More people want to be Michael Jordan than want to work like he did to arrive where he is, and work like he does to stay there.

PLANNING TO ACHIEVE GOALS

One of the best teachers I ever had was a diminutive, gentle man named Manley Howe Jones, Ph.D., mentioned in the chapter on case studies. It was nearly 30 years ago, but I still remember his Executive Decision Making class. He taught students that "one test of a good decision is whether it still looks like a wise one when we re-examine it later."

That's sound advice in recruiting. It is also the reason for a teenager to try to imagine being 50 years of age, in order to look back at a college decision before making it. We can't see the future, but by going into the future we can look back on the past.

Jones said, "a decision can only be as good as the best of the alternatives taken into consideration." He also stressed the importance of asking questions, advice echoed by so many people in the first section of this book. Most important to this book was Dr. Jones' concept of Goals and the Means-Ends Staircase.

He taught that ultimate goals only take place if satisfactory preliminary goals have been achieved. For example, every college graduate graduated from high school, was admitted to a university, took required courses, passed required courses and met other criteria in order to graduate. To graduate with a degree in business, the university might have required admission to a College of Business, based on satisfactory performance in the first year or two. At some point along the academic way, the student would have had to develop writing and analytical skills, study habits, etc..

The staircase approach to goal achievement applies to sports as well. A softball or baseball player begins on the sandlot, gets into some form of little league, then gets into school sports programs. All the while the athlete was building a base of skills, like running, batting and throwing, and knowledge, such as hitting the cut-off and watching the coach while running the bases.

By learning and competing, the ball player may be on the high school freshman or reserve team before playing varsity, developing skills and knowledge at each step on the staircase. The player good enough to skip a traditional step, for example playing varsity as a freshman, has to compete with older, more experienced players.

The very best high school players move up the staircase to college, some to play, some to star. Climbing the staircase, in school, athletics or life, is a matter of ability and planning. Ability will never be maximized without planning, but good planning can only take limited ability so far.

As a young boy I loved basketball. I even had a plan to play it in college. My plan was to be like Jerry West, then a great college player at West Virginia University. Now he is the General Manager of the Los Angeles Lakers; as an All-Pro he was the model for the NBA emblem. My plan was to be 6-foot-3 like Jerry West, and develop a jump shot like Jerry West, in order to be as good a player as he was.

I worked on my jump shot, ate vegetables and slept, in order to grow. Eventually I grew to be 6-foot-4. I met one goal. Unfortunately, my jump shot reminded more people of Mae West than Jerry West. Planning only goes so far.

Though I enjoyed playing competitive basketball long after college, I was not as good at my sport as sub-par high school athletes are at theirs. Part was lack of athletic ability, but, looking back, I didn't work very intelligently toward my goal either. The model of Jerry West was fine, but there was a lot more to him than his jump shot. A good staircase would have been thousands of foul shots, miles of running every week, weight lifting (nobody did that then, so it would have been a big advantage), more playground ball, and plenty of drill work. Just doing what I enjoyed, shooting, did not turn out to be much of a plan.

Development of clear goals which will necessarily lead to larger, future goals is essential to having a good plan. Write goals down. Make them precise. "Run faster" is not as good as, "Run a mile in 5:20." What sub-goals must be established to get there? What has to be done to achieve them? How long will they take? Build a "Means-Ends Staircase," with small goals providing the means to larger goals, which lead to success, which is defined by ultimate goals.

Because goals and the plans made to reach them will form the framework of life, goals are very personal. It is a waste of time to list a goal because someone wants you to do it. If it is right for you, make it your goal. If not, you will not carry it out. It may be necessary to help the other person understand why it is not right for you, but then go about constructing your own life.

"What you do speaks so loudly that I cannot hear what you say," wrote Ralph Waldo Emerson, the famous American lecturer, essayist and poet of the 1800's. Goals don't have to make sense to everyone to be sound goals for the person who has to carry them out.

GOALS IN SPORTS AND BEYOND

When Sandy Koufax refused to pitch for the Los Angeles Dodgers in the opening game of the 1965 World Series, the issue was not money. The game was being played on Yom Kippur, the holiest holiday of the Jewish year. Though he had become the best pitcher in baseball through tremendous dedication to his sport, the goal of serving his God was more important. Few understood the conflict he faced between religious faith and vocation.

Los Angeles lost the first game of the series without Koufax, but he returned after the holiday to pitch shut-outs in two later games and lead the Dodgers to the championship. Koufax was able to serve God and man. Sometimes a choice must be made which excludes one or the other.

Eli Herring was a 340-pound offensive lineman for Brigham Young University who loved football. However, as a Mormon, he believed playing on Sunday dishonored the Sabbath. Herring turned down a likely multi-million dollar contract in the NFL and became a teacher.

These men had clearly defined goals in athletics, but higher goals in life. They acted on their convictions.

College athletes may not have to resolve a conflict between professional sport and religion, but they will have to resolve the conflict between education and athletics.

Bill Bradley was the epitome of a student-athlete. Heavily recruited as a basketball player, he went to Princeton where he could not receive an athletic scholarship. There he was College Player of the Year and a Rhodes Scholar. After studying in England for two years, he played ten years in the NBA before entering public service, including serving as U.S. Senator from New Jersey.

Bradley was able to achieve athletic and academic success by having clear goals and concentrating his efforts toward achieving those goals. He often quoted something he heard 1950's NBA star Ed Macauley say at the age of 15.

"Just remember that if you're not working at your game to the utmost of your ability, there will be someone out there, someone with equal ability, who will be working to the utmost of his ability, and he'll have the advantage." Bradley took those words to heart, applied them to the classroom and the basketball court and excelled at both.

Adonal Foyle is a modern day Bill Bradley. His desire to play in the NBA may be higher than Bradley's was as a high school senior 30 years earlier. Yet ranked in the Top 10 high school basketball prospects in 1994, Foyle turned down Duke, Syracuse and other traditional powers to enroll at Colgate in the Patriot League, which does not give athletic scholarships.

Asked about a future in the NBA, Foyle said that it is a very high priority. He simply believed that hard work on his part had more to do with making the NBA than playing on television. He also wanted an excellent education in a quiet location, near Joan and Jay Mandle, his legal guardians who teach at Colgate. When questioned further, Foyle said, "I know what I want." That ended the questions.

As a 6-foot-10, 255-pound sophomore, he ranked among the nation's leaders in rebounds and shots blocked while averaging 20 points per game. Professional scouts who had expressed concern about Foyle's level of competition raved about his improvement from freshman to sophomore year.

English biologist Thomas Huxley believed "perhaps the most valuable result of all education is the ability to make yourself do the thing you have to do, when it has to be done, whether you like it or not." Thomas Huxley would have appreciated Wake Forest student-athlete-father Rusty LaRue.

As the first Atlantic Coast Conference athlete in 42 years to play basketball, football and baseball in the same year, LaRue serves as an example that people can achieve more if they expect more from themselves.

A National Honor Society student and North Carolina Athlete of the Year in high school, LaRue was just getting started. As Wake Forest's quarterback, he set eight NCAA passing records and became the school's best percentage passer for a career in football. He was a valuable reserve on Wake's first ACC championship team in 32 years as a junior in 1995, then started and ranked among the top 3-point shooters in the country on another nationally ranked team as a senior. Though the NCAA tourney and football spring practice cut into the baseball season, he pitched in relief.

Off the courts and fields, he was a Dean's List student in computer science and the only married member of the basketball team. When son Riley was born, Rusty was not worried about the added time being a father would require. "Riley's going to be there and not know if I missed three or four jumpers. It's a pleasant distraction," he said.

Not very many student-athletes can balance both priorities with the success of Bill Bradley, Adonal Foyle and Rusty LaRue, or

Katie Smith from the first section. But all student-athletes can challenge themselves to set meaningful personal goals, organize a plan for achieving those goals, and draw motivation from the accomplishments of examples like Bradley, Foyle, LaRue and Smith.

Besides having something to tell coaches when they ask, there are other benefits to goal setting. For one thing, while concentrating on obtaining an important objective, other good things can happen.

By deciding to improve grades to qualify for a college scholarship, your chances of graduating from college improve. By getting stronger to play a sport, your clothes fit better. By playing soccer, footwork for every sport improves, whether or not a career in soccer develops.

(By writing this book, I developed a strong interest in women's basketball. Though comfortable talking with coaches of most sports, I didn't feel I knew enough about women's basketball. To address that shortcoming, I made a point of watching Big Ten basketball in Columbus, seeing the top women's teams on ESPN, reading about and watching the National team, and seeking out top high school coaches, players and games.

Hopefully I did justice to the exciting sport. I did try. But I definitely enjoyed the education, and look forward to seeing many more games in future years. What began as a sense of obligation to readers and the sport of women's basketball developed into a new hobby. The sport may have been great a long time ago, but now I have discovered it!)

Another benefit to setting goals is that temptations along the way don't seem as desirable as they do to someone who is just hanging out. High school students with athletic or academic goals are more likely to avoid problems with alcohol, drugs and unwanted pregnancies.

"My dad always told me that prisons and cemeteries are full of people who made bad three-second decisions," said MCI Coach Max Good. People with clear goals are more likely to avoid mistakes which can impact a lifetime.

OBSTACLES TO GOALS

In addition to temptations, obstacles will arise on the way to reaching goals. Not all student-athletes are able to overcome those obstacles, yet there are many stories of athletes who were not recruited by the universities they had loved all their lives, but who still found a way to become college athletes.

Chris Doering grew up in Gainesville, Fla. His father graduated from the University of Florida and taught there. Chris went to the Gator games, then their football camps. He dreamed, thought and, in an English assignment, even wrote about playing there. An All-Florida selection in basketball, baseball and football, he would have been the easiest recruit the Gators ever signed, but they didn't want him. Neither did other Division I teams, which labeled him, "Too slow for wide receiver, too skinny [160 pounds] for anything else."

Without scholarship offers, Doering had to enroll somewhere as a walk-on. He swallowed his pride and went to Florida. After a redshirt season and one reception for 13 yards as a freshman, he earned a scholarship for the 1993 season. By the time Florida played Nebraska in the 1995 National Championship game, Doering had more touchdown catches (31) than any receiver in Florida or SEC history.

Harold Deane loved Virginia basketball as much as Doering did Florida football, but Virginia did not share Deane's interest. Instead of accepting a scholarship to another school, he went to Fork Union (Va.) Military Academy after high school. Virginia Coach Jeff Jones began to like his game, signed him and Deane was starting point guard for Virginia as a freshman on a team that went to the NCAA.

Dion Cross grew up in Woodson, Arkansas, and wanted to play basketball for the Razorbacks. They didn't recruit him. Cross went to Stanford, where he joined Brevin Knight. Knight was a New Jersey kid rejected by Seton Hall, where his father had been an assistant coach. They formed one of the best backcourts in the country in 1996.

The Naismith Women's Player of the Year in college basketball in 1996, Saudia Roundtree, wanted to play for Georgia and they wanted her. The problem was one-half point on the ACT. Rather than miss a year of competition, Saudia decided to attend Kilgore Junior College in Texas. Then she went to Georgia, where she scored 37 points to lead her team past No.1 ranked Louisiana Tech on the way to the NCAA tournament final game.

Jon Stark went to Florida State to play quarterback, but found himself behind Charlie Ward and Danny Kanell. Rather than lose a year by transferring to a Division I school, Stark went to Trinity, an NAIA school. In 1996, he was selected in the NFL Draft by Baltimore.

Brian Schottenheimer, son of Kansas City Chiefs Coach Marty, quarterbacked his high school team to the Kansas state championship as a senior. After a year at Kansas, Brian decided his future was in coaching rather than on the playing field. To learn the "Fun-n-Gun" offense of Coach Steve Spurrier and to begin to establish his own identity, he walked-on at Florida, with the promise of a scholarship if he became third string quarterback. He achieved that goal as a redshirt junior in 1995, while working toward becoming a coach.

Different athletes have different goals, and find different ways to achieve them. Not everyone could have gone to Florida after being rejected, like Chris Doering did, or enrolled in prep school like Harold Deane. It was not easy to cross time zones to go to college like Dion Cross and Brevin Knight, or take care of academics in junior college like Saudia Roundtree. Transferring from Florida State to play quarterback, or virtually giving up the chance to play quarterback by walking-on at Florida, both took commitment to clear goals.

Most athletes encounter problems during recruitment. The "dream school" may not want a player, grades may be a problem, exposure can be difficult at times or conflicting personal goals may be difficult to weigh. The problem may be deciding between several great opportunities. The challenge is to set clear goals, to expect the inevitable obstacles and to remain determined to find a solution to reach those goals.

As the Greek philosopher Epictetus wrote, "On the occasion of every accident that befalls you, remember to turn to yourself and inquire what power you have for turning it to your use."

Abraham Lincoln overcame nearly three decades of defeat in political elections, business ventures and his personal life to become one of the greatest American presidents. He said, "I am not concerned that you fail; I am concerned that you arise."

SPECIAL TREATMENT

Having goals creates a power all its own. When goals are real, they tend to happen. That is not always a good thing.

Many athletes are given special treatment early in life.

"(Former NBA player) Garfield Smith told me, 'I became a slave to laziness as an athlete,'" said Max Good at Maine Central Institute. "The athlete doesn't have to grow up because the coach lives his life for him," according to Merlin Olsen, former defensive lineman for the Los Angeles Rams who became an actor and media personality.

Without necessarily realizing it, an athlete can seek a college which continues the special treatment begun before high school. Some athletes intentionally covet such a situation. According to biographies of former University of Oklahoma football players, Barry Switzer created the ultimate laissez-faire atmosphere when he was coach there.

"We'll take care of you," was the recruiting pitch to the best football players in the country, and reality matched the promise. Players had no problems with parking tickets, spending money, drunkenness, drugs, tests, homework or anything else. "If you were a star on the University of Oklahoma football team, you could do just about anything you wanted. You had no rules," wrote All-American linebacker Brian Bosworth in his biography, *The Boz.*

Being taken care of sounds good. It worked to bring players to Oklahoma, where Switzer won three national championships before being forced out. But it didn't work for the players. Instead of college being a time to learn about life, about dealing with responsibilities, about growing up, it was a time of prolonged adolescence. Rather than helping boys become men, being taken care of retarded the process.

Bosworth, now an actor, sees that today. He wrote, "Somehow nothing I could do was enough to get Switzer [now coach of the NFL Dallas Cowboys] pissed off at me. I wanted him to discipline me. I wanted to know that he cared what happened to me, that I wasn't just a big piece of meat ... But as it was, Switzer never helped me grow up. I had to do it on my own, and it took me, I'll admit, a long time."

As mentioned, special treatment of athletes starts long before college, and has similar negative results. At times colleges have to do the work high schools should have done, both in the classroom and on the athletic field.

"William Foster" enrolled at a Division I school. He was skilled enough to receive a basketball scholarship, but ineligible to play because he was not academically qualified under NCAA rule 5.1 (j), commonly known as Proposition 48. Since he will be referred to as a "Prop 48" for the rest of his career, his name was changed to prevent further embarrassment.

Proposition 48 became effective in 1986 because the NCAA, under the leadership of the President's Commission, determined that athletes were not being prepared to do college work in high school. One study showed that in 1983, fewer than 100 of 16,000 school districts in the United State required a minimum C average for participation in extra curricular activities.

In a way, the NCAA decided that college sports were a type of high school extra curricular activity. Prop 48 stated that athletes without a C average in 11 core courses and a minimum test score, 700 on the SAT or 15 on the ACT, would be ineligible for athletic competition as college freshmen.

Compared to admissions requirements for non-athletic students, those standards were very low. At schools not supported by the state where the student lived, a B+ average and a score of 1000 on the SAT might have been acceptable. The SAT is scored in the range of 400-1600; 700 was well below the mid-point of incoming college students. Yet there was concern about Prop 48 limiting athletic scholarships to black athletes.

Based on an NCAA study of football and basketball players examined in the class of 1981, the concerns were valid. If Prop 48 had applied to that class, 83 percent of black male basketball players and 75 percent of black football players would have been ineligible at the largest schools. The same study showed 33 percent of white male basketball players and 50 percent of white football players would have been ineligible.

By the time Prop 48 went into effect in the fall of 1986, high school teachers and athletes had largely responded to the challenge of higher standards. Less than 10 percent of football players and 13 percent of male basketball players were ineligible to play as freshmen. Whereas the 1981 NCAA study had shown 69 percent of all black male athletes in the 1981 class would be ineligible, fewer than 20 percent actually were in 1986-87.

Foster is a real, though anonymous, individual in a sea of statistics. He is a very pleasant, personable guy, who seemed to be well above average in intelligence. His problem was lack of preparation for academics. His family life was difficult, and there was little emphasis on school in the home. At school, his teachers let him slide by. If he had received appropriate preparation from the adults in his life, he may have qualified. They short-changed him, and not just academically.

Foster sat out his freshman year. Under the rules of the time he couldn't receive financial aid or practice with the team. Despite being separated from organized athletics, he adjusted well to college. After freshman year he appeared to be on a path toward graduation.

As a sophomore he finally got to play basketball. On the first day of practice, the players were told to form three lines and run a three-man weave, something first done in midget basketball. Foster was lost. He couldn't get the hang of the drill, which consisted of the player who threw the pass cutting behind the player who caught the pass. He looked foolish while others ran the drill easily. An assistant took him aside and said he looked like he'd never run that before. Foster said, "My coach always told me I didn't have to do it with the rest of the team."

Because Foster was so talented and so pleasant, the high school coach had given him special treatment, excusing him from drills which he would have quickly mastered. For the same reason, teachers let him slide by in class. All these adults thought they were being

THE RECRUITING STRUGGLE

kind to someone they liked. In fact, they were sentencing him to unnecessary embarrassment by not helping him develop the academic and athletic tools he would need for future success.

In college, Foster had to compete in class and on the court with one hand tied behind his back. If his coaches and teachers had required that he excel early, he would have excelled the rest of his life. Because they encouraged him to slide by, he was spending a lot of time and effort catching up.

The moral of this story is that there really are no short cuts. To play sports in college, athletes have to run the miles and do the drills. To get a meaningful college degree, students have to prepare to do college work, then have to do it. The kindest thing an adult can do for an athlete or a student is expect the most he or she has to offer, not the least.

Good luck to "William Foster," and all the rest of the young people like him who are trying to make up for the "kindness" of adults who should have known better.

SEEING YOURSELF AS A "DUMB JOCK"

Some athletes are brilliant students. Most are true student-athletes, able to mix easily with the university population on an intellectual basis. A few, who gave in to the label "dumb jock" at some time in their lives, are tempted to try to find a college which will take care of them academically, at least enough to keep them eligible with little effort.

Unfortunately, some colleges try to do that for athletes who can meet requirements for admission. Athletes must accept the responsibility to see themselves as being worthy of a college degree, and of being capable of doing the work necessary to earn one. Just as goals begin in the mind, so does lack of self-respect. A student accepted to a university is capable of earning a degree there. Once an individual gets beyond the mind set of "I'm not smart enough to do that," it is possible to find a college which shares a commitment to education and graduation.

Many young people go to school without having been read to by their parents, or even talked to (as opposed to talked at). Chances are one in three that a given home is headed by a single parent. She (usually the mother) has to do the work of two people, leaving no time for everything the child needs, or the children need. Maybe English is the second language in the home, at least compared to the type of English taught in school. Without preparation for education, there is no early interest. Unless arithmetic and verbal skills are far above average, the students start behind and have to struggle to · catch up. They lose interest in the whole idea of school before discovering their form of intelligence, and decide they have none. Or they find their strength, but it isn't sufficiently academic to impress the teachers.

Coaches, parents and athletes who are reading this book are concerned about kids who are gifted in athletics, a mental/physical kind of intelligence. That gift may be a blessing or a curse, or both.

Athletics is a blessing because it is one more area where a child can excel, where self-worth can be reinforced. Exercise strengthens their bodies, lessons of team work and individual sacrifice can last a lifetime, a good coach makes learning fun . . . there are many benefits to athletics.

The curse comes when athletics is an escape from education, an alternative. A child struggling in the classroom is naturally going to gravitate to an area which makes him/her feel good (sports) over an area which makes him/her feel bad (class). Hopefully adults in education will tie the two together, so one strength is used to create two. That is not always the case.

Tim Brown and his wife Karmen Fields-Brown established TAKE/ABC, a non-profit youth organization in Columbus, Ohio, in 1985. The name stands for Talented Athletes and Artists Kompeting for Excellence/Achievers, Believers and Challengers. The organization uses basketball to teach girls life skills, beginning with the importance of education.

"As a middle school teacher, we had a discipline problem with a player on the football team," said Brown. "We wanted him to miss a game as a penalty, to get his attention. His father wouldn't let us do it. As coach of the team, he didn't want to lose one of his best players."

If a father refused to put his son's best interests ahead of athletics, it is not surprising that other coaches look past an athlete's long term needs at times.

During recruiting, many people talk about the importance of education. Some speak a sincere belief, proven repeatedly. Others know it is the right thing to say. But no one can make an athlete care about overcoming obstacles to get an education and a meaningful degree. Like every other goal, that has to come from within the individual.

Bowling Green basketball Coach Jim Larranaga takes an interesting position.

"It bothers me that coaches get praise for players who do well academically. That praise belongs to the parents, who developed study habits long before college. Likewise," he continues, "coaches shouldn't be blamed for poor performance if a student didn't learn to study in elementary school or high school. That doesn't mean they shouldn't be recruited. Recruitment is to help the team win. Duke, North Carolina, Virginia—they can get the complete package. Mid-majors get the great athlete who is a marginal student, or great student who is a marginal athlete."

Some athletes are afraid to try in the classroom. Maybe too many teachers criticized, maybe not enough cared. Maybe parents never talked about school, maybe athletic acclaim became more intoxicating than academic challenges. Perhaps it's time to recognize that avoiding the classroom is a type of "fear of failure," and to decide to face that fear. In his cartoon strip, *Pogo,* Walt Kelly wrote, "We have met the enemy, and he is us."

F. Scott Fitzgerald, author of *The Great Gatsby,* said, "I never blame failure—there are too many complicated situations in life—but I am absolutely merciless toward lack of effort."

Besides his legacy of basketball greatness brought about through hard work, Michael Jordan serves as a model to young and old of someone who was not afraid to fail. When he was the best basketball player in the world, Jordan had a goal to be a major league baseball player. Many said it didn't make sense. But the thing about dreams is, they don't have to make sense to anyone except the dreamer.

Some say he failed in baseball, but that is wrong. He just did not succeed.

Failure is when someone is afraid to try to achieve something he or she wants. That person then spends a lifetime wondering, Could I have done that? How would my life have been different? Why didn't I try? The regret may never subside.

Trying and not succeeding results in disappointment, there is no getting around that. But the disappointment soon gives way to a peaceful feeling of having given an effort in a worthwhile quest. Sometimes there is another opportunity to try again, with added knowledge. Often a new goal appears, one which was not clear before the first attempt.

After his "failure" with baseball, Jordan had a contentment at having tried to achieve his dream. He also had a renewed interest in basketball, which helped him quickly reclaim his status as the pre-eminent player in the world. He did not just survive his "failure," he thrived because of it.

If Michael Jordan could do that, under worldwide media pressure, a student can succeed in a school situation, where people are there to help.

For someone who has been afraid to try to succeed in school, here's a suggestion. Go to a teacher and say, "I want to do better, will you help me?" The teacher will probably be pleased to find a newly dedicated student and anxious to help. If not, ask somebody else. Teachers have "fear of failure" too. After being rejected by students, some quit trying to teach, just like students who are rejected quit trying to learn. Finding someone who wants to succeed will help teachers get excited about the profession they chose years ago. Helping you will help them, and other students as well.

Whether in class, doing homework or even finding a teacher to help you get serious about school, don't be discouraged if things are less than perfect at the start. You fell down the first time you tried to walk. Now you are an athlete college coaches want to recruit. That same kind of growth and improvement can take place academically. As Wilson, the knowledgeable neighbor on television's *Home Improvement*, said, "True nobility lies not in being superior to another man, but in being superior to one's former self."

Or you can find a school which will arrange easy courses with preferential treatment. You will not get a meaningful degree, maybe no degree at all, but you can stay eligible with very little effort. That opportunity has been around for years.

A high school classmate, a National Honor Society student who went to one of the best colleges in the country to study nursing in the 1960s, told me about getting the autograph of the school's All-American star outside an astronomy class. "You were a good student, but why was he taking astronomy?" I asked. "You don't know the professor. On his scale, A was for athlete, B for boy and C for coed," she replied.

For those who truly want an education in college, two findings from NCAA Research Report 91-07 can help evaluate colleges.

Finding 8 reads, "There are extremely large differences among Division I colleges in the student-athlete graduation rates." Finding 9 says, "The best college-level predictor of the student-athlete graduation rate is the graduation rate of the entire student body at that institution."

Emerge Magazine has begun to publish articles based on NCAA Division I Graduation Reports. In 1996, the magazine reported that, in the preceding four years, 25 schools failed to graduate a black student-athlete from their basketball program and four schools failed to graduate a black football player. In a separate report, of student-athletes receiving scholarships over a period from 1985-88, 37 cross-country/track men's programs graduated zero African-American athletes within six years, and 14 women's programs graduated none.

According to the 1996 NCAA report released in June 1996, 58 percent of Division I scholarship athletes who entered college in 1989 graduated in six years or less. Among revenue sports, women basketball players graduated 64 percent of the time, men 44 percent and football players at a rate of 55 percent. As expected, rates at individual schools varied greatly, by school and by sport.

Though there are universities which do not deserve serious consideration by athletes who want an education, their coaches may still sound like everyone else during recruiting. The athlete must ask questions, compare answers and conduct research to separate the good programs from the others.

Ask to see data for student-athlete and student body graduation rates during college visits. Review the student-athlete handbook. Find out about missed class policy and tutorial assistance. Ask how many athletes are in your field of interest. If you want to study business, for example, do not settle for a grouping like "business related courses." Schools are not identical. It is possible to determine which ones are truly concerned about your best interests, if you are truly concerned about them yourself.

As President of the University of Notre Dame, Rev. Theodore M. Hesburgh said, "A decade after graduation, almost everyone will have forgotten where and what they played. But every time they speak, everyone will know whether or not they are educated."

In the words of President Theodore Roosevelt, "Far better it is to dare mighty things, to win glorious triumphs, even though checkered by failure, than to rank with those poor spirits who neither enjoy much nor suffer much because they live in the gray twilight that knows neither victory nor defeat."

"I WANT TO START AS A FRESHMAN"

Besides seeking to be taken care of, another dangerous goal is placing too much importance on starting as a freshman. It's not always a good thing, according to former Ohio State quarterback, Art Schlichter. He should know. He did it twice.

Writing for *People* magazine from a federal prison in Terre Haute, Ind., where he was serving a prison sentence for bank fraud, Schlichter discussed the pressure of being the first freshman to ever make his high school's football team, and the resentment of upperclassmen who felt they deserved more attention than a newcomer.

He also wrote about going to nearby Ohio State in 1978. Coach Woody Hayes had promised him the starting quarterback position.

To keep the promise, Hayes moved returning starter Rod Gerald to wide receiver. Since a white freshman was given the most important position on the team over a proven black senior before practice began, resentment wracked the team. Feeling isolated, Schlichter took refuge by gambling at the race track. Though he became a record-setting college quarterback and high NFL draft choice, the gambling problem grew. It finally led to his suspension from the NFL.

No one knows how critical the promise of a starting position was in Schlichter's difficulties, but it did not help. He didn't have the respect of his teammates because he did not earn the position. Something given is not appreciated as much as something earned. The goal of starting as a freshman, or even playing as a freshman, might be better stated earning playing time as a freshman. Once playing time is earned, earning more playing time, and starting, become reasonable goals. Use of a word like "earning" reminds the athlete that he or she starts all over in college, with, at best, a fair chance to begin to carve out an entirely different niche than high school.

Many recruited athletes have a goal of starting as a freshman. Most are too intelligent to say that to the media, but express the expectation to friends. Some are so naive about the difficulty of college athletics that they just assume they will start their first year. "Why else would a coach recruit me?" Not unlike assuming a career in pro ball, immediate college success may happen, but the odds are against it.

Samuel Johnson, one of the framers of *The Constitution*, wrote, "The mind which has feasted on the luxurious wonders of fiction has no taste for the insipidity of truth." Recruiting is not real, it is an aberration of life. College is real, in academics and athletics. The acclamation is over, at least for a while. The work, at a higher level of intensity than high school, remains.

"SPIN" CONTROL

For athletes with clear goals and plans to meet those goals, recruiting can be an enjoyable experience. However, even the most organized and focused athletes will have to deal with the ability college coaches have to "spin" a story.

The heavily recruited athlete must understand that coaches are, among other things, salesmen. As such, they have developed the skill of turning every negative into a positive. In essence, they will say, "Nothing bad ever happens at State U., only good things and things which turn out to be good."

This trait of finding the silver lining in everything is desirable in an adult the athlete will be around for several years. One goal may be to find a coach with this ability. However, beware during the recruiting process. If everything is good, how is it possible to decide which school to select? The answer is, with a cautious eye and clear goals.

Here are some examples of turning a negative into a positive from college basketball.

In 1996, Kentucky went through the Southeastern Conference season undefeated, then lost in the conference tournament. Could the team be struggling with the NCAA Tournament starting in five days? Wildcat Coach Rick Pitino said, "I don't think we could make a serious run [at the national championship] without this happening to us because things have been so easy."

Bad was good. Kentucky won their next six games and the national championship

In a more amazing story, in the early 1990s Tennessee Coach Kevin O'Neill was at Marquette, recruiting Kevin Seckar to play basketball. The subject of Jeffrey Dahmer came up just after the serial killer was arrested living near the Marquette campus. O'Neill immediately said, "The way I look at it, every campus has one weirdo walking around. We caught ours."

While Seckar ended up having a fine career at Vanderbilt, O'Neill got high marks for what the political people call "spin control".

If Coach A from California is recruiting a Los Angeles athlete, the story will be, "stay close to your family and friends, be able to get a home-cooked meal when you want, make a name in the community to help you get a good job after graduation. Coach B from New York will say, "Strike out on your own, prove your independence, be your own man (or woman)."

Those two approaches are guaranteed. The coaches do not know what is best for you, they only know they want you at their college. If the coaches traded jobs, they would exchange stories, and do it without missing a beat.

By the way, that is not a criticism of coaches. They have to be effective salespeople. They are not supposed to decide your life, that is your job. The way to do it is to set goals, then evaluate what the coaches have to offer based on what you want.

While filtering out the "spin doctors" during evaluation of schools, learn the skill for use throughout life. It might even be helpful during recruiting.

After former Penn State basketball Coach Bruce Parkhill resigned to become Assistant Athletic Director, he was asked how an athlete should deal with rejection in recruiting. "When a school decides another player is better, athletes have to put a positive spin on it," said Parkhill. "See it as an opportunity to find the level where they can achieve their goals."

Spoken like a coach, but also very sound advice.

Chapter VIII

NCAA RULES, RECRUITING AND OTHERWISE

"Sometimes I wonder what dishonesty is. Is it

dishonest for a kid to be paid ... or is it just against

the rules?"

John Thompson
Coach, Georgetown basketball

When told about this book, a Division I coach who makes a commitment to operate within the rules said, "Good. Parents and athletes need something that clearly and logically explains NCAA rules."

What a compliment. Unfortunately, a better writer than Hemingway, who was more intelligent than Einstein, couldn't begin to do it.

NCAA rules, the good and the bad, change every year. Even if a situation could be explained properly once, it would be obsolete almost immediately. The purpose of this book is to present expert recruiting insights formed over many years, observations which do not become useless within months. Also, many current rules defy logical explanation.

Three vital points overshadow anything else in this chapter:

1. *The NCAA Guide for the College-Bound Student-Athlete,* in its latest edition, is an absolute must for a recruited athlete and his or her parents. Since rules change every year, it is essential to have the current edition. High school and college coaches have copies, or call the NCAA (913-339-1906, or 800-638-3731 for a recorded message).

2. It is a waste of time, not to mention very risky, to look for logic or reason in any rule. Doing something clearly "in the spirit of the law" may be outside the letter of the law. The NCAA is very literal in rules interpretations. Logic may help in a lawsuit, but it may

not help in an NCAA appeal. Stay within the strict parameters of the current law to avoid problems.

3. A college coach who says, "That's a dumb law, don't worry about it," is asking for trouble. That school could be on probation at any time, and a recruited athlete could be punished without even being involved. Trust the coach who walks by a recruited athlete during a "non-contact period," not the one who sneaks in cute conversation. The first coach is merely trying to stay within the rules; the second may be one step away from a violation.

INHERENT INCONSISTENCIES AND IMBALANCE OF POWER

In baseball or softball, if the ball hits the line it is considered "fair" or "in," like tennis. In football or basketball, a ball or foot on the line is considered out of bounds. In football, the offense keeps the ball, but in basketball the team loses possession. In golf, the player who hits the ball out of bounds gets to keep it, but receives a penalty.

Combined, the rules of sports do not make much sense.

While true, that is not a problem because each game is separate. Inconsistencies from sport to sport are irrelevant.

The National Collegiate Athletic Association is not charged with combining all sports into one. Actually, the NCAA has the more difficult task of meeting the needs of revenue and non-revenue sports; priorities of both sexes; the interests of an array of educators and bureaucrats, teachers and coaches, including people ranging from egotistical and selfish to caring and concerned; dealing with millionaire adults and impoverished teenagers, some of whom will soon be millionaires while the vast majority will not; and students who either desperately want an education, don't care about an education or don't know what they want.

Colleges created the Intercollegiate Athletic Association of the United States (IAAUS) in 1906 in response to President Theodore Roosevelt's demand for reform in the sport of college football. Long an advocate of the value of athletics, Roosevelt felt the events of the 1905 season, when 18 boys were killed and 149 seriously injured, damaged the credibility of the sport. Federal intervention was at least implied.

The IAAUS was formed and significant rules changes were adopted. Loose balls could no longer be kicked. Hurdling, or flinging a small back over the line of scrimmage, was prohibited. The length of the game was cut from 70 to 60 minutes, and first down yardage increased from five to 10 yards. The National Collegiate Athletic Association, as it was named in 1910, saved the colleges from governmental regulation.

Another fundamental change began in 1972 and continues today with Title IX.

Title IX is a stipulation in the Educational Amendments of 1972 stating "No person in the United States shall, on the basis of sex, be excluded from participation in, be denied the benefits of, or be subjected to discrimination under any education program or activity receiving Federal financial assistance."

When Title IX passed, about seven percent of the high school athletes in the United States were girls. Though it did not become effective until July 21, 1975, and complaints were not answered until late 1980, by 1994 the proportion of girls in high school athletics had increased to approximately 38 percent. By then, seven times as many girls played high school sports as did in 1971.

Athletes, parents and coaches have had many struggles along the way, and more remain, but drastic changes have taken place.

Title IX, and a December 1979 policy ruling emphasizing that scholarships be proportionate to the female population at a university, is the reason for the imbalance of scholarships in basketball (15 for women, 13 for men), volleyball (12 to 4.5), swimming (14 to 9.9) and several other sports.

By individual sport, the differences do not make sense. In basketball, for example, top women's coaches may not award all their scholarships to avoid having unhappy players on the bench.

However, the differences are considered a lesser evil. At colleges which have football and, to a smaller degree, wrestling (which has 9.9 scholarships to football's 85), allowing women more scholarships in common sports, reduces the imbalance in total scholarships.

While the benefits of Title IX far outweigh the problems, it has caused changes in the way the NCAA operates.

Today, in a brochure titled *The NCAA*, the organization lists its purposes as follows:

> "To initiate, stimulate and improve intercollegiate athletics programs for student-athletes . . . To uphold the principle of institutional control of, and responsibility for, all collegiate sports . . . To encourage its members to adopt eligibility rules to comply with satisfactory standards of scholarship, sportsmanship and amateurism. To formulate, copyright and publish rules of play governing intercollegiate athletics. To preserve intercollegiate records. To supervise . . . regional and national events . . . To legislate . . . upon any subject of general concern to the members related to the administration of

intercollegiate athletics. To study in general all phases of competitive intercollegiate athletics and establish standards whereby the colleges and universities of the United States can maintain their athletics programs on a high level."

Like any bureaucracy from the federal government to a local school board, the NCAA responds to power. Colleges established the NCAA, fund it and pass all the measures the NCAA is required to enforce. Though coaches like to distance themselves by referring to the NCAA as "they," colleges direct all activities of the NCAA.

Lack of power is a concern when priorities of the colleges conflict with those of students, whose only influence is what the colleges grant them.

History teaches that two groups do not mutually benefit when one group makes all decisions for both. Americans rebelled against Britain for taxation without representation, then relied on the concept of Manifest Destiny to repeatedly break treaties with Native Americans. From slavery through "Jim Crow" to "separate but equal" education until the Civil Rights Act, African-Americans received deplorable treatment until they became a part of the political process.

In professional sports, National League President Warren Giles spoke the owners' party line decades ago when he said, "The players can do much more for themselves than any outside representative. By delegating someone else to negotiate for them, the players are surrendering a privilege." Now professional athletes with agents and a union have to struggle along making more money in a month than they ever expected to make in a year.

Dick DeVenzio, often referred to as an "activist" for the rights of athletes in revenue-producing sports, said, "Major college revenue-producing athletes are exploited because they are too transient. They are too busy, too unorganized to do anything about their rights."

The issue of power is important for two reasons. One, athletes don't have any, so finding a coach and an athletic director and a university president with a strong sense of propriety is critical. Two, when interests of student-athletes conflict with interests of colleges, colleges will win. This is the case on the subject of distribution of revenue to athletes who produce it.

MONEY

Nineteen NCAA Division I-A football bowl games made total payments to participating teams of over $100 million in 1995.

Four bowls, the Fiesta, Orange, Sugar, and Rose, accounted for

$66.8 million. Assuming all that money came from people wanting to see players perform, 85 scholarship players on eight teams generated almost $100,000 a piece. In return, the players received $300 in gifts from the bowl people and $300 in gifts from their school. Nothing in cash, of course, because the players were amateurs. Just off hand, $600 spent to generate $100,000, that's a better return than most investments produce. Amateurism is good business.

But wait. "Those players get a college education, worth hundreds of thousands of dollars in earning power," cries a university spokesman. Hopefully that is true, but only if the athlete earns the degree. However, football players on the teams which did not qualify for bowls, as well as athletes in other sports, get the same scholarships.

University of Massachusetts basketball Coach John Calipari signed a 10-year contract worth at least $4.5 million in 1995. It included a $132,000 base salary, nearly a quarter million dollars per year in radio-TV guarantees, an annuity and a job for 24 years if he decided to quit coaching and stay at the university. Based on what he had done to build a national program before signing the contract, and the fact that UMass won its fifth straight conference title and went to the Final Four in 1996, the two parties apparently negotiated a good business deal.

Giving one great talent a scholarship to play basketball might mean an added 5,000 fans per game, resulting in an extra million dollars in ticket sales, increased television licensing and NCAA tournament revenue. Another good business deal.

Nike signed a $9.2 million contract with Ohio State to supply the athletic department with footwear, apparel and cash. Since it is Nike's tenth agreement with a university on an all-sports contract, and Ohio State officials were very pleased, probably another good deal.

The NCAA men's basketball tournament brought more than $6 million in gross receipts in 1977, through ticket sales and television revenue. Nine years later that figure had increased over seven times; nine years after that it was almost $185 million. That's impressive growth in any business.

A school which makes the Final Four can count on selling $3 million in merchandise during the tournament. Michigan, the annual leader in merchandise, sold more than $250 million in 1995.

Among the reasons for Michigan's windfall was the popularity of the "Fab Five," which included NBA star Chris Webber. When he saw "#4 Webber" jerseys in Ann Arbor stores, and everywhere else the Wolverines played, he asked, "We're making a lot a money for the university, why can't I get a percentage of the sales? Why can't I work a camp in the summer?"

The issue of money can distract a student-athlete from accomplishing his or her goals. "Why do we travel on buses when they fly? Why do we stay in a hotel like this, when they stay in a hotel like that? Why do we have to spend so much time with the media?"

All fair questions and all, like Webber's, tied to money. Why would colleges share, if students will wait until their eligibility is over to benefit from capitalism and free-market enterprise?

As the 1996-97 school year began, there was talk of change to the NCAA definition of amateurism. The early exit of basketball players to the NBA, with nine of the top 10 selections in the NBA Draft being underclassmen or high school students, threatened to undermine the incredible cash cow NCAA basketball has become to athletic programs at all universities. While it might be preferable for colleges to share the money with athletes who produce it because this is America and money is really not a dirty word, action based on enlightened self-interest would be something.

As was the case with amateurism in the Olympics, the concept will be redefined by the NCAA. The question is when, and after how many different approaches?

If nothing happens before a student-athlete signs a scholarship, or if what happens doesn't seem fair, the financial inequity in college sports is something for the teenager to face, then decide to accept or fight.

Fighting means believing that unorganized, unfunded students could defeat organized, heavily funded bureaucrats, within a time frame which could benefit the students who began the battle. The risk may be loss of the scholarship. It would be difficult to recommend such a struggle.

The alternative is to work within the system, not let it be a distraction, and get an education and a degree which will be beneficial for a lifetime. Channeling efforts toward achieving goals will not make the system better, but the key is to be too busy to notice the inequity most of the time, and smart enough to ignore it the rest of the time.

Besides, sometimes the system does work. It did in the case of Pell grants, although the process took 40 years.

PELL GRANTS

One of the saddest episodes in the history of changing NCAA rules concerns a long period when colleges kept federal money from poverty-level students on athletic scholarship.

The concept of the "full-ride scholarship" was developed 40 years ago. Like so many NCAA rules, it was in response to abuses by coaches and boosters. In this case, the concern was the original "jobs" programs for athletes.

Until the mid-1950s, athletes were required to "make sure nobody steals the stadium," given credit for working two or three jobs during the same hours of the same days, or paid multiple times the going rate for a job they may actually have performed. Colleges decided to give athletes the same room, board, books and tuition rather than try to police the cheaters. In addition, athletes received $15 a month "laundry money," for incidentals incurred by a student during the school year.

Since the scholarship was covering "everything," any federal or state money available to the students resulted in a like amount being subtracted from the athletic grant. The student received all the government's money, just not as much of the college's. The net result was no change in benefits to the needy student, more money for the college.

At first ROTC and National Guard training were the only exceptions. During the 1960s, such programs as the War Orphans Educational program, Social Security and the GI Bill of Rights were also excluded.

In the 1970s, colleges stopped paying athletes $15/month in laundry money as a cost cutting move. While many college students think clean clothes are overrated, incidentals such as snacks, dates and transportation have a place in the college experience.

Still looking for new sources of funds to comply with governmental requirements that women receive equal opportunities for athletic scholarships, colleges noticed an expanding federal program called the Basic Educational Opportunity Grant (BEOG). When the value of the grant nearly tripled to $1,400 in 1975, administrators began suggesting that coaches fill out forms for eligible athletes. Since NCAA rules caused a dollar-for-dollar reduction in scholarship funds, the athlete never received the benefit of the money, which went to the school to reduce scholarship costs. BEOG grants were later named Pell grants, after Senator Claiborne Pell, Democrat, Rhode Island.

Over a 20-year period, amid a multitude of cries that athletes should be paid; and pleas that athletes should at least be allowed the opportunity to produce income for themselves; and the fact that $15 a month would be inadequate today, restrictions on Pell grants have loosened.

In a series of NCAA conventions, when administrators on healthy expense accounts argued whether a college student really needed a few hundred dollars for an entire school year, the portion of the Pell grants withheld from scholarships was reduced. In 1982, the schools decided to withhold half of the maximum $1,800 meant for the students. In 1990, Division I schools retained $600 of a maximum $2,300, while D-II and D-III schools retained $900. There were other steps along the way.

Finally, after much public pressure to compensate athletes, and the necessary lawsuits as well, students receive their scholarships and the Pell grant money intended for them. At Division I schools, 100 percent of the Pell money goes to the athlete; at D-II and D-III, athletes receive the full Pell grant up to the cost of attendance at the university, a figure calculated by the financial aid office which includes transportation and certain incidentals.

DARNELL AUTRY, RUNNING BACK/ACTOR

Logically, one of the NCAA's stated purposes would be "to prepare student-athletes for success after graduation." Isn't that obvious? Wouldn't athletics supplement the university's academic challenge? In fact, that is not a stated purpose, nor is it deemed nearly as important as "competitive balance," a high priority of the organization.

Within limits, competitive balance must be maintained. Teams should not be allowed to have extra players, take extra time-outs, make extra recruiting visits or mail more colorful brochures. There are necessary standards in place to prevent those kinds of things from happening.

On the other hand, certain geographic advantages will always exist. Some schools are located on oceans, some have better weather, some have better medical or law schools, maybe one has a parent as the head coach. To one recruit, being close to home would be an advantage, to another it would be a disadvantage. Such circumstances are unavoidable. A better concern might be the idea of "unfair advantage." After eliminating unfair advantages there will inevitably be competitive imbalance.

As important as it is to eliminate unfair advantages, preparing the student-athlete for success should be at least as important. So, teams should not be allowed to mislead recruits regarding their role on the team, undermine the education of an athlete by putting eligibility ahead of a worthwhile degree or require a four year commitment in return for a one year scholarship. These things happen all the time.

The best interests of a scholarship athlete versus competitive balance, not unfair advantage, was the essence of the Darnell Autry story which surfaced in the spring of 1996.

Autry gained national fame as the star running back of Northwestern's Rose Bowl team in 1995. After a sophomore year in which he rushed for 100 yards or more every game and became a Heisman Trophy finalist, Autry was offered a summer job in line with his major. The NCAA ruled he could not accept it.

In his real life, Autry was a theater major, like Ann-Margret and Charlton Heston before him. At Northwestern, theater is top shelf stuff.

William Bindley, a 1984 Northwestern graduate, offered Autry a bit part as an "audience member" in a movie he was directing, *The Eighteenth Angel*. The supernatural thriller would be filmed in Italy during the summer.

Maybe Bindley wanted to give a fellow Wildcat a break, maybe to receive a little free publicity. He would also avoid one salary, because Autry could accept only expenses under the rules of NCAA scholarships.

Regardless, it was a big opportunity for a theater major. It is difficult to get that first break in show business; thanks to football, this might be Autry's. It was definitely something for the resume and a chance to learn about the business and make contacts. Score one for student-athletes?

No, said the NCAA, can't do it. Bylaw 12.5.2.3.4. prohibits student-athletes from appearing in feature films. A business major can work on Wall Street in the off season, a prospective attorney can work in a law office, a med student can work in a hospital but no movies. Modeling is off limits, too.

The rule came about in the 1960s as a result of UCLA and USC athletes receiving pay above scale to act in movies. "For years, studio tour directors said, 'There's the hill many UCLA athletes ran down during the filming of *Spartacus*.' In fact, Mike Warren got his start in Hollywood because of his reputation as a basketball player and the work he did as an extra while attending UCLA," according to a compliance director at another university.

Aren't there two different things going on here? Paying more than scale is an unfair competitive advantage. Paying scale seems reasonable; or, don't pay anything. But why can't a kid who wants to act try acting? Michael Warren, Renko's partner Bobby on *Hill Street Blues*, is still on television. Acting became his career. Why is that a bad thing?

"Not all schools are as close to Hollywood, so that constitutes a competitive advantage," an NCAA official might say.

Sure, and there must be a way to help Iowa compete against California schools for football players who like to surf, or Alabama to attract gymnasts who snow ski.

Autry was denied an opportunity to prepare for his vocation. In a better world, the NCAA would have acted in the best interests of the student-athlete. Maybe the bureaucrats wanted to do that, but were prohibited by a rule book the size of a small car, a rule book filled with phrases, clauses and points which restrict student-athletes. But this isn't a better world and Autry did what you do in this world. He went to court.

Cook County Circuit Judge Thomas Durkin issued a temporary restraining order on Autry's behalf and suggested that the NCAA "take the higher road" in handling the problem. Then the NCAA Administrative Review Panel decided to overturn its original ruling and grant a waiver so Autry could appear in the film. That prevented him from the difficult choice of giving up what he had the right to do or putting his teammates at risk of a suspension of their offensive star for violation of NCAA rules.

The priority of the colleges is not to restrict student-athletes, but rather to maintain competitive balance. Even cost containment has secondary importance to competitive balance.

Costs could be sharply reduced by requiring schools to award a certain percentage of scholarships to in-state students. In 1995, a full athletic scholarship to Ohio State cost $14,700 for an out-of-state athlete, compared to $8,500 for in-state, 42 percent less.

Since the measure would not be fair to states with small populations it will not happen, but it would save money.

Colleges will not have a reasonable NCAA until presidents take responsibility for the actions of the group they established, and make the best interests of student-athletes a priority. In the words of Autry's father, Gene, "The NCAA has a responsibility to look out for the big picture."

Until that happens, athletes must go to the university compliance officer for a rules interpretation before taking actions open to any other citizen, like taking a job. To show how absurd the situation is, Autry could have been in a made-for-TV if it had been filmed within 30 miles of campus, just not a feature film. Go figure.

EVOLUTION OF RECRUITING RULES

Long before Jackie Robinson broke the color line in organized baseball he was a highly recruited athlete. At Pasadena Junior

College, he was excellent in baseball, better in track and field and basketball, and a legend in football. While colleges sought his services, coaches at each college argued about which sports Robinson would play if he attended theirs. Some coaches decided they would be all right as long as Robinson didn't play against them. Recruiters offered to pay his full tuition and expenses to attend, or, alternatively, to cover his costs at a school outside the state if he did not want to attend, their schools. He ended up at UCLA in 1939.

Before Chet Walker scored 18,831 points in his 13 year NBA career, the native of Benton Harbor, Mich. had to choose a college scholarship to accept. He chose Nebraska, which got him a summer job and obtained a job for his brother. In his autobiography *Long Time Coming* he wrote, "I just wandered into the decision."

In September 1958, Walker was leaving for Nebraska. His mother sent his trunk ahead, his brother was going to drive him to the airport in Chicago to fly to Lincoln. At 6 a.m., a Bradley assistant coach stopped by the Walker house, said he was driving to Chicago and would be glad to take the young athlete to Midway Airport. Having been heavily recruited by Bradley, Walker accepted. When they stopped for breakfast, other school representatives happened to be there. When Walker wanted to call his mother, the phone was out of order. When the trip resumed, Walker was slipped several hundred dollars. In Chicago, the car ended up at Meigs Field. There the Bradley athletic director and head coach shuffled him onto a plane which took them to Peoria, Ill., home of Bradley University.

Eventually Nebraska returned Walker's clothes. He led Bradley to national prominence and made All-America. In 1976 he was inducted into the Bradley Hall of Fame.

There are hundreds of other such stories about college sports which help explain why the NCAA has so many rules. For readers who want to know more about problems the NCAA has had in dealing with creative coaches, several books are identified in the Bibliography.

USING THE NCAA GUIDE - ACADEMICS

Prop 48, discussed in the Chapter VII, was instituted for the fall of 1986. In January 1989, the NCAA voted to adopt Proposition 42, which meant students who did not meet Prop 48 guidelines could not receive a scholarship. They would have to pay for their first year of college, not the athletic department. This measure was widely condemned as racist, because most Prop 48 students were black.

In only two years, limited data showed that Prop 48 students were doing as well as those who qualified initially. About 80 percent of each group was eligible. Whether the measure was based on prejudice or on cost cutting, Prop 42 was in place until the 1996-97 school year. Then Proposition 16 raised academic standards and introduced the "sliding scale," which emphasized grades over test score, or test score over grades, depending on the academic strength of the student.

Currently, colleges look for high school courses which prepare a student to do college work. The term given these college preparatory courses is "core courses." They include English, math, social sciences, natural or physical sciences and other approved courses. Each high school is required to keep a list of core courses updated with the NCAA Clearinghouse annually, so the student can know which courses are "core" through the guidance counselor.

A student must take a minimum number of courses in English, math and the sciences, and at least 13 in all. It is a good idea to take more if the student can do the work. Not only is the student better prepared for college, the 13 best grades in core courses count for college qualification. A low grade in one course can be replaced by taking a 14th course.

The grade average of the core courses, not the overall high school grade point average, is an important part of qualifying with the NCAA. A minimum of 2.0 is necessary. Higher grades mean a lower test score is required, under the sliding scale.

While a minimum test score is necessary to be eligible to compete athletically as a freshman, a student with grades above 2.5 may still be a "partial qualifier," and receive a scholarship even though not able to compete. High school grades are very important.

Coaches and guidance counselors cite students who mistakenly expect to pull their grades up as juniors or seniors. Some, like Youngstown State football Coach Jim Tressel, believe later grades would be better indicators of college success.

"The students should be more mature at 18 than 15, but senior year and freshman year count the same," Tressel said.

As the 1997 school year begins, core courses count the same, regardless of when they are taken. The time to begin concentrating in school is no later than freshman year.

Goal: Begin taking core courses early and aim for a "B" average. By getting close to that, the student will be at the top of (current) NCAA requirements.

The other part of the academic sliding scale is the standardized test, either the SAT or the ACT as required by a particular college. Under the sliding scale, students with the minimum high school grades of 2.0 must have 86 on the ACT or 1010 on the SAT. The minimum test score to compete as a freshman is 68 or 820; the minimum to receive a scholarship, with grades at 2.75, is 59 or 720 as a partial qualifier.

There has been a lot of talk about standardized tests being racially biased. Administrators of the testing services maintain that they study every question, dropping those which produce biased results. Still, a white guidance counselor at an upper-middle class high school in the Midwest told me, "My experience is that college boards are culturally biased. High school performance is a better indicator of college success."

A 1992 survey of the American Association of College Registrars and Admissions Officers found that grades and class rank were much better indicators of academic success than test scores. Since then more than 200 schools have dropped the requirement of a standardized test for admissions.

Test taking is a type of intelligence. Some have the skill, others don't. For colleges, standardized tests provide a way to evaluate students for their ability to succeed in college, regardless of quality of the high school or laxity of its grading scale. These tests have been a part of the admissions process for a long time; some educators believe in them, some don't.

The athlete with an eye on getting a scholarship is working too hard to qualify to worry about fairness. If changes come, they will not be the result of his or her actions. The best strategy is to take the test at the end of sophomore year, or fall of the junior year. If the first test goes well enough to qualify, that is one more goal achieved. If not, the extent of the problem becomes clear and steps can be taken to solve it. Maybe high school classes in certain areas will help. Maybe study courses. Maybe taking the test again will be enough, because learning how to take the test can make the difference of several points. A good guidance counselor will be able to help the athlete and the parents develop a strategy. The sooner the athlete faces the problem, the more time and alternatives there are available to solve the problem. Or the sooner there is no problem.

The third and final segment of academic qualifications involves the Initial-Eligibility Clearinghouse. Even if the student's grades, course work and test scores are acceptable, nothing counts until the proper papers are filed with the Clearinghouse.

"In the summer of 1994 there was a backlog of 24,000 forms," remembers basketball analyst Tom Konchalski. "Qualifiers missed games their freshman year because their paperwork was delayed, or because courses had not been approved."

Though the fairly simple process is far from smooth, things are getting better. Future athletes will benefit from the problems of their predecessors. Still, it makes sense to file the Student Release Form as soon as possible, leaving time to solve problems if necessary. (For information, call the Clearinghouse at 1-319-337-1492. To order forms from a touch-tone phone, call 1-800-638-3731.)

The NCAA is committed to the function, brought on by adults tampering with grades and high school courses not preparing students for college. Plans are for the NCAA to be spending $1.5 million per year to operate the Clearinghouse by its fifth year of operation.

"Parents who think, 'If they want my son bad enough, they'll get him in,' are wrong," advises one football recruiter. "We have enough trouble getting in kids who qualify. With the higher standards, quite a few players won't be eligible. This could mean a chance for less talented players with grades and paperwork in order."

USING THE NCAA GUIDE - RECRUITING

It is impossible to summarize rules for being recruited, since times and dates vary by sport, by division and change every year. Before doing anything, the student must obtain the *NCAA Guide* and review it with the high school coach, who can point out important details. However, here are some warnings:

A student being recruited for more than one sport must follow the rules for each sport. For example, five paid visits is the maximum per athlete, not per sport. Also, phone calls and personal contact is permitted at different times for football than other sports. If two coaches from two sports are involved with one athlete, they must coordinate the contact which the university is allowed with each recruit.

The student may contact the university, and is encouraged to do that. It would be wise, however, to read the *NCAA Guide* before even taking that step. If a rule is broken, a common penalty is that the school may not continue to recruit the student. For the student who has a serious interest in the school, possibly having dreamed of playing there, that can be a harsh penalty.

No alumni or boosters may recruit athletes, nor is contact permitted after enrollment. This is another example of young people being penalized because adults caused problems.

"We used to have a 'Hoop Family,'" said Ohio University women's basketball Coach Marsha Reall. "Families would sort of adopt a player, give her a home cooked meal once a week, a place to do laundry, hang out off campus. The families came to our games, gave the player another support system.

"When UNLV's men's basketball players showed up in a hot tub with bookies, the rule came for no alumni contact. I had to stop the program. Violations by alumni are reduced, but so are future employment opportunities. I don't know if there is a hot tub in Athens, Ohio," she concludes.

Mike Gottfried of ESPN has a similar story:

"At Pitt we had 30 alumni in for a luncheon every year, including most of the business leaders around town. It led to future summer jobs and sometimes careers, but schools can't do that anymore. I think the emphasis should be on what's best for the kids, not the schools. There are so many sad stories about kids transferring, being unhappy, not graduating."

TRANSFER PENALTY

In recruiting, the assortment of rules colleges require the NCAA to carry out is illogical, burdensome and a threat to eligibility. After the athlete arrives on campus, things do not get any better. But student-athletes have to adjust, like they do when an official is calling to tight game. Unable to effect meaningful change, recruits have to prepare to follow the rules and make a good choice.

In the sports of D-I basketball, DI-A football and D-I men's ice hockey, athletes who wish to transfer colleges must sit out one year of competition, two years if their formal school refuses permission for the athlete to transfer. In all other sports there is a "one-time transfer exception," which allows the athlete to compete immediately as long as it is the first transfer, the athlete is in good academic standing and making satisfactory progress at the first school and the first institution releases the athlete in writing. By refusing to authorize the transfer, an institution can assign a one-year penalty to the athlete.

When Rick Pitino was 34 years old he said he expected to remain the coach of Providence College for the rest of his life. "I truly felt that in my heart," Pitino stated weeks later, when he was coach of the New York Knicks in the NBA.

Pitino was an adult, nearly twice as old as a recruit, yet he changed his mind. What adult hasn't? People commit to each other "for better or worse, in sickness or in health, as long as we both shall live," and half the marriages end in divorce. Adults change jobs, careers, even religions. Everyone changes their mind, sometimes for substantial reason, sometimes from immaturity, sometimes because they were deceived.

In 1996, John Calipari went to the NBA within one year of signing a 10 year contract to coach University of Massachusetts.

Yet adults who are in charge of college athletics have decreed that if 17-18-year-old student-athletes change their minds, either because they made a mistake, or because the coach left, or because they were intentionally misled, the young adult is penalized. This may be the single most unfair rule in college athletics. Making it even more unfair is the fact that the rule was placed in effect when athletes received four year scholarships. Now scholarships are reviewed annually. If a college coach says, essentially, "You aren't as good as I thought you were, please leave," D-I athletes in football, men's ice hockey and basketball are unable to compete at a new school for a year.

The rationalization is that it takes an athlete time to adjust to a new college and to be representative of the student body. A year away from competition allows him/her that time. Strange that athletes in revenue sports need that time when others do not.

The truth is that the transfer rule is a way for coaches to prevent other coaches from tampering with their players. Colleges don't trust each other, so they make rules. In this case, the weight of the rule falls on the student-athlete.

If it takes a college student a year to adjust to a new college, wouldn't it take a high school graduate at least as long to adjust to college? Of course, that brings up freshman eligibility.

FRESHMAN ELIGIBILITY

Except for brief periods during World War II and the Korean War, freshmen were never eligible for NCAA varsity competition. The need for a time to adjust to being away from home, to a different social life, to more rigorous academic work and to bigger, stronger teammates and opponents was considered obvious.

In 1968, a movement began to make freshmen eligible for all sports except football and men's basketball (women's basketball was not under the jurisdiction of the NCAA). Proponents of the measure wanted to save money. They excluded football and basketball thinking the uproar would prevent passage. The measure was adopted, 163-160. Four years later, football and basketball were added.

With redshirting widespread, most football players have not competed as freshmen. Players gave up their first year in college for a fifth, and adjusted to school while practicing but not competing. They also gave up the opportunity to play four years if they later transferred.

For very talented athletes, this practice is ending. Now players can apply for the NFL Draft after three years in school, regardless of eligibility remaining. There is no reason to trade an athlete's first year of eligibility for a fifth year if he might be gone by then. Sadly, the logic sounds more like an engineer maximizing machine utilization than an educator guiding a student.

With few exceptions, talented athletes have played basketball as freshmen. With freshmen, and even high school seniors, entering the NBA Draft, that tendency is more likely to accelerate than be reversed. Yet the National Association of Basketball Coaches has proposed that freshmen eligibility be repealed, citing deterioration in performance on the court in addition to academic problems as reasons. Current high school coach and athletic director Joe Petrocelli agrees.

"I have seen so many players unhappy about not being able to play as freshmen, I'd make freshmen ineligible for varsity. They would have to increase the number of scholarships, but if they gave four a year and added a couple of walk-ons the kids could adjust to college while playing a freshman schedule. That would be a big help," he said.

Retracting freshman eligibility is not an easy issue. Where does the money come from for freshman teams? Do athletes lose a year of eligibility, having only three as they did previously? What about redshirt years? Would student-athletes anticipating varsity glory as freshmen be outraged?

These are important questions. The best interests of the student are important too.

Since NCAA colleges place requirements on incoming freshmen, it would be reasonable to anticipate colleges placing requirements on themselves regarding academic growth and graduation. Minimum grade points must be maintained for a student-athlete to play, but there is no loss of scholarships if athletes do not graduate. In fact, one independent study concluded that male football and basketball players score significantly lower in reading comprehension and mathematics *after their freshman year in college.*

"Intercollegiate Athletic Participation and Freshman-Year Cognitive Outcomes," published by the Ohio State University Press and reprinted in *The Journal of Higher Education,* July/August, 1995, came to that conclusion after studying 2,416 freshmen at various colleges in 16 states. The study also showed scores in critical thinking lower, though the disadvantage was not statistically reliable. The effects on women were negative, but less pronounced and not statistically significant.

Four professors from three different universities found that in a group of males with similar reading skills before freshman year, if the nonathletes were 50th percentile after the year ended, football and basketball players would be 40th percentile. In math, athletes in revenue producing sports would be 42nd percentile. The difference between revenue and non-revenue athletes would be almost as wide, 7.7 percentile points in reading comprehension, 6.8 in math.

Women athletes in all sports were about four points behind their nonathletic peers.

The study speculated that the results could be due to "extensive time commitment required of intercollegiate football and basketball players . . . a possible subculture that may not always value reading or study . . . (and athletes taking) a greater portion of their freshman year course work in applied/professional areas, such as physical education, speech pathology, or child and family studies."

It was only one study. Still, the possibility that competing as freshmen causes students to fall behind their peers intellectually would seem to be of great concern to anyone in the field of education. Is the study accurate? What other evaluations are necessary? How soon can the appropriate extensive studies be initiated? What is true? If the causes are found, what changes are necessary? How much of a student's intellect can reasonably be sacrificed to play as a freshman? How can parents and athletes be warned of the dangers, if there are any?

NCAA colleges have a responsibility to student-athletes to see that the reality fits the label. Costs and competitiveness are concerns, but not as valid as a true college education, graduation and preparation for a meaningful job. The schools can improve; hopefully, they will.

Because change is slow, by being aware of current problems, athletes have a better chance to make a good choice during recruiting. Before the final, critical decision on an athletic scholarship is made, there are some other thoughts which deserve special consideration.

Chapter IX
FINAL CONSIDERATIONS

"Preparedness is the key to success and victory."

Douglas MacArthur
American military leader

Recruited athletes think about a free education, national championships, maybe All-American honors, possibly a pro career. While these are all worthy goals, there are other facets of the college decision and the college experience that are more common, and probably more important. This chapter explores considerations which impact the kind of recruiting decision which will look wise a decade or two in the future.

RELYING ON AN EXPERT

Some athletes become overwhelmed by the recruiting process, and do what an "expert" suggests. Even if that person is a truly knowledgeable parent or coach, it is almost always a mistake to give this decision to anyone.

My mother used to say, "You have to be your own doctor." The first time she said it, I argued, "But a doctor is highly educated, current on medical changes and experienced." She replied, "Yes, but no one knows your body better than you, and no one cares more about you than you do. You have to tell a doctor about every symptom, and ask many questions, then decide what to do about the recommendation."

Not only was that valuable advice regarding medicine, it applies throughout life. The phrase "be your own doctor" became part of our shorthand communication. It has been applied to education, career, social, family and other types of decisions. Get expert advice, understand it, question it, consider it, but do not give the decision to someone else.

No one knows what is important to you as much as you do. College coaches are primarily concerned with improving their team;

your interest in playing two sports or going to medical school may not hold the same priority. High school or AAU coaches may have their own agenda, possibly a coaching position for themselves as a condition for you accepting a scholarship.

For anyone, particularly an athlete who has been taken care of since athletic ability became apparent, there is a real temptation to have someone take care of this recruiting decision as well. There are people to cut the grass, do taxes, go to the grocery and other unpleasant tasks, why not just ask an expert what school to attend?

Relying on an expert, whether a coach, a parent, an older brother or sister or a family friend, is one of the biggest, and most common, mistakes athletes make in selecting a college.

To explore the foolishness of this approach, consider the most popular, most visible media personality in college sports, Dick Vitale. In addition to his media impact, as a former high school and college coach, he is well qualified. Plus, he truly cares about young people. Imagine having him decide what college is best.

The problem is, despite his credentials, Vitale might make a mistake. It might be as bad as the mistakes he made as head coach of the NBA Detroit Pistons.

After finishing 30-52 in his first season, Vitale chose local star Gregory Kelser from Michigan State instead of Sidney Moncrief of Arkansas in the 1979 NBA Draft. Moncrief had an 11-year career, and played in five All-Star games, while Kelser was a role player for six years. But that was not Vitale's biggest mistake.

He put together a trade with the Boston Celtics, who needed to rebuild after a season even worse than Detroit's. Vitale sent M. L. Carr and two first round draft choices to Boston for Bob McAdoo, a player General Manager Red Auerbach disliked.

The next year, Vitale was fired after 12 games. Detroit finished 16-66, still the worst season in team history. Detroit's position of first choice in the NBA draft had been traded to Boston along with Washington's pick, No. 13.

The Celtics sent those two draft choices to Golden State for an established center in Robert Parrish and the rights to Kevin McHale of Minnesota. For many years they teamed with Larry Bird to form possibly the best front line in NBA history.

In a 1990 poll, NBA general managers voted the Golden State-Boston trade as the most lopsided of all time. But that's only part of the picture for the Celtics. In actuality they traded McAdoo for Parrish, McHale and Carr. McAdoo's play declined sharply and he was soon traded. McHale and Parrish totaled 16 All-Star appearances, and Carr was a valuable player for six years.

The poor Pistons were 143-267 in the five years from the time Vitale was hired until Chuck Daly was brought on board for the 1984 season. Daly turned things around and the Pistons were world champions in 1989 and 1990. By then, the Celtics had battled the Lakers throughout the decade, and won three championships. Vitale's mistake had influenced Boston's joy, and Detroit's pain, for a decade.

Dick Vitale's incredible popularity makes him the perfect example of an expert who does not have all the answers. (Not that he pretends to have them. He often pokes fun at himself over "getting the ziggy in Detroit." In addition, he repeatedly challenges young athletes to "make your own decisions and be accountable for them." He is too smart to tell athletes what school to attend.)

Along with Vitale, every person, expert or not, has made decisions which look bad in hindsight. Consider Bear Bryant's handling of Ken Hall. Bryant called himself "a fool."

It may seem like turning an important decision over to an expert would be a good idea, but it is not. The person who has to live with the decision must make it, after seeking counsel from many others who raise different types of concerns and insights. No coach, or even parent, can properly decide which scholarship an athlete should accept. As much as they may genuinely love and care for the athlete, they are all subject to biases and prejudices. No one is totally objective. So the athlete must try to be unbiased, and very selfish, because the decision will influence his or her life far more than anyone else's in the next 70 years or so. In selecting a college, one mistake can last a lifetime.

FIND MENTORS TO HELP WITH RECRUITING

While essential for athletes to make the final decision, it is just as important that they have help in gathering information.

"Too many athletes fall into the trap of letting coaches control the conversation," said ESPN's Robin Roberts. "I think it's good for the parents to be involved, to see that the athlete asks questions about what is important. My parents had a strong background in education and were very involved in my college choice."

Athletes with two parents participating in recruiting start with a big advantage. Even then, it may be wise to bring other points of view and experiences into the discussion. Without two parents, someone—coach, teacher, counselor, pastor, athlete—has to put together a team to provide guidance. The decision is too big for a teenager to make without help.

Roberts is an advocate of mentors, not just during recruiting, but for life.

"Here at ESPN," she said, "Chris Berman is doing the kinds of things I want to do, and I go to him for advice all the time. I needed an accountant, I asked Chris. My older sister was in television. She didn't have a choice about being a mentor, I tagged a long. Chris Myers worked with her, and agreed to critique a tape I sent him. Now we work together. I sent letters to broadcasters early in my career. Some I didn't even know were helpful. My parents were always mentors. And the late Arthur Ashe was very important in my life. He told me, 'If you are just remembered as a broadcaster, you haven't reached your full potential.' I've been very fortunate."

Yes, and no. She was fortunate in having some of those mentors available, but made her own luck by seeking out the rest. Many people enjoy helping others. By asking, Robin Roberts found several people to help her.

The student-athlete without mentors can find good ones, by understanding the importance of mentors and asking for help.

CAMPUS VISIT

Coaches prepare for an official visit as thoroughly as they do for a game, making sure recruits see what they are supposed to see when they are supposed to see it, so that the school appears in the best possible light. They take special care to match the player most like the recruit as the team host.

One Division I basketball program put together a good recruiting class in 1995 by using well-researched information to plan the visits to two recruits. For the first player, "A", the approach was, "Get him drunk, then get him to sign." That might have put the young man in the correct frame of mind, but he didn't sign until he received a promise of a starting position and specific minutes as a freshman, regardless. "A" signed, and started as a freshman. Though his performance tested the limits of "regardless," he stayed in the line-up. For "B," a good student from a solid family which had many contacts in the world of college athletics, the recruiting approach was, "nothing at all shady, send him around campus with our born-again Christian." After enrolling, "B" consistently outplayed his teammate, but didn't play nearly as many minutes their freshman year. On the other hand, if "B" had asked about guaranteed playing time as a condition for signing, at some schools the scholarship offer might have been withdrawn.

At another school, a valued recruit told his teammates he really enjoyed his campus visit, having had sex twice while he was there. Maybe he was just talking, maybe it was a game plan successfully implemented. Anyway, he started, and produced, as a freshman.

If the campus visit is the sole basis for selecting a school, chances are high that a mistake will be made, because the school can stage the events which take place. A player can easily sign with the wrong school, or reject the right one if things don't go well. Al McGuire used to say, "If it rains, I won't get the kid," when he coached Marquette. Instead, independent research and fact-finding must be combined with what happens on the visit. If a couple of informal visits can be added, so much the better. The more information gathered from different sources, the more likely the best decision will be made.

A potential red flag should pop up if you are unable to speak with all players on a visit (except football, where there are too many). It could be that the player who "is out of town," or who "has to study," is exactly the player you need to meet. Get a phone number and call on your own. Schools hide things, so do some investigating.

During the 1996 school year, two developments in recruiting raised additional issues to consider regarding the campus visit.

As a virtually unanimous choice for prep All-America linebacker at Los Angeles Dorsey High School, Na'il Diggs had plenty of opportunities to make campus visits. He went on four before deciding that the University of Southern California was the place for him. Allowed five visits, he did not think another one was necessary.

Many athletes take all their visits, necessary or not. It's fun having people tell you how good you are, what you can do for their program. Diggs was mature enough not to want that attention. When something happened to change his decision, he had a visit in reserve to use in making a new decision.

Since his mother died three years before, Diggs had lived with his sister Roslyn Simpson and her husband, Charlie Parker. The fact that Parker was USC basketball coach influenced Diggs toward committing to the Trojans. When Parker was fired the day before colleges could sign football players to letters of intent, Diggs decided he did not want to go there to school.

In looking for an alternative, Ohio State, located thousands of miles away, came to mind. The Buckeyes were in the news because a local star running back, Durell Price, had renounced an earlier commitment when a drug store attendant had incorrectly faxed the wrong page of his signed letter of intent. His mother, who had always disagreed with her son's decision, called it "an omen" and convinced him to stay close to home. He chose UCLA. Because Ohio State lost Price, would they have a scholarship available for Diggs?

Parker had graduated from high school in Columbus and his mother still lived there. Roslyn Simpson knew Coach John Cooper from her college days at Arizona State, when she dated one of his football players. The school now seemed logical, though it would not have been considered without reports about Price.

When Diggs and Simpson flew to Columbus together, he decided Ohio State would be right for him. He told *The Columbus Dispatch*, "Columbus is a big city; it really shocked me. I thought it would be more of a country town; cows walking through the streets, things like that. I didn't expect a big city-type school."

If his career goes well, Buckeye recruiters and writers will be telling that story for years. For the purpose of this book, Diggs benefited from his ability to say "No" to all the coaches who said, "Why not use your last visit to see us?" By retaining his fifth visit, Diggs was able to make a decision with a minimum of confusion, then, when he felt a new decision was necessary, have the flexibility to do that.

When an athlete is heavily recruited, why not first seek to reduce the list of schools to three or four, visit them and make a choice? If there is still some indecision, take another visit. If that is not necessary, nothing significant has been lost. Athletes with one signing period could take most of their visits early, the remainder later if required. Athletes with two signing periods could take three early their senior year and still have two for the later period if they are not sure, or if they want to see if a coach or star player leaves.

Another important development occurred during a visit in February 1996.

When Mateen Cleaves of Flint Northern High School in Flint, Mich. visited the University of Michigan, he accompanied five players to Detroit for a party at the home of freshman Robert Traylor. At around 5 a.m., while returning to campus, Maurice Taylor drove the car off the road. Traylor broke his arm; the others were shaken-up but not injured. Michigan Coach Steve Fisher was quoted as saying, "If we hadn't had a recruit in for a visit, this probably wouldn't have happened."

Any parents could reasonably wonder, "What takes place when my child is in the care of a university's athletic program? Does the coaching staff know what is happening when they are not present? What limits are placed on the athletes who entertain my child? How are they selected?" Questions which may not have been considered in the past suddenly became very important.

Interestingly, Mateen Cleaves chose to attend Michigan State. The NCAA decided Michigan had committed a minor rule violation by taking the recruit more than 30 miles from campus, and accepted as adequate punishment the university's decision to suspend efforts to recruit him.

COACHING EXPERTISE AND PLAYING TIME

When the time comes that ESPN televises 1,000 college football, basketball, baseball, volleyball and softball games in the same year, one thing is certain: there will be two outstanding representatives of the coaching profession at every game.

According to all national media, every coach we ever see is a "genius, legend, superb strategist or brilliant leader." Local broadcasts are worse, particularly in regard to the hometown coach. When you hear "announcers of this game are approved by ————," take that very seriously. The announcers do.

Announcers won't say this, but some coaches are better than others. An objective listing of coaches by their ability to formulate a game plan would be different than one based on ability to recruit, organize a team, communicate with players, react to game conditions or any other phase of their craft. Half are below average, at any particular skill or overall. Others are relatively poor.

To any thinking reader, such a revelation will border on the obvious. There is a bell-shaped curve for evaluating performance in any group, from sixth grade softball players to MIT graduates. Some are simply better than others.

Purdue's Gene Keady touched on this while campaigning with the media for his senior point guard Porter Roberts to be named first team All-Big Ten.

"If Porter is not the best point guard in the league, then I don't know much about basketball," said the man about to win his third straight Big Ten championship and be selected national coach of the year. "Now, if you are going to go on stats, which is what you guys usually do, then he won't get it." At the time Roberts averaged eight points, five assists and four rebounds a game.

When a writer said he would wait to see how the coaches voted, Keady said, "You know what they'll vote. They're like you guys. Maybe that's why we're winning. Some of them don't understand the game."

Keady arrived at Purdue in 1981, winning six conference championships and going to the NCAA 12 times. In that time there have only been five years when either Purdue or Indiana did not have at least a share of the conference title. It is safe to assume Keady was not talking about Indiana Coach Bob Knight's lack of understanding.

One complication in evaluating coaches is, what is the standard? Is the Joe Paterno way superior to the Tom Osborne way? Both have resulted in national championships, but fan loyalties and recent results would influence the voting.

For the recruit seeking to evaluate coaches, the evaluation does not have to be objective. A personal bias can become a criteria. If the athlete is a quarterback who likes to run the ball as well as pass it, Tom Osborne should have an edge over a pro-style coach. Since the athlete has to live with the decision, for four years as a student and 40-70 as an adult, he or she benefits by applying the criteria fairly to make a sound choice.

Try to imagine playing for a team that is not well-organized, suffers a disadvantage in coaching strategy most of the time, or where the coach is never available to the players because the latest endorsement opportunity is too good to pass by. That happens in college. It results in a frustrating experience for the athlete.

All coaches have strengths and weaknesses, a fact the recruit must recognize, investigate then evaluate. While that is a lot to ask of a teenager, those strengths and weaknesses will be a reality to the college athlete in the fall. It would be advantageous to know what is coming before then.

One way to get objective information is to ask players individually, "What do you like best about Coach, and what do you like least? What do you like best about practice, and what do you like least? What do you like best about the trips, and what do you like least?" Individually players do not have to worry as much about what they say being repeated. By being asked for a positive and a negative, they are more likely to express a range of feelings.

Comparing coaches is a difficult, but essential, part of choosing a school. The information is difficult to collect, but by ignoring this you run the risk of being frustrated by having to outplay a team, their coach and your coach for four years.

The negative aspect of playing for a good coach can come up regarding early playing time.

Most high school athletes exaggerate their potential for playing time as college freshmen. It's not totally their fault; high expectations are largely the result of recruiting attention.

"When their daughters are sophomores, parents worry about them playing at certain schools. After listening to coaches for two years, they expect them to start," said Melissa McFerrin, assistant women's basketball coach at Ohio State.

Playing time is a function of the skill of the individual and the competition on the team, as evaluated by the head coach. Skill is a combination of the ability the athlete had in high school and the improvement which has taken place through experience in college. The better the coach, the more valuable that experience will be. At a program like Purdue, for example, good high school players have become better Big Ten players than great high school players at other universities. Yet Purdue recruited only four McDonald's All-Americans since Keady arrived, compared to 15 by Michigan, 10 by Indiana and eight for Illinois and Iowa.

The "Fab Five" at Michigan was an example of athletes with great ability going to a university where the skill level was low at the time. The result was immediate, extensive playing time. The success and media attention made a unique circumstance seem reasonable to many high school athletes, who now expect similar results in their career.

Say there is a sophomore on the team who you played against in high school. He, or she, was not as good as you were, so there should be no problem starting ahead of her or him, right? However, that player will have had the advantage of playing two years for a good coach, in practice if not in games. Experienced players improve more under a good coach than under a weak one. You will learn more with a good coach, but it will be more difficult to catch up to what the upperclassmen already know.

"A good coach will make his players see what they can become rather than what they are," former Notre Dame football Coach Ara Parseghian once said.

Neither Shawn Respert of Michigan State nor Brian Evans of Indiana was very highly regarded in high school, and both sat out their freshman years as redshirts. Yet after five years with Coaches Heathcote and Knight, respectively, both became Big Ten Men's Basketball Players of the Year as seniors.

Some players recoil at the mention of a redshirt year.

"If we tell a kid she's a redshirt candidate, it's an eliminator in women's basketball," said Ohio State's McFerrin. "She may redshirt, but it will be somewhere else. Players don't see the talent and experience gap. It's perceived as a put-down rather than something that would help down the road."

There are times when a redshirt year is not good. Redshirts who later transfer lose a year of eligibility from the four they would have had. Also, redshirts who later lose a season to injury will be left with only three years of play. The NCAA allows five years to play four.

Because the importance of early playing time varies with the athlete, there are three things to consider in examining that aspect of the entire situation. First, how much can you reasonably expect to play as a freshman and sophomore, based on returning players, incoming players, your talent and work ethic? Second, can you adjust to that? Third, if you were overly optimistic, can you adjust to less time? Usually, the third point is the most important. For example, McDonald's All-American Luther Clay played sparingly his freshman year at Purdue, when the seniors dominated court time in 1996.

MORE TALENTED TEAMMATES AND PLAYING TIME

More than 30 years ago, Ron Maciejowski went to Ohio State as a freshman quarterback. He probably would have had a good career except a better quarterback, Rex Kern, enrolled the same time.

"It didn't bother me that he was going too," remembers Maciejowski. "Lee Corso was the coach at Navy, and he said, "You could sit behind Rex Kern for four years.' I said, 'Yes, and I could go to Navy and sit behind Roger Staubach [Heisman Trophy winner from the Naval Academy who later led the Dallas Cowboys to three Super Bowl victories] too. What's the difference?' Publicity doesn't matter. Some guys can't play. Of course, it turned out Rex was a great football player.

"As freshmen we talked about having too much talent, but I was never serious about leaving. I even thought I might beat him out. By sophomore year I knew my fate, but I was having so much fun, we were national champs (in 1968) and it never came up again," Maciejowski remembers.

Then a quarterback who did transfer came to mind.

"Gary Zetts from Youngstown got discouraged about playing time and transferred to Virginia Tech after his sophomore year. That should be safe, Ohio State to Virginia Tech, right? When Gary got there he sat behind Don Strock [who played for the Miami Dolphins for over a decade]. Those things happen."

While Maciejowski did not have the career he might have wished, he was an important "relief pitcher" at times. For example, he directed a 70-yard scoring drive which won Ohio State's first road game of the 1968 season at Illinois.

Months before receiving his engineering degree, Maciejowski

was drafted by the Chicago Bears. After being cut before the season started, he tried out with Cincinnati the next year but was cut again. What seemed to be bad news turned out to be very good, very soon.

"I made twice as much money in sales at Worthington Industries as I would have with the Bengals," he recalls. Today Ron Maciejowski is Vice-President of Marketing at Worthington Industries.

Whether athletes put sports behind them or go into coaching, many remember thoughts of transferring. When Indiana's Knight was at Ohio State he thought he should have played more and often spoke of transferring.

"One night he came to my room on a road trip," remembers former *Columbus Dispatch* writer Dick Otte, "and said, 'I'm going home, I'm quitting the team.' I said, 'Why are you here?' He said, "I don't have any money. I want you to give me an airplane ticket.' I said, 'You're in Champaign, Illinois, and you want to fly to Orrville, Ohio. What kind of an airline do you think makes that flight?'"

After graduating from Ohio State and becoming an assistant high school coach, Knight sent college coach Fred Taylor a note saying, "I think every player should have to be a coach before being allowed to play."

THE COLLEGE COACH AS MENTOR/PARENT/FRIEND
FOR A LIFETIME

When Doug McDonald thought about being recruited to play basketball in college he recalled eating lunch with Taylor. "I was eating Waldorf salad and flipped a wedge of lettuce right out of the bowl onto the table. What a klutz."

Despite his nerves, and despite the presence of a group of outstanding and heavily publicized freshmen, McDonald enrolled at Ohio State. By his junior year he worked his way into the starting line-up. As a senior he was captain of the conference champions. Because of Taylor's recommendation, McDonald was hired as a high school teacher and head basketball coach immediately after graduation. He has since retired as a high school principal.

In April 1995, McDonald attended a 35-year reunion celebration to honor Ohio State's only NCAA championship basketball team. He listened to Hall-of-Famers John Havlicek and Jerry Lucas talk about the impact that team, those teammates and Coach Taylor had on their lives. He listened while their teammates, who had gone on to success after athletics, said much the same thing.

When college recruiters are on the trail, everyone they meet is "Coach." It's easier than learning all those new names. But for the college athlete, the title belongs to the adult in charge, the boss, "the man," even if she is a woman.

With effort, and a little luck, that college coach will always be "Coach," in the highest sense of the name. "Coach" will also be a role model, mentor, advisor, surrogate parent, best friend, job reference, psychologist, and more, for a lifetime. The value of that multi-faceted relationship may rival the value of the college degree. McDonald, in his mid-50s, said "I tried, but I can't call him Fred. No matter how old I get, he'll always be 'Coach' to me."

There are many college head coaches who deeply believe that long term relationship is simply part of the job. Most of the time they cherish it as a benefit of the profession. Occasionally, when the swamp is filled with alligators and time is short, it is a responsibility. In any case, it's always present. Not only that, it continues beyond the job, to the next job and well into retirement.

Most coaches feel that way. Many of them also act that way, but not all. Some coaches have priorities which stretch no further than the present—today's recruits, today's team, today's game take all their attention. For them, the record setter of years ago is history, not to mention the third-stringer.

The recruit with an awareness of the future will look for a coach who cares about athletes as people, who teaches what Purdue's Keady calls "the basics of life." Examples include, "eat breakfast and go to bed at night," as well as, "if you want to play, get a rebound." Keady mentioned both while winning his third consecutive Big Ten championship. Beyond the present, the recruit will seek a coach who has had an impact on players' lives after graduation, one who knows where past players are and what they are doing. The coach who was and is involved with his past players is likely to care about today's recruits years later. History is a better indicator of the future than mere promises.

At North Carolina, Dean Smith has lost many outstanding players to early entry in the NBA Draft. When he thought they were ready, he advised men like Michael Jordan and James Worthy to pass up college eligibility. Of course, that meant he lost an All-American each time. That can't make a coach too happy, but Smith was concerned about their best interests.

At Kentucky, Rick Pitino almost ordered Jamal Mashburn to leave college after his junior year. A former NBA coach, Pitino was certain his player was ready. Other coaches have done the same. They are the kind of people who can be relied upon to provide counsel, or make a job recommendation.

Having a good coach helps assure a pleasant college experience, but having a friend and mentor for life is even better. It is possible to have both, though it does not happen all the time.

GUARANTEED PRO CAREER

After the many examples of men who did not play pro ball as they aspired, either due to inability to perform college work, or insufficient skill, or injuries, the logic is compelling to heed Dick DeVenzio's advice, to pick up the money (get an education and a degree) on the way to the game (pro career). There are more than 3,500 Division I basketball players every year, plus D-II, D-III, junior college, players overseas and even some coming out of high school. There are 29 NBA first round draft choices. More than 10,000 D-I college football players, plus smaller school stars, get squeezed into seven rounds and 254 selections in the NFL draft. The average NFL career lasts less than four years. The odds are very steep.

However, assume that you know you will be one of the lucky ones. Of course, that means college no longer matters, right? If you had a guaranteed pro career of several years, why would those classes be important?

Here's why. College offers a degree as proof of an education, so an employer will consider an applicant for a job. The degree is only the first step in the door. After being hired, the degree provides no advantage, because everyone has one. This is where the education that generated the degree starts to matter. Some people learned more than others on their way to graduation ceremonies, so they produce more at work. They get promotions, others get left behind.

Many a young athlete thinks college doesn't matter if the NBA or NFL beckons. Granted, the degree may not matter as much to him. It is possible he will never have to go to a corporation to interview for a job. Yet a college education probably matters more, not less, for the young man who will earn millions of dollars in pro sports. He has more to lose, between the money he will earn as an athlete and the money he could earn in other opportunities which may be presented to him.

The pro athlete doesn't have to work for a corporation; he already has a job in charge of ME, INC. It could be a multi-million dollar business. The good news is, he doesn't have to worry about being fired, or the victim of a hostile takeover. The bad news is, if he doesn't know what to do with his opportunities and makes poor decisions, he could lose everything. Many others have.

Yes, he will have advisors, but he has to set goals, establish priorities, plan and prepare time tables, speak effectively and persuasively. He has to know enough to check on his advisors. He has to make the final decision. He has to "be his own doctor."

Even assuming a guaranteed pro career, and there is no such thing, a college education in areas like business, personal finance, income tax law, accounting, decision making and investments would be helpful. A knowledge of history and sociology would help him avoid mistakes others have made. Public speaking courses, writing classes, media laboratories would be valuable, particularly to the athlete who hopes to be involved with endorsements. Many will want to be involved in broadcasting after their career, making such courses essential. Seldom does a pro career last past 35, less than half a lifetime.

There is a great deal of talk about the college degree, and rightfully so. It is a requirement for most desirable jobs, and becoming more so all the time. It is almost as necessary to operate in our society as a driver's license. But for the athlete who is sure he won't need a degree because he will be in the pros, the college education becomes more important than most athletes seem to realize.

There are many examples of athletes who went into pro sports early, were successful, and still went back to school to graduate.

Isiah Thomas had a brilliant career in the NBA following his sophomore year in college, but found time to complete his degree at Indiana. Now that his playing career is over, he is using his mind as General Manager of the NBA Toronto Raptors.

Juwan Howard left Michigan one year early but graduated with his class. His hard work on the court has made him one of the budding stars of the NBA, and his hard work academically has prepared him for the time when that phase of his life is over.

On the other hand, it would be unfair to leave this consideration without stating that a guaranteed pro career is not always what it appears to be. Consider the case of Luther Wright, the 7-foot-2, 270-pound player who decided he would declare for the 1993 NBA Draft rather than spend his senior year at Seton Hall.

Despite his size, most observers questioned his decision at the time. Wright had only averaged seven points and five rebounds as a college junior. But when Utah made him a first round selection and

signed him to a five-year, $5 million contract, it seemed he (
lose. He had plenty of time to make the league, at a far bett
ing salary than most college graduates enjoy.

As a rookie in the 1993-94 season, Wright appeared in 1_
playing 92 minutes and scoring 19 points. He had two blocked shots
and ten rebounds. Justifiably, the Jazz expected more.

Cut before the next season, Wright agreed to an annual pay-
ment of about $150,000 per year for 25 years. While most Americans
live and raise families on much less than that, after life in the NBA it
was not enough for Wright. He couldn't afford health insurance. In
March 1996, he was committed to a public psychiatric hospital with
manic depression. For anyone who has ever seen a hospital bill, it
was a frightening development to consider.

Maybe Luther Wright would have been better prepared to succeed in the NBA with another year in college ball, maybe not. Maybe
he would have signed a larger, more secure contract, or learned better life planning skills with more schooling. Maybe not. But he
unquestionably serves as a reminder that even a signed, $5 million
contract is no guarantee. He wasn't able to run ME, INC.

HIRING A COLLEGE SCHOLARSHIP MARKETING ORGANIZATION

For over a decade, parents of athletes have been approached by
organizations which provide exposure to colleges for a fee.

Tracy Jackson is the president of one of the first such organizations, College Prospects of America (CPOA), in Logan, Ohio. The
company opened its doors in 1986 and has representatives in over 40
states, as well as Canada, Great Britain, Australia and several other
countries.

"I was talking to someone in the athletic department at a
Division I university the other day," said Jackson. "The school has 20
athletic programs. I asked, 'How many coaches have recruiting budgets under $5,000?' The answer was 'eight or nine.' And four were
under $1,000. Those coaches can't hear about athletes unless they are
nearby. If the athlete plays a position which is filled at the local
school, there can be a problem getting a scholarship.

"Parents in the work place know there is a big difference
between being qualified to do a job and being hired. In much the
same way, there are athletes who could play in college who do not
get scholarships because they are not marketed properly," he adds.

"In 1991, Georgia Tech had the largest athletic recruiting budget in the country, based on 203 D-I schools self-reporting their expenditures. It was about $770,000, not counting telephone and postage. Yet something like $712,000 of that was spent on men, mostly football and basketball, only $58,000 on women. By the way, that year Northeastern Illinois had the lowest reported budget, under $10,000 in all sports. Even the best coaches have trouble finding players without money," he said.

CPOA screens athletes for their college talent, and targets the colleges where they can succeed. "We offer credibility to the colleges," Jackson maintains. That limits their potential market to "10-12 percent of the high school athletes," but leaves room for some interesting anecdotes.

"One wrestler had won two state championships but hadn't been contacted till he signed with us. He ended up at Stanford with $29,000 in academic and athletic aid . . . a United Kingdom tennis player, Paul C. Robinson, is the top rated singles player in the nation at Texas Christian . . . I have a list of several dozen United Kingdom and Australian athletes who will have scholarships in the United States in 1997 in front of me . . . a player on Katie Smith's AAU basketball team, which went to the National's every year, didn't have any offers until she worked with us. She got a scholarship to UNC-Ashville two months later."

CPOA is not the only marketing organization with interesting stories about recruiting exposure. Here are some considerations for parents who are evaluating their need for this type of service:

- Before talking with anyone, have the student-athlete develop goals for the recruiting process. For the athlete who wants to stay in-state, has a small list of schools which would be acceptable, has poor grades, or has a very high profile already, this service may not be necessary. If he or she is not good enough to play in college, such a service will not fool any coaches.
- Next, talk with the high school coach. How does he or she promote athletes? How is your child different? What does the coach know about local marketing organizations? What needs to be done? Who can do it?
- Now that you know what you want and have an idea of the support which is available, if hiring someone to provide exposure still might make sense, schedule a meeting. During the meeting, learn what the service can do that will be valuable in your case. Mailing information to schools where your

child would not be admitted, or could never play, is not valuable. Get names and phone numbers of past customers so you can check references. Ask about the risks, and request a copy of NCAA rules which relate to the transaction.

- Afterwards, check the references by asking probing questions. Were you happy? Why? What didn't you like? Would you do it again? Could you have done it yourself? Why not? What kind of athletic honors did your child receive? How many offers (not letters) did your child receive? Get the people talking, not just answering 'Yes' and 'No.' Also, call the Better Business Bureau. They may identify an individual you will want to avoid.
- Talk with competition and compare capabilities of each company.
- Compare what needs to be done to what you can do yourself. Libraries have directories of colleges which offer various sports, colleges can be reached by phone or mail, this book is full of ideas of ways to market athletes, but what can and will you do for your child? It could be that an organization offers a great deal which a family could not do for itself. Maybe you have the time, talent and interest to do everything without paying a fee. A major concern would be that parents could find the time to do almost everything on their own, but that small other part might mean a college scholarship. Or it might not be worth the money.
- Scholarships in most college sports are "equivalent," which usually means athletes get partial assistance. For those sports, the real question is, "How much will it cost to go there?" With various kinds of aid, expensive universities can be reasonable. Does the marketing organization have expertise in analyzing financial aid? If so, Division III athletes can benefit from such a service.
- Finally, discuss what you have found with the high school coach, who may have some new ideas, or friends to ask, before a final decision is made.

RISK OF INJURY

According to the National Athletic Trainers' Association (NATA), over one-half million injuries in high school football take place in an average year, and over 22 percent of all high school basketball players sustain a time loss injury each year.

In 1967, John Brockington, Jack Tatum, Leo Hayden and Tim Anderson enrolled at Ohio State to play football for Woody Hayes. All became first round NFL draft choices. Nine other members of that recruiting class were also chosen by pro teams. Yet in remembering his teammates, Brockington, 1971 NFL Rookie of the Year at Green Bay, said, "Tim Wagner was a heck of a player before he got hurt."

Tim Wagner was a 5-foot-10, 175-pound tailback who made second team All-Ohio, then suffered a career ending injury his freshman year. "He was at running back in a scrimmage," recalls one teammate. "His leg was taken three different ways, and he never made it back." Few fans of the 1968 Buckeyes remember Tim Wagner, but, nearly 30 years later, John Brockington still did.

In any sport, injury can rob a player of the athletic experience he or she hoped to have. Anyone can be a "Tim Wagner," by being in the wrong place at the wrong time.

Considering the effects of football, females seem to have an advantage in avoiding sports injuries. However, the knee injury, particularly tears of the anterior cruciate ligament which provides support to the knee, causes disproportionate problems for women.

In the February 13, 1995, issue of *Sports Illustrated*, an article titled "Out of Joint" addressed the disparity, citing studies showing women basketball players are between four and six times as likely to suffer an ACL injury as men. A separate study of active players in six major conferences showed 83 ACL's for women, 26 for men.

Dr. Rod Harter of Oregon State University, Chairman of the NATA Research Foundation, called the *SI* study "anecdotal, and not controlled in any way." Harter is trying to set up a national study, and said grant applications to study the problem were pending.

"We are looking to experience, conditioning, hormonal change and the width of women's hips [which allows child bearing], among other things. Women's injuries seem to stand out compared to men in two areas: the ACL in basketball and the kneecap in repetitive motion sports, like swimming and running," he said.

"There are studies which suggest excessive exercise can produce the reverse effect of expected, that bones become weaker rather than stronger. This causes repeated stress fractures," Harter concludes.

Dr. Ray Tesner, D.O., played football at Penn State and is Medical Director of Sports Medicine Grant in Columbus, Ohio. He mentions the same two problem areas for females, ACLs and knee caps. "We think the higher percentage is due to wider pelvises, causing a steeper angle to the knee cap, and less muscle in the female than the male. There is not much to do, except to be in shape, have weight under control and work on strengthening the area around the knee."

In a follow up article April 10, 1995, *Sports Illustrated* quoted Dr. Donald Cooper, team physician at Oklahoma State for 35 years. He believes young people of both sexes will have an increasing number of ACL tears, with girls at greater risk than boys because girls are encouraged to be less active. "Muscles will grow, but once you go past puberty, you can't go back and stimulate the tendons and ligaments to get that strength," said Cooper.

So it's better to have kids running around the house than sitting in front of the television, especially if they are going to want to play sports in college.

By high school, athletes think they are invulnerable, but the risk of injury in sports is real. That risk is small compared to the benefits of participation. In particular, the Women's Sports Foundation (1-800-227-3988) has extensive literature on the benefits of exercise, which include building confidence and self-esteem in children, avoidance of drugs and early pregnancy, higher graduation rates and reduced likelihood of breast cancer in adults. Still, parents and coaches must work with doctors and trainers to learn about new developments which can reduce the likelihood of injuries. At a minimum, obtain the brochure "Minimizing the Risk of Injury in High School Athletics" from a trainer, who can get it from NATA (214-637-6282).

One other thought from NATA. More than 60 percent of game-related basketball injuries (59 percent boys, 63 percent girls) occur in the second half of high school games. Proper conditioning might minimize that imbalance.

It would be comforting if doctors had a perfect understanding of the reaction the human body has to exercise. The frightening truth that they do not was pointed out by the collapse of UMass basketball player Marcus Camby in 1996, and the earlier deaths of college player Hank Gathers and Boston Celtic Reggie Lewis. All of these incidents were heart-related, but none could be fully explained even in hindsight.

Because the unknown is so vast in the area of sports medicine, it is prudent to seek to evaluate the medical expertise of trainers and doctors at a college, not only by talking with them but also asking questions of athletes they have treated. It is also prudent to ask, "If I go there and get hurt, will I want to stay there and get my education?"

ISSUES FOR THE FEMALE ATHLETE

Female athletes have two more considerations than males in recruiting. The decision to play for a male or female coach is seldom available to boys. To girls it is either an added opportunity or an increased burden, depending on how they approach it. The other decision has to do with the possible presence of sexual pressure within the athletic program.

The question "What is the coach like?" takes on a different dimension in female athletics. Parents worry about their daughters being protected, college coaches have to be ready to answer blunt questions during discussions with parents, all coaches are concerned about being quoted on such an emotional issue and most journalists, particularly those with close working relationships to athletic programs, are reluctant to acknowledge that the concern exists.

The best written discussion of the subject which I found, and one which several coaches referenced, is *The Stronger Women Get, The More Men Love Football,* by Mariah Burton Nelson. From the review of the first women's basketball game in April 1896, which men were not allowed to watch because seeing public female sweat was deemed indelicate, to the end, the former Stanford basketball player provides an unconventional look at male-female relationships in a variety of sporting roles. (I suggest it as leisure reading for anyone interested in sports beyond the scoreboard, and strongly recommend it to anyone whose daughter is an athlete.)

The chapter entitled "My Coach Says He Loves Me" is a discussion of incidents when male and female coaches have taken advantage of their positions of power over female athletes, as well as the need for concern for the welfare of girls and boys competing long before high school.

Gender issues at the university surface during recruiting. "Every parent brings it up," said one female college coach. "I'm a father of two grown daughters, and I recruit the fathers," said another college coach. "Let's face it," said a veteran girls high school coach. "Colleges want girls who play like boys."

What the parents and athletes have to decide is, is the important issue the sexual orientation of the coach, or the impact on the athlete? In the words of the Women's Sports Foundation, "leaders have a professional responsibility, regardless of their personal beliefs, to ensure the safety and fair treatment of all participants." Male or female, coaches who fail in that regard should be dropped from consideration. Beyond that, what constitutes an important issue is a matter for each family to determine, then to research with appropriate diligence.

Chapter X

EXECUTIVE SUMMARY

"Some men see things as they are and say, 'Why?' I

dream things that never were and say, 'Why not?'

George Bernard Shaw
Irish dramatist

"Pressure is something you feel only when you don't

know what the hell you are doing."

Chuck Knox
Coach, Four-Time Super Bowl Champion Pittsburgh Steelers

In business, an executive summary accompanies a lengthy report so the boss doesn't have to wade through all the information which led to the conclusions. Time is too important for all that reading.

It may not be a bad idea, because the experts are just down the hall. Something comes up, the answer is an intercom away. The boss doesn't have to be an expert.

With recruiting, the athlete, or the parent, or the coach, or the mentor who is helping the athlete, those people have to be experts. For that reason, this summary is at the end of the book. If you have read this far, you are aware of all the insights from the experts which came before. If you ignored the advice to read every chapter, that's your loss. You may have missed what Anson Dorrance said about "forces of fortune," or Ken Hall said about closing the book on a high school career, or Nancy Fowlkes said about going to camps. Those thoughts apply to any sport. Why not go back and read what you missed now, before forgetting about it?

Whether you returned or just kept reading, here is a summary of some of the key issues for a young athlete to address during the recruiting process:

1. Practice setting and attaining goals. Write down the goal, then monitor your progress. Run for time and try to improve, even if track is not your sport. Set weight lifting goals, and exceed them. Study a certain number of hours every day. If your homework is done, review it. If there is more time, read a book. The more goals you set, the more you will achieve, the better you will feel about yourself. And, the closer you will be to those larger goals which don't happen every day, but which don't ever happen without the smaller ones.

"Set goals for yourself and work your hardest to achieve them," Beth Daniels, pro golfer, once said. "Some goals you will achieve and some you won't, but at least you will have the satisfaction of knowing where you are going."

2. Each year, write down your goals as if you were looking for a college. Even though you are a sophomore, act like you will be recruited. What is important to you? Playing time? Pro career? Distance from home? Your major? What job do you want to have at age 30, and how will you prepare for it? By doing this before it is necessary, you will get practice. Think your high school coach wants to play a game before the first practice? No way, and you shouldn't try to go through recruiting without some practice either. Each year your goals will be more sophisticated, as you get older and have practice setting them. By the time you have to explain your goals to coaches, you will be ready.

3. Read for fun. Indiana University professor Murray Sperber, who wrote *College Sports, Inc.: The Athletic Department vs. The University,* said, "What I noticed in the movie *Hoop Dreams* is not seeing a single book in the home of either player." Reading about sports now will help students learn Shakespeare later.

4. Take school seriously. Challenge yourself to get good grades. Not only will that increase your chances of getting into college with a scholarship, statistics show the higher the high school grades, the better the odds of college graduation. Also, develop study habits. The students who get good grades without knowing how to study eventually get to course work where intelligence and organization are required. In college, particularly for the student-athlete, time is precious. The ability to plan and maximize the use of what time is available often means the difference between success and failure.

Outside the classroom, be the kind of person your coach will be able to recommend when college coaches ask about character.

Columbus (Ohio) DeSales football coach Bob Jacoby remembers addressing that question about his star back, Gary Berry, in early 1996.

"When Notre Dame got his transcript, their assistant called and asked what kind of person he was. After I said how much regard I had for him, the assistant said, 'On this transcript there's a notation for G.F. What's that about?' I told him that stood for gum fine, for chewing gum. He laughed and said, 'I used to teach in a Catholic school. Little things become big things.' When he knew the 'worst' about Gary, he knew how much they wanted him."

5. "Get to know your guidance counselor in ninth grade," said LSU track coach Pat Henry shortly after leading the women's team to its tenth consecutive NCAA outdoor title in 1996. "Understand what core courses are, the difference between courses like social science and natural science and what g.p.a. [grade point average] means. The academics of the athlete has been taken out of the hands of the college coaches; 100 percent of the responsibility is on the athlete and the parents."

Concerned, Henry wants athletes to be aware of the difficult challenge so they have the best chance to meet it.

"How many ninth graders have a perception of what they want in five years? Studies show the average college student changes majors three times in college, yet we expect ninth graders to have their lives planned out. Athletes can't rely on anyone except themselves, and they can't wait," he said.

"Good coaches have always emphasized grades," said Bob Beutel after 16 years as girls basketball coach at Eastlake North, near Cleveland. "Now, you have to be very technical with core courses and everything."

6. If you did not start working in school early, don't give up. There are examples of high school drop-outs owning their own businesses. Just start now.

7. Do not be impressed by letters. A letter only means you're a name on a list. In fact, try to get beyond the glitter of recruiting. Kent Miller, former assistant boys high school basketball coach now women's assistant at Eastern Kentucky, said, "It seems like girls are interested in education, the boys are concerned with the bright lights. Still, more and more girls are talking about televised games." Focus on your goals, not the glitter.

8. Get a copy of *The NCAA Guide for the College-Bound Student-Athlete* now! Read it, digest it, discuss it, with your coach and with other, older athletes. Do not wait until your senior year to find out how the system works. Get a copy each year. It will change, but adjusting to the changes is easier than learning the whole thing under the pressure of being recruited.

9. At the end of each season, talk with your coach about realistic goals for playing in college. What looks like the right level? What skills do you need to develop in the off-season? What camps, AAU teams or other forms of exposure make sense?

Toni Roesch, a highly recruited basketball player who coached in college before deciding to coach in high school, said, "Colleges put their computer lists together based on AAU and exposure camps, then go see the high school team play." In your sport, how will coaches at the right level see you?

10. Former Penn State basketball Coach Bruce Parkhill said, "Quite a few high school coaches don't have exposure to the college game, with bigger, stronger athletes." Does your high school coach have a college contact? Do your parents? Even for a Division III athlete, a Division I coach's opinion would be very helpful, and vice versa.

11. Keep your options open. Return information to every school you might be interested in. Do not close the door on one sport over another unless you are absolutely certain.

NFL wide receiver Cris Carter of the Minnesota Vikings was ready to drop football his junior year until his high school football coach Bill Conley, now an assistant at Ohio State, said, "There are a lot of 6-foot-2 kids playing basketball, but not a lot of receivers who can do what you can do. Plus, you can play defensive back in college. Why not play both sports and keep all three options open?" Carter became an All-Pro receiver.

High schools handle the multi-sport issue differently. One girls basketball coach said, "Some can't play more than one sport. We tell them what is required, then they decide what they can get done." Another coach said, "We don't do much with basketball in the summer; 31 of our 32 players are out for fall sports and have volleyball or or field hockey conditioning."

Athletes need clearly defined goals before deciding what sports to play.

12. If your coach does not seem very helpful, try to understand. Many want to do more but cannot find the time. Take responsibility for what needs to be done. Ask the coach for names of other adults who could help, and don't be afraid to explain what you need. They may be glad to help someone as pleasant and sincere as you are.

13. Take the ACT and SAT as soon as you can, no later than early junior year. There is no penalty for taking either several times, and you benefit from the practice. Don't just aim for the minimums. Most good schools have higher requirements than the NCAA. If you don't have satisfactory scores by the beginning of your senior year, you will not be allowed to accept paid visits in the fall. Depending on the sport and the schools you wish to consider, that may cost you a scholarship to the school which is best for you.

14. As soon as you register to take the ACT or SAT, talk with your guidance counselor about getting records to the NCAA Initial-Eligibility Clearinghouse. If the Clearinghouse does not have your records, fall visits can be delayed.

15. If you go to camps where college coaches are allowed to be present, understand that you are auditioning. Imagine being a college football player at an NFL tryout. Arrive in the best shape of your life, have a great attitude at all times and aim to make a good impression on everyone from the coaches to the ball boys/girls. Tell coaches before the camp starts that you would like to receive an evaluation after camp. Would they do that? Not only will you get an informed opinion, you will greatly increase your chances of being noticed and remembered.

16. If possible, take unofficial visits during your sophomore and junior years and the following summers. Plan visits which could lead to official visits. If the unofficial visit doesn't go well, figure out why. Maybe your goals need to be reconsidered. The worst thing that can happen is you will know one school you definitely do not want to visit, which is an important step in deciding where you do want to go.

17. The recruiting process can be fun; hopefully, it will be for you. However, it will also be "a struggle," according to Archie Griffin, the only football player to win two Heisman Trophies.

After setting the NCAA record for 31 consecutive 100-yard games rushing, and playing eight years in the NFL, Griffin returned to Ohio State to work with the athletic department. In 1994 he was ed Associate Athletic Director. From that vantage point, he said, ruiting is a struggle. It's a struggle for the university to know the ent-athlete, it's a struggle for the student-athlete to know the university. The best way to overcome the problem is to ask questions. Ask players what they like and what they don't like. Talk with teachers, counselors. Find out if players graduate, and in what field. Ask what tutoring help is available. Is the fifth year paid? If you want to play a certain position or a second sport, get that settled with the coach up front, before you sign."

18. No later than the end of junior year, develop your goals for the final time. When schools which cannot meet important goals contact you, politely thank them for their interest and say good-bye. For other schools, return forms and applications as soon as possible.

At the age of 70, Bob Stuart had 245 victories in 41 years as a high school coach in central Ohio. When he gave advice on recruiting to athletes he went beyond his great players, and he had many All-Americans including Archie Griffin, to himself.

"Don't prostitute your dreams. I wanted to study art, but went to Maryland to play football. They didn't have art, so I switched to physical education." Despite an outstanding coaching career, Stuart still felt a void from not working in his "dream" field.

At the same time you dream, be honest with yourself. For example, most successful coaches are very demanding. Is that a positive or a negative for you? Ask high school and AAU coaches for an honest appraisal of your work ethic. Is it as high as your talent level?

LSU track coach Henry, who had coached 16 NCAA champions in men's outdoor, women's outdoor and women's indoor after nine years at the school, stressed the need to "find the right balance between athletic and academic goals. The average high school student may have to pull away from athletic goals to meet academic goals, or change a major to meet athletic goals. Those who excel in both are the exception. You have to find the right balance, which is different for everyone. Then it is a challenge to find the school with the right balance for your future."

19. Don't be afraid to market yourself. One high school basketball player in suburban Columbus, Ryan Pedon of Bexley, sent a letter to about 80 coaches before his final summer in high school. It had personal, educational and athletic information, as well as times and places his AAU team would play during evaluation periods. He sent it to Division I, II and III schools. After agreeing to go to D-III Wooster, Pedon said, "It didn't work for me. I ended up at the level I would have without it." In fact, it did "work," because he was observed by more coaches. Those coaches just did not evaluate him highly enough to offer a scholarship. Contacting schools helps the athlete be seen; being selected is another challenge. Pedon was smart to find a good D-III situation in case his D-I dream did not develop.

20. If unable to market yourself effectively, consider a marketing organization. Find one with a proven record of meeting needs of athletes like yourself.

21. When you begin to speak with colleges, remember that coaches are trained to be good sales people. They know how to find your "hot buttons," saying what you want to hear. You've heard the expression, "take it with a grain of salt"? Fill up the whole shaker.

Also, be careful in expecting impartial information from recruiters. Not only do they want you to attend their school, most are very loyal to their friends in the profession. When one coach called a prospect to tell him the school decided not to offer a scholarship, the player said, "I understand. Coach ... [from your conference rival] just called to say the same thing. But could you tell me why [a more nationally known school] has offered me a scholarship?" The answer was that the coach at the larger school was desperate, but this coach did not fell comfortable saying that. Instead he tactfully said, "good luck." The athlete never played at the bigger school.

At the same time, treat the coaches with respect and honesty, exactly as you wish to be treated. Not only is it the right thing to do, most players who transfer go to schools they initially considered. If you don't meet these coaches later in school, you may meet them in a job interview or a sales situation. Begin to build an array of friends in the business.

22. At all times, be aware of the grapevine among assistant coaches. Bob Stuart said, "They all travel at the same time of the year. They meet at Bob Evans for breakfast and talk about the players. If someone fails a test or has a bad game, they all know about it by breakfast. The phone can stop ringing immediately."

23. As a senior, approach your English teacher, or maybe a Sociology teacher, with the idea of writing about your college selection process for class. It could replace another assignment, or might count for extra credit. You would benefit from writing down events and justifying decisions; your teacher may ask some thought provoking questions; and you will have an interesting record of the process. At the very least, do a book report on this book. It will help you digest the many ideas, and decide which ones pertain to your situation.

24. Listen to the thoughts of parents, coaches and other mentors. If they have a concern, it is because they want what is best for you. Evaluate their thoughts, don't just accept or ignore them. At the same time, remember college coaches are trying to determine who influences your thinking.

"In every recruiting situation the coach wants to identify the decision maker," said ESPN's Mike Gottfried. "It could be Mom, Dad, the high school coach, the girl friend. The coach has to sell the player and the decision maker."

25. If phone calls are a problem, set limits on time, number and length. Schools will be glad to honor your requests, especially if you are fair. If you don't like a school enough to be fair, you have eliminated them from serious consideration, so tell them. If they are not willing to be fair, you don't want to go there.

26. Coaches will ask you about other schools. When he was the Michigan football coach, Bo Schembechler said, "If my son wanted to play football, I'd have him drive to East Lansing and see a movie, drive to South Bend to see a movie and drive to Columbus to see a movie. When recruiters called he could say, 'I've already been to Lansing, South Bend and Columbus.' Immediately they would want him, because everyone else does." You want to shift the conversation back to the school which called, to learn what it can do for you.

27. Try to decide whether it is better to be a big fish in a small pond, or a small fish in a big pond. There are risks to both. Which is more risky to you?

28. Set targets for reducing the list of schools, if that is a problem. "The biggest problem I see kids have in recruiting is that they have too many schools," said Purdue's Keady. "Narrow the list quickly, clearly and diplomatically tell the others you aren't interested. Then concentrate on the four or five that are left."

On the other hand, do not be too disappointed when schools reject you. Since the coach didn't want you, you probably would have been on the bench there. You wouldn't want that, so the rejection really is an opportunity to find a better place to go.

29. Many years ago, Indiana's Knight talked about wanting his players to be "In the game, with the game and ahead of the game." He wanted the players to be concentrating on the game at hand, adjusting to changes in circumstances and even anticipating those changes. A similar approach would be advantageous to an athlete being recruited. Schools lose interest, as their lists go from hundreds to only a few. Others become interested as they learn about the athlete. The recruit who concentrates on what is happening and adjusts to change, hopefully anticipating it, has the best chance of making a good decision.

30. If there are not enough schools interested, discuss ways to increase the interest with your coach. Not only can you recruit colleges, they want people who want to attend. If you are good enough to be a borderline athlete, sincere interest and a great attitude can make you a recruit.

31. Develop an evaluation method before going on your first visit, so you know what to find out on campus. A plus/minus system, or a weighted scoring system (like five points for the coach, six for the value of the degree in your field, etc.), might be helpful.

High school football star Gary Berry did not have an evaluation system when he took visits. He decided Penn State and Florida were too far from home, but could not choose between Notre Dame, Michigan and hometown Ohio State. Each was strong in important areas. National signing day came and went, and he still did not have an answer.

A longtime family friend suggested selecting important criteria, rating each school from 1-10, then comparing the total scores. Aided by his parents and the friend, Berry did.

After considering and rejecting "position availability," 11 categories remained. Location referred to distance from and accessibility to Columbus. Out of 10 points, Ohio State got 9, Michigan 7 and Notre Dame 5. Campus lay-out, the impression of the 48-hour visit, interest from each school in recruiting him, academics and graduation rate, reputation of the football program, history of producing NFL players, opportunity for a national title, and Berry's relationship with the head coach, the running backs coach and the defensive backs coach were the other criteria. Each school had at least two scores of 10, each scores as low as 7.

The final totals were Ohio State 92, Michigan 90 and Notre Dame 83. Gary decided to sleep on the figures and see how he felt in the morning. When nothing changed, he had made a difficult decision in an orderly way. "If he hadn't come up with an approach like this, he may not have made a decision yet," said Coach Jacoby later. "For Gary, this was very helpful."

There are no easy answers, but a thoughtful approach like Gary Berry used resulted in an answer which made sense to him. For another athlete, a similar approach might produce an entirely different conclusion. Sometimes a good process is more important than the result. (For more thoughts on evaluating choices, see Appendix.)

32. Apply a simple formula: A+B+C+F = Good college choice

A is for Athletics, which is why you have the opportunity for a free education. What goals are important? Essential?

B is for Books, standing for the education you will receive. That will be the basis for your career. What will that career be? What degree do you need to get? Is the school strong in that field? How about related courses? What grades are necessary for the job you want, or the graduate work?

C is for Community, what goes on at college besides sport and class. What about the teachers? The other students? The social life? The distance from home? The campus? As Sharon Taylor asked, "How is the fit?"

F is for Future, which is a reminder that we will all live there. As important as it is to enjoy your four or five years in college, don't forget the 50, 60 or 70 years you will live afterwards. The color of the uniform and the size of the locker room will not matter then. Think about Athletics, Books (education) and Community for the joy and rewards they will provide, now and in the future.

33. On your visits, ask plenty of questions. Also, be sure to take notes. If you don't write things down, you will forget important impressions. Do not hesitate to ask for verbal assurances in writing. If the coach hesitates, say, "It would mean a lot to my mother," or even, "I read this book that said that would be a good idea." The fact is, a recruit has to sign a document without being able to draft it, so coaches can confirm their own promises. Just be pleasant when you ask.

34. It may take some time, even some visits, but eventually you will decide that it is either good or bad to stay close to home. After reaching that decision, the choice of a college becomes easier.

Most athletes want to stay close to home, some want to leave regardless of where they go. The smartest pursue the best situation for them, with distance one of the many factors.

Twice all-state basketball star 6-foot-9 Lamont Barnes chose

Temple, over 700 miles away from Hopkinsville, Kentucky, ar clear on his reasons.

"The coaches showed a lot of interest in me. They talked about grades than basketball, the players were friendly and Coach [John] Chaney has a reputation for getting the best out of his players," Barnes explains.

Asked about Chaney's reputation for early morning practices, Barnes laughs and states, "You've got to get up and get ready to go," then adds more seriously, "That's all I have to say about that."

35. After your visits, apply the evaluation method you have chosen. Do not necessarily pick the school with the most points. It is more important to reject those schools which do not compare to the others. If one school has 92 points and another one has 91, do what you want. Just don't go to the school with 65 points.

"Go where you'll be happy," in the words of 1995 NBA lottery pick Gary Trent, who played at Ohio University. He said, "You have to like the environment and have fun playing ball. It's a lot of work. In the off season, we had to be at the track at 6 a.m. for conditioning, pre-season and post-season. If you aren't happy, the work is not worth it."

36. Be sure it is your decision.

"I think parents and high school coaches should be less involved in the recruiting decision," said Purdue's Keady. "The player is the one who has to go through it [being a student-athlete], he should go where he feels comfortable." While students benefit from advice, they have to make the eventual choice.

37. When you think you have a decision, what was the most important factor? If it was the head coach, what if the coach leaves next week? Still want to go there? If it was because of a boyfriend or girlfriend, assume you break up. If it is the expectation of playing time, what if they recruit a better player next month? Next season? The point is, find the biggest strength of the school where you think you want to attend and eliminate that advantage. Does it to remain a good choice? Coaches leave, couples break up, players are recruited over . . . stuff happens.

38. After deciding, talk directly with the head coach and review every understanding you believe has been reached. **Agreements with assistants carry no weight**. If you think you will be able to play a certain position, wear a certain number or have a specific roommate, talk with the head coach to confirm the agreement. Assistants who would not lie to an athlete might get carried away with their enthusiasm, or be hesitant to correct a misunderstanding.

"Too many assistants worry that this is their last year in coaching. They are short-sighted, which leads to misleading recruits," according to one talent evaluator.

39. Write down why you decided to go there. Write the truth, because this is not for public consumption. This is something you will want to pull out during your freshman year, when you will be discouraged about academics, homesickness, lack of playing time, too much pressure from early playing time, lack of sleep or whatever. You will be wondering how in the world you ended up in this place, so have the facts ready to remind yourself.

THAT CONCLUDES THE RECRUITING STRUGGLE

40. The last point is to go to work and make your decision be the right one.

Anticipate a difficult adjustment to college. Ron Mercer's freshman year at Kentucky came after he was selected the best high school basketball player in the country. He said, "I didn't understand just how tough it would be when I came here." Rebecca Lobo was National Player of the Year in 1995 while leading Connecticut to the NCAA championship. When she moved to the USA Basketball Women's National Team, she received very little playing time at first because she was not as good as her teammates. To overcome a lack of international experience, she had to learn more about the game.

When it seems like every player on the team is too good, think of the 6-foot-2, 150-pound high school basketball player who went to Central Arkansas because his coach convinced the coach there to let him be a manager. While working out with the team, the youngster grew and became more skilled. He became a star, and caught the attention of NBA scouts. The fifth selection in the 1987 Draft, Scottie Pippen is now one of the best players in the world.

By playing hard and improving, Pippen surpassed almost every highly acclaimed high school star in more than a decade. The press clippings and acclaim from high school do not matter in comparison to performance on the court, or the field, or in the pool, or on the track.

Each step up is a big one, but others have done it and you can too.

APPENDIX

HYPOTHETICAL EVALUATIONS

"There is always an easy solution to every human

problem—neat, plausible and wrong."

H. L. Mencken
20th Century American critic

The following are hypothetical evaluations, intended to require the athlete or parent or advisor to address some questions which will arise during recruiting. Unlike formal schooling, the answers are not the point. It is not important whether the student wants to stay close to home or not, wants to study physical education or physics, plays soccer or tennis, or prefers the country or the city. Each person answers these questions differently. What is correct for one is not for another. The important thing is to ask enough of the right questions, answer them honestly to yourself, consider what is important and make an orderly decision. Set goals, reject situations which do not meet those goals, then evaluate the remaining choices.

"Get into the skins" of these people. Serve as their advisors, urging them to ask more questions on matters they seem to be overlooking. Question their values, and evaluate their decision. Does it make sense for you? Why not? If they did not consider as many issues as they should have, what did they omit? Do you understand what they did? If not, find someone to help you. These tools will be useful in making your decision. So will the experience of going through recruiting many times, even if that experience is only on paper.

"CAROLYN JONES"

By the time she was a sophomore, 5-foot-9 Carolyn Jones had received dozens of letters and information packets from basketball coaches at Division I colleges. With the help of her parents, her coach and other adults she trusted, she began to think about college. Not all the ideas in this chapter were hers initially, because she was smart enough to listen to the advice and questions of others. But everything she did was her decision. It was her life.

First, she had discussions with people about her personality, her character strengths and weaknesses, and her abilities, including but not limited to basketball. She established these goals for her life, for use in selecting a college:

Vocational Either teach math in high school and coach, or study business and go into sales.

Personal Single until age 25-27; married, no children until 30-32; then children. Live within 300 miles of parents after graduation.

Academic 2.8 grade point average or better as freshman, 3.0 by end of sophomore year. Carry double major, math and business, until certain which to choose. Graduate in four years with over a 3.0 average.

Athletic Play at least 10 minutes a game as a freshman. At least first substitute as a sophomore, start as a junior and senior. Win league championship twice, go to NCAA two or three times. Learn the game from outstanding teachers. If possible, play pro after college.

Social After freshman year, possibly join a sorority or some other non-athletic college activity.

Then Jones began to consider schools as the letters arrived. She filled out every application, knowing that most schools make hundreds of contacts to recruit two or three players. It was too early to know what her real choices would be.

She worked with her guidance counselor to have her grades and test scores sent to the NCAA Clearinghouse as soon as possible. She also found out about the math and business departments at the schools which contacted her. Some programs were rejected based on weak academic programs in her field.

"I better eliminate them early, before the coach starts telling me all the good things. I don't want to spend my life with a weak degree," she decided.

She adopted a two-phase approach to considering schools. The first phase would be to "veto" schools which were deficient academically, or not competitive athletically, or obviously not able to meet her needs. After the "veto" phase would be the "evaluation" phase, when a few schools could be compared for their strengths and weaknesses.

There were still several schools remaining, but she was organized when the phone calls started. She and her parents decided to ask all coaches to call on either Sunday, Tuesday or Thursday night, from 7 p.m. to 9 p.m., for no longer than 15 minutes at a time. Jones would make an effort to be available, but the times might have to be changed when the season started. The Jones' were very pleased at how cooperative the coaches were: in fact, the coaches thanked them for organizing the calls.

When one coach called he said, "If you don't sign with us I'll lose my job." At first, she felt a strong obligation to the coach. Then she thought, "If that's true, I would go to a school where the coach is liable to be fired for anything, at any time. If it is not true, anyone who would lie to me once would lie again." Despite a good academic program, she crossed them off her list.

Three schools had NCAA violations in recent years. Jones asked for the NCAA press releases of those situations, so she could decide how important she thought they were. In two instances they were about things she did not want to be associated with, so she rejected the schools. The other finding did not seem so bad, so she prepared questions for the coach about what happened, and why. If the coach addressed the matter directly, she would consider them.

One of her most difficult questions came about the setting of the school. Her high school experience, in fact her whole life, had been suburban. That was more comfortable to her. Yet she might teach or live in an urban setting after college. Even if she did not, wouldn't college be the perfect time to experience something different? Did she want a college that was like high school, or not? She decided not to eliminate schools based on their location at first. As she narrowed down the list, hopefully some of each would remain. If she felt comfortable with the people, and their answers checked out, and the program met her needs, any setting might be good.

Some schools were eliminated because they made claims about graduation rate, or jobs after graduation, or academic standards, and never backed them up. When Jones asked for documentation of claims, she expected it to arrive within three weeks or assumed it did not exist. Even if it was true, the coach was not well enough organized to obtain it, which might indicate a basic lack of organizational skill.

Several schools located far from home sounded great, but she rejected them because of travel costs. Sure, the school would pay for her official visit, but how could she get back and forth during the year? What about visiting friends she expected to make at school?

Would she want to live there after graduation? How could her parents, friends and coach ever see her play? However, she did not eliminate every school over 300 miles from home. One stayed on the priority list because she had always admired the coach, another because the school was so highly regarded in her fields of academic interest.

She eliminated another school because the coaches implied that money for a trip home would be available in an emergency. She knew that was not within NCAA rules, and did not want to be punished for any sort of violation. Even if she never accepted anything, the team could be penalized if a teammate did, or even a recruit.

Jones questioned another school because the coach talked about "the percentage of seniors who graduate" all the time. Seniors should graduate; she would be a freshman and was more concerned about her chances to graduate. So she asked the coach, "What percentage of freshmen graduate?" After several weeks, and a few reminders, the coach finally had the answer. Of 75 recruits, 35 had dropped out of basketball, dropped out of school or transferred. Of the other 40, 38 had graduated, 95 percent. Of the original 75, 38 graduating was 51 percent. Carolyn saw why the coach always talked about seniors rather than freshmen and made a point of asking her remaining schools about incoming freshmen.

One school sounded good when the coach said, "We may not have a great history, but we're bringing in good players and you will be our star. We are going to run our offense around you. You'll be all-conference as a sophomore, and probably score 20 points a game as a junior. Come be our star."

Then she checked on the coach's record at the school he just left. In his first year he signed eight players, in his second year he signed six. Three players left after one year, opening extra scholarships. The next year he signed six more players, partly because four more players left. By then the team was doing well, but seven of his recruits had left. It seemed that he had a great sales pitch, then sorted through the players, getting rid of the ones he didn't want. "Even if I stay, some of my friends on the team will probably leave," she concluded. Her decision was to look for another coach.

She eliminated four schools close to home, which she decided was within 150 miles, for various reasons. Her high school coach had a problem with one of the coaches with another player, she did not like the style of play at two schools and the fourth had a reputation for dissension on the team.

Her AAU coach called two current Division I players he had coached to find out what he could about remaining schools. Then

Jones sat down with her AAU coach and her high school coach. They talked about her ability, her potential, her college position and the talent at some of the remaining schools. She dropped two schools because she just did not think she could play soon enough.

About that time, two schools called to say they had commitments at her position and would not be recruiting her any longer. She knew that might happen, but it hurt anyway.

Jones and her parents took a long weekend to visit the campuses of four schools left on her "first choice" list. She had questions to ask at each school, some for the coaches and some for professors she would meet. When she saw the campuses she eliminated one of them.

By the end of August, Jones had reduced her list to five schools, which she scheduled for "in-home" visits. Three coaches would be from schools she saw in August, two others were too far away. Her plan was to reduce the number to two or three official visits in October, then see if she could decide. If she was sure, she would sign early. If not, she would have two official visits left for the spring, plus she could visit more schools informally if she needed to do that.

During the "in-home " visits, one coach made a poor impression, so that school was easily dropped. Of the other four, one coach could not offer a scholarship, but wanted her to visit anyway. They had two positions open and she was their third choice. It was likely that at least one of their top choices would go elsewhere. Jones was a bit offended, but decided not to let her pride get in the way. This school had a lot to offer, so she asked the coach if they could talk again after the early signing period. If she did not decide on one of the other three schools, and the coach had a scholarship left, she would like to visit. They agreed on this approach.

That ended the "veto" phase. Three good schools, with no glaring weaknesses but a combination of various strengths, remained. She scheduled her visits, and decided how she would compare the three offers. She listed the criteria, defined each so she was sure she knew what each term meant and decided the relative importance of each. Then she wrote questions to ask at each school so she could score each one. When she returned, she compiled the chart on the following page.

Evaluation Criteria	Schools		
	A	B	C
Basketball			
Strength of team (4 point maximum score)	4	4	3
Early playing time (3)	2	2	3
Coach (5)	5	4	3
Players as friends (4)	3	4	2
Practices (2)	2	2	1
Personal development (3)	3	3	2
Freedom on court (1)	0	1	0
Facilities (1)	1	1	1
Fan Support (2)	2	2	2
Tradition (2)	2	2	1
Academic			
Math Dept. (4)	3	3	2
Business Dept. (4)	4	4	3
Tutoring and Support (2)	2	2	2
Scheduling problems (games, travel) (2)	1	1	0
Grade average on team (2)	2	2	1
Grad. majors/rates in program (4)	4	3	2
Overall reputation of school (5)	5	5	3
Personal			
Campus atmosphere (3)	3	2	2
Campus layout (2)	2	2	1
Distance from home (4)	2	4	3
Social activity (3)	3	2	2
Vocational			
Availability of jobs after grad. (2)	2	2	1
Career planning programs (2)	2	2	1
Pro players from program (2)	2	2	1
Desirability of working close to school (2)	1	2	1
Totals	62	63	43

After checking each score, Jones added the totals. She was surprised C rated so low compared to the others, then realized what had happened. She was so infatuated with the idea of playing time that she overlooked everything else. It was important, but should she

THE RECRUITING STRUGGLE

change the weights she had established to give it more importance? No, she decided. C was no longer a consideration.

That left A and B. She liked both, well enough to go to either one. That meant she would sign early. But which one? If the difference had been 10-15 points, that would be one thing. But this was so close. They were identical in many areas, so she decided to concentrate on the differences. What would be more important to her goals? When she turned 30, 50, or 60, what would she care about the most? A's coach, graduation rate in strong degrees, campus atmosphere and social activity? B's players, freedom on the court, closeness to home and the fact that it would be a nice place to live and work after graduation?

Some readers would prefer one place, others the other. Make yourself happy with the story, and write your own ending. As a case study, the important thing is Carolyn Jones took a very complex issue and brought it down to two good choices. She had followed her head as long as necessary, now she could follow her heart and do what she wanted.

But there was one more step. After deciding and informing the coaches, she wrote down the reasons for her final decision. Why were the other schools rejected? Why was A or B chosen? She knew that during her freshman year she would face unhappiness and want consider transferring. When (not if) that happened, she would remind herself why she made her choice, why it was the best, and go about making it work.

While Carolyn Jones had a difficult decision, she also had a great situation. Many schools wanted her, and she got to choose from among a group of full scholarships. The "goals/veto/evaluate" approach worked for her, but what about someone comparing a partial scholarship for baseball at one school to a full scholarship at another, or a partial soccer scholarship to A compared to walking-on at B? Let's see what happened with her friend and classmate, Joe James, who wanted to play soccer in college more than colleges seemed to want him to play soccer for them.

"JOE JAMES"

James had a good, but not great, high school career. His coach made some contacts to colleges, and asked opposing coaches for ideas and references, but there was not a great deal of interest. Maybe the colleges were underestimating James, maybe he wasn't good enough, but it came time for a decision. His choices were: 1), walk-on at a near-by state school, D-I; 2), accept a 25 percent scholarship to a D-II school 2,000 miles away; or, 3), choose from among several D-III schools where he would have to work during the year to pay the bills.

His parents asked him to consider some questions before he decided on his goals. They wanted him to ask himself: 1. Is soccer critical to you over the next four years? 2. Will soccer have any impact on your life after college? 3. How will you repay loans after college? (Because they had three younger children to educate also, they told James exactly how much money they could contribute each year. The rest would have to be up to him.)

As he thought about their questions, James realized how much he wanted to play soccer. It would probably not impact his future, but it was very important to him to continue with the sport as long as he could. He enjoyed the competition. For now at least, he identified himself as, among other things, a soccer player.

On the financial side, his parents had taught him to control money rather than letting it control him. They were raising four children on a very ordinary income. They did it by limiting expenses and saving for purchases rather than putting everything on their credit cards. This eliminated the interest charges everyone else seemed to have, and made their money stretch farther. At first, James had resented not having as many things as fast as his friends did. However, as his parents explained what they were doing, he saw the wisdom in it. He planned to live his financial life the same way.

The nearby state school would be the least expensive, but would offer the least opportunity for playing soccer because of the competition. The D-II school would have the prestige of the scholarship, but would be the farthest away. It would also be the most expensive, considering out-of-state tuition and travel costs. Both were very different from the various D-III situations, which were similar to each other. James decided to evaluate the D-III schools, then compare the best one to the D-I and D-II choices. That two step process seemed to make more sense than trying to compare several schools at once.

After talking with his coach, his parents and some of his teachers, James decided on the following goals:
- Not be more than $10,000 in debt after graduation
- Graduate in accounting and work for a large corporation
- Live within 300 miles of home
- Have a family very much like his own

- Enjoy college by participating in soccer, getting good grades (which he would need to get that corporate job), working part-time and having a social life.

As James looked at his goals, his reasonable choices became clear. He quickly eliminated several Division III schools for a variety of reasons, then used the evaluation technique his friend Carolyn had explained to choose the best D-III school. The D-II offer really didn't make any sense except to tell people he had a scholarship. It would not have met any of his goals.

What seemed like a very confusing question became a simple one. James could meet his long-term goals with an accounting degree from either the big state school or the excellent smaller school. Both were close to home. The question became, "Do I go further into debt than I wanted in order to have a better chance to play more of the sport that I love, or do I make a sound financial decision at the risk of only being a practice player on the team?" After establishing exactly how much money was involved by the time he graduated, well, what would you have done? Joe James doesn't exist, so it's your decision.

ACKNOWLEDGMENTS

I was unable to interview everyone who could have contributed to this book. Some I did not know about, others were unable or unwilling to participate. Yet, according to an early television show, "There are 8 million stories in the naked city; this is one of them." Well, to paraphrase that, there are probably more than 8 million recruiting stories, but this book includes a few dozen of the best.

My deep thanks go to everyone who gave time and expertise to this effort. Because of those contributions, every young athlete in every sport with any ability level now has much more expert advice available to utilize than had previously been the case. Not only were all 173 experts who will be listed interviewed on the specific topic of recruiting, many also took the time to review their story and make sure I did not misunderstand what they said.

To Paulette Angilecchia, Jennifer Azzi, Sharron Backus, Lamont Barnes, Jim Bauer, Bob Beutel, Tracey Beverly, Mac Bledsoe, Dave Bones, Ruthie Bolton, John Brockington, Delray Brooks, Jim Brown, Ron Brown, Tim Brown, Chris Burgess, Bob Burton, Andy Burneson, Dave Butcher, Lynn Cadle, Bill Chupil, Kristen Clement, Eddie Clinton, Elores and Jim Chones, Jeff Collier, Bill Conley, Tuck Connor, Dick Corbin, Elbert Couch, Duane Crenshaw, Helen Darling, Brian Deal, Dick DeVenzio, Don DeVoe, Pat Diulus, Marilyn Dixon, Anson Dorrance, Carolyn Doughty, Teresa Edwards, Mike Elfers, Dave Esterkamp, Chrissy Falcone, John C. Feasel, Sharon and Pat Fickell, Mike Flynn, Nancy Fowlkes, Carly and Katy Funicello, Howard Garfinkel, Jayson Gee, Deb Gentile, John Gillis, Max Good, Damon Goodwin, Mike Gottfried, A. J., Dawn and Joe Granger, Susan Green, Archie Griffin, Jake Grunkemeyer, Ken Hall, Dr. Rod Harter, Melissa Hearlihy, Jud Heathcote, Beth Heiser, Greg Henley, Pat Henry, Kirk Herbstreit, Archie Herring, Frank Howe, Bill Hoyer, Larry Hunter, Wendi Huntley, Tracy Jackson, Bob Jacoby, Betty Jaynes, Dixie Jeffers, Gene Keady, Howard Keene, Rick Kimbrel, Tom Konchalski, Bobby Kortsen, Bill Kurelic, Jim Larranaga, Reggie Lee, Jami, Sherry and Stan Lewis, Nancy Lieberman-Cline, Janet Lipp, Rebecca Lobo, Carl Love, Bob MacDougall, Joe Machnik, Ron Maciejowski, Bill Mallory, Greg Marsden, Mike Marshall, John McCallister, Ray McCartney, Kelly and Tanya McClure, Nikki

McCray, Doug McDonald, Carla McGhee, Linus McGinty, Al McGuire, Melissa McFerrin, T McFerrin, Gene Millard, Greg Miller, Kent Miller, Jeff Moore, Steve Moore, Clair Muscaro, Brick Oettinger, Bruce Parkhill, Steve Pederson, Felix and Ryan Pedon, Rocky Pentello, Dan Peters, Joe Petrocelli, Jim Place, Rene Portland, Mike Price, Semeka Randall, Marsha Reall, Dick Reynolds, Linda Rice, Kate Riffee, Robin Roberts, Toni Roesch, Larry Romanoff, Jimmy Salmon, Gene and Kathy Schindewolf, Bob Sheehan, Roy Simmons, Jr., Doug Smith, Katie and Dr. John Smith, Steve Smith, Vince Speciale, Murray Sperber, John Spravka, Dawn Staley, Jim Stillwagon, James Stocks, Jim Stone, Bob Stuart, Aaron and Mike Stumpf, Pat Summitt, Fred Taylor, Sharon Taylor, Ed Terwilliger, Dr. Ray Tesner, Bob Todd, Gary Trent, Jim Tressel, Alex Vergara, Dick Vitale, Bobby Wallace, Kevin and Scott Weakley, Steve Williman, John Wooden, Larry Zelina and Greg Zimmerman, I say, "Without you this book would not have been possible."

Since there are so many stories from which athletes could benefit, and new stories take shape every day, there may be a sequel to this book. To anyone who would like to participate, send me your name, address and phone and fax numbers to me (address on page 273). Parents, coaches, mentors and athletes are invited, but please do not volunteer other people's involvement. Feel free to recommend to them that they contact me, but let them speak for themselves.

I'm looking forward to the next edition already.

Several other people helped with this project. This is an opportunity to thank Peg Antle, Liz Cook, Dave Golowenski, Kris Hammer, Mary Havener, Gary Hoffman, John Israel, Dave Jones, Stu Mathewson, Bruce Peterson and Jeff Phillips for their assistance at different times and in various ways. Thanks also to the secretaries who helped arrange interviews, the sports information people who provided sent so much research material and several NCAA staff members who answered my many questions.

Also, this is the time to express appreciation to the people at Doubleday & Co., Grove/Atlantic, Inc., Harcourt Brace & Co., *People* and *Sports Illustrated* who kindly provided permission to use excerpts of their work which appear in the book.

Finally, I would like to thank my parents for everything they have done and continue to do for me. This may not be the most appropriate way to do it, but I usually forget at other times.

Lee Caryer
September, 1996

BIBLIOGRAPHY AND RESOURCES

Among books which discuss the college athletic experience and/or the recruiting process are: Patricia A. Adler and Peter Adler, *Backboards and Blackboards: College Athletes and Role Engulfment* (Columbia University Press, 1991); Brian Bosworth with Rick Reilly, *The Boz - Confessions of a Modern Day Anti-Hero* (Doubleday, 1988); Kenneth Denlinger, *For The Glory* (St. Martin's Press, 1994); Kenneth Denlinger and Leonard Shapiro, *Athletes For Sale* (Thomas Y. Crowell Co., 1975); Dick DeVenzio, *Rip-Off U.* (The Fool Court Press, 1986); Carolyn Doughty and Jim McGrath,*The Winning Edge - A Guide for College Bound Athletes* (Sports Planning Consultants, 7570 Northfield Lane, Manlius, NY, 13104, 1995); Jud Heathcote with Jack Ebling, *JUD: A Magical Journey* (Sagamore Publishing, 1995); Ben Joravsky, *Hoop Dreams - A True Story of Hardship and Triumph* (Turner Publishing, 1995); Richard E. Lapchick with Robert Malekof, *On The Mark - Putting the Student Back in Student-Athlete* (Lexington Press, 1987); Richard E. Lapchick and John B. Slaughter, *The Rules of the Game: Ethics in College Sport* (MacMillan Publishing Co., 1989); Nancy Lay, *The Summit Season* (Leisure Press, 1989); Nancy Lieberman-Cline with Debby Jennings, *Lady Magic—The Autobiography of Nancy Lieberman-Cline* (Sagamore Publishing Co., 1992); Carolyn Stanek, *The Complete Guide to Women's College Athletics* (Contemporary Books, Inc., 1981); Charles Thompson and Allan Sonnenschein, *Down and Dirty - The Life and Crimes of Oklahoma Football* (Carroll & Graf Publishers, 1990); and John Wooden as told to Jack Tobin, *They Call Me Coach* (Bantam Books, 1973)

Books which address problems within intercollegiate athletics, often dealing with recruiting, include Walter Byers with Charles Hammer, *Unsportsmanlike Conduct* (The University of Michigan Press, 1995); Francis X. Dealy, Jr., *Win At Any Cost* (Carol Publishing Group, 1990); Tom McMillen and Paul Coggins, *Out of Bounds* (Simon & Schuster, 1992); Mariah Burton Nelson, *The Stronger Women Get, The More Men Love Football* (Harcourt, Brace & Company, 1995); Hank Nuwer, *Recruiting in Sports* (Franklin Watts, 1989); Randy Roberts and James S. Olson, *Winning Is the Only Thing: sports in America since*

1945 (The Johns Hopkins University Press, 1989); Murray Sperber, *College Sports, Inc.: The Athletic Department vs. The University* (Henry Holt and Company, Inc., 1990); John Thelin, *Games Colleges Play - Scandal and Reform in Intercollegiate Athletics* (The Johns Hopkins University Press, 1994); Alexander Wolff and Armen Keteyian, *Raw Recruits* (Pocket Books, 1990); and Don Yaeger, *Undue Process: The NCAA's Injustice For All* (Sagamore Publishing Co., 1991)

Books and articles otherwise valuable in writing this book include *At The Rim - A Celebration of Women's Collegiate Basketball* (Thomasson-Grant, 1991); *Eliminating Homophobia: Resources for Use in Women's Sports and Fitness Settings* (Women's Sports Foundation, 1996); John Gillis, edit., *National High School Sports Record Book* (National Federation Publications, 1995 and 1996 Editions); Nancy Lieberman-Cline and Robin Roberts, *Basketball for Women* (Human Kinetics, 1996); Douglas S. Looney and Carlton Stowers, "Whatever Happened To The Sugar Land Express?" *Sports Illustrated,* September 27, 1982; Jack McCallum, "Out of Joint" *Sports Illustrated,* February 13, 1995; Ernest T. Pascarella, Louise Bohr, Amaury Nora and Patrick T. Terenzini, "Intercollegiate Athletic Participation and Freshman-Year Cognitive Outcomes," published by the Ohio State University Press and reprinted in *The Journal of Higher Education,* July/August, 1995; Michael Ryan, *Five Star: Celebrating 25 Years of History, Legends and Instruction from the Nation's Premier Basketball Camp* (Masters Press, 1990); Judith Valente, "A Long Road to Daylight; a fallen football hero fights to break free of a gambling addiction that sacked his career- and drove him to prison, *People* Weekly, January 15, 1996; and Chet Walker with Chris Messenger, *Long Time Coming: A Black Athlete's Coming of Age in America* (Grove Press, New York, 1995).

For the reader interested in reading periodicals or newsletters mentioned in this book which may not be readily available at newsstands or libraries, addresses follow: *BLUECHIP Illustrated,* 22900 Ventura Blvd., St. One, Woodland Hills, CA 91364; *Buckeye Sports Bulletin,* PO Box 12453, Columbus, OH 43212; *Cage Scope,* PO Box 18, Waterville, OH 43566; *HSBI Report,* 104-40 Queens Blvd. Apt. 19D, Forest Hills, NY 11375; *Ohio Girls Basketball Magazine,* 373 Enterprise Drive, Westerville, OH 43081; *Ohio Roundball Prep,* PO Box 141153, Columbus, OH 43214; *Prep Stars Recruiter's Handbook* or *ACC area Sports Journal,* 121 S. Estes, Ste. 103-A, Chapel Hill, NC 27514; *Reidel's Roundball Review,* PO Box 23466, Jacksonville, FL 32241; and *South Bend Football Recruiting News,* 281 Bruce Court, Westerville, OH 43081.

Addresses of camps mentioned in the book include "Blue-Chip" Basketball Camp, PO Box 155, Shepherdsville, KY 40165; Drew Bledsoe Foundation & the All Northwest Football Camp, Mac Bledsoe, 8311 Summittview, Yakima, WA 98908; Five Star Basketball Camp, 500 Kimball Ave., Yonkers, NY 10204; Nancy Lieberman-Cline Basketball Camp, Box 790054, Dallas, TX 75379-5054; and No. 1 Striker & Goalkeeper Camp, 19 S. Main St., P.O. Box 107, Branford, CN 06405. For information on high school or college camps, write to the school.

The following addresses and phone numbers may be valuable to high school athletes involved in college recruiting: National Association of Intercollegiate Athletics (NAIA), 2 Warren Place, 6120 South Yale , Avenue, Suite 1450, Tulsa, OK 74136 (918-494-8828); National Collegiate Athletic Association, 6201 College Boulevard, Overland, KS, 66211-2422 (913-339-1906); NCAA Initial-Eligibility Clearinghouse, 2255 North Dubuque Rd., P.O. Box 4044, Iowa City, Iowa 52243-4044 (319-337-1492 or 800-638-3731); National Junior College Athletic Association, P.O. Box 7305, Colorado Springs, CO 80933-7305 (719-590-9788).

Finally, the Women's Sports Foundation, Eisenhower Park, East Meadow, NY 11554 (800-227-3988) is a useful contact for anyone involved in female athletics.

ABOUT THE AUTHOR

Lee Caryer is the former editor of *Midwest Basketball News*, a newsletter founded in 1978. He wrote about recruiting because so many fans wanted to know who the best basketball players were and where they were going to play in college.

Interest in basketball and football recruiting has grown exponentially since then. So has the number of "expose'-type" books on the evils of recruiting and the problems the NCAA has had in overseeing college athletics. He decided there was a need for a third type of recruiting analysis. The idea was to take the knowledge of coaches, athletes and parents who had been through recruitment, and provide their insights to high school athletes and their parents, as well as fans and high school coaches who wanted to learn the process

Nothing of that type existed in 1983, when he tried to help Steve Smith, his Little Brother in the Big Brother/Big Sister Association, decide on a college. Smith's story was in the chapter on Case Studies. Later, in writing *The Golden Age of Ohio State Basketball: 1960-1971* and *Bobcat Pride,* which chronicled Ohio University's 1995 basketball season, Caryer found that athletes have vivid memories about being recruited, whether it happened 30 years or 30 months before.

He decided to match the need athletes, parents and coaches have for information about recruiting with the experiences of men and women who would be able to provide guidance. This book is the result.

If you have comments about the book, including points of view which may be reflected in future editions, or require a speaker on the subject of recruiting for the student-athlete, please contact Lee Caryer at 975 Atlantic Ave., Ste. 676, Columbus, OH, 43229.

ADDITIONAL COPIES

To buy additional copies of *The Recruiting Struggle*, send $18.95 per book (plus 5.75 percent tax in Ohio). For Big Ten basketball history buffs, *The Golden Age of Ohio State Basketball: 1960-1971* is available at the same price. Make the check out to Caryer Enterprises, add $3 shipping and handling per order and send to: 975 Atlantic Ave., Suite 676, Columbus, OH 43229. Feel free to request that books be signed if you wish.

High school booster organizations, AAU groups, camps, coach's organizations, athletic clubs, etc., wishing to use this book as a promotional or fund raising project may order in quantity at wholesale prices. Cost is $11.37 per book for orders of 20 books or more, plus $5 shipping and handling. Groups are welcome to purchase cooperatively to obtain this price, and also may offer the book to athletes and parents at a reduced price. Please include explanation of tax-exempt status or intent to resell, or include sales tax in Ohio.